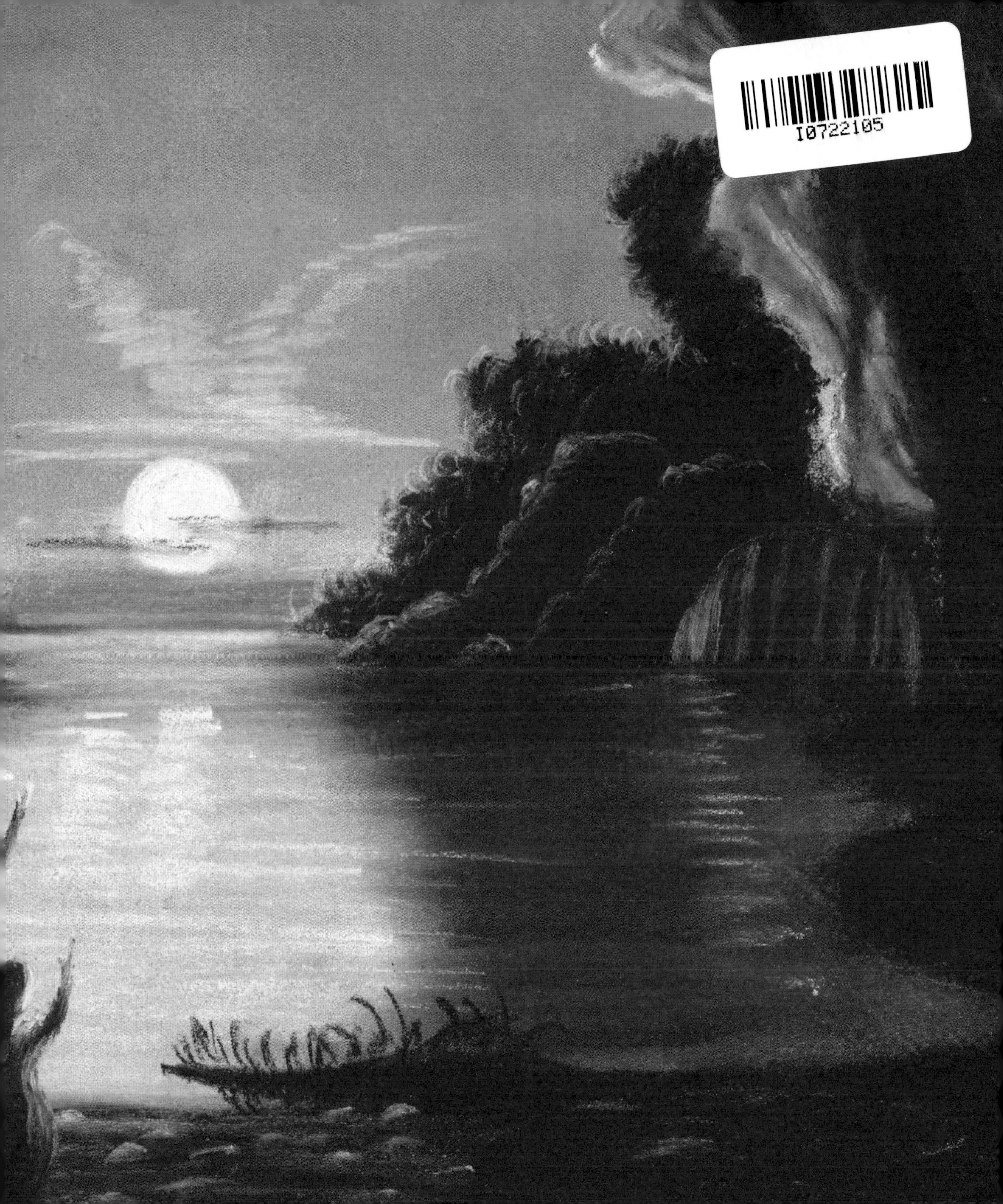
I072210S

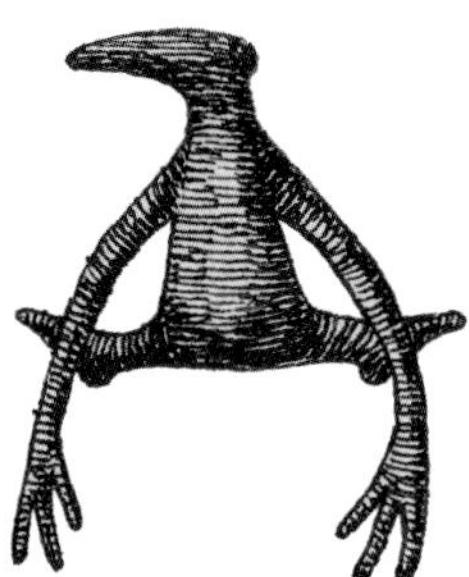

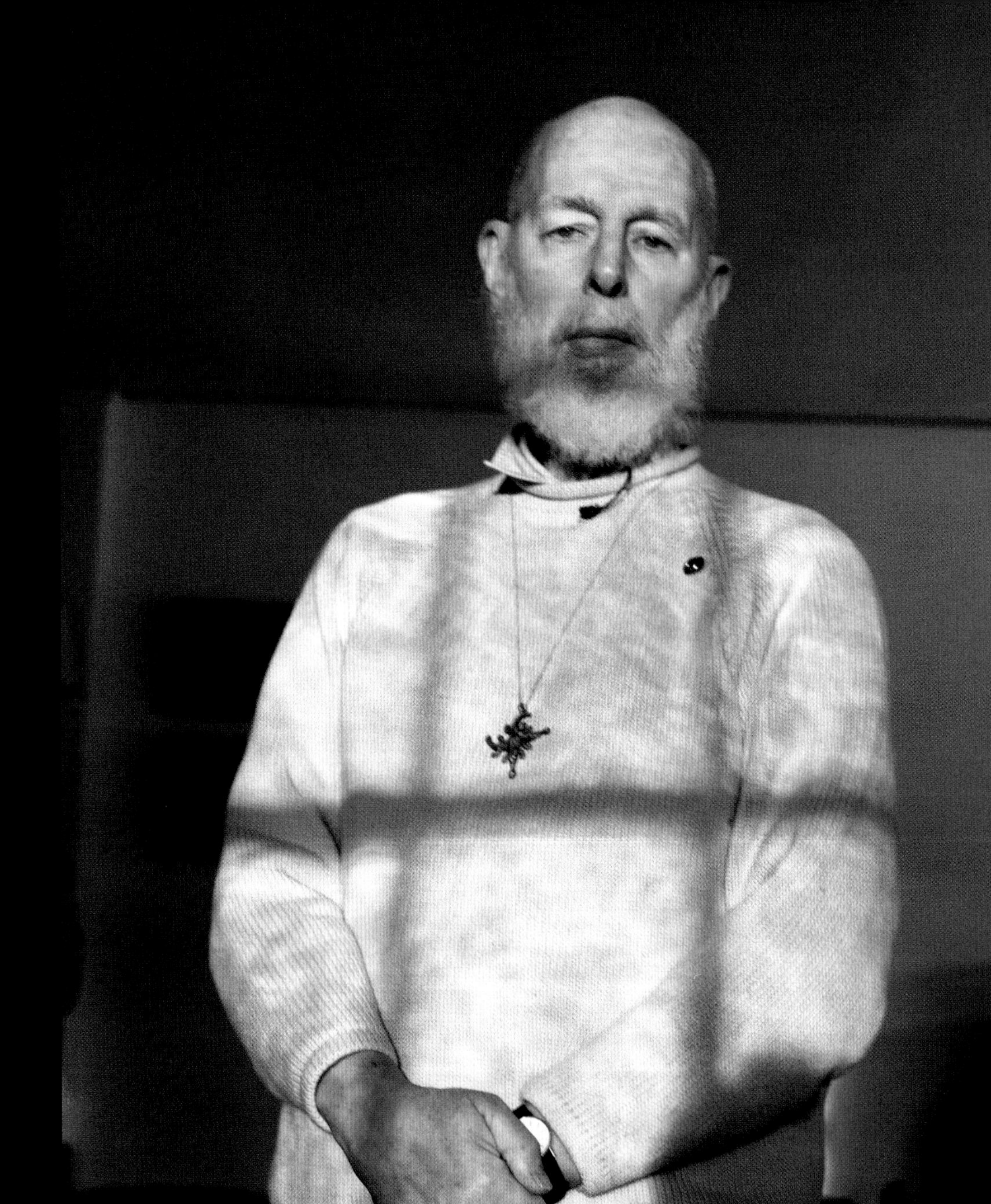

GOREY'S WORLDS

Erin Monroe

with contributions by
**Robert Greskovic,
Arnold Arluke,
and Kevin Shortsleeve**

Wadsworth Atheneum Museum of Art
Hartford, Connecticut

in association with
Princeton University Press
Princeton and Oxford

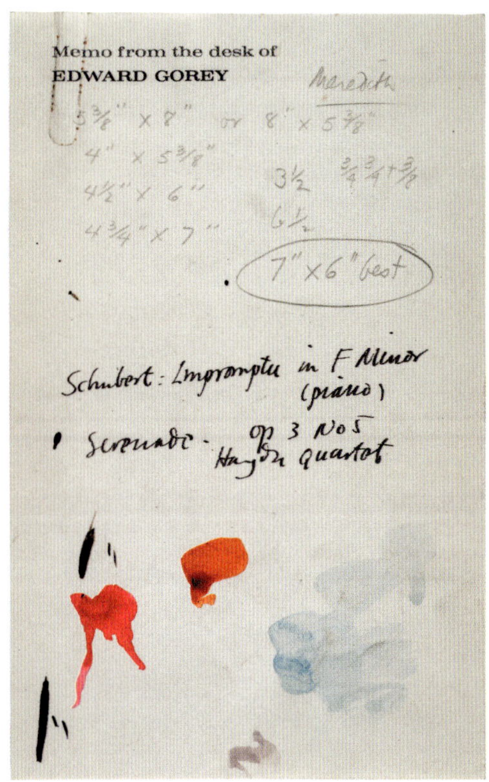

Copyright © 2018 by Princeton University Press and the Wadsworth Atheneum
Museum of Art

Requests for permission to reproduce material from this work should be sent to
Permissions, Princeton University Press

Published by Princeton University Press, 41 William Street, Princeton, New Jersey
08540

In the United Kingdom: Princeton University Press, 6 Oxford Street, Woodstock,
Oxfordshire OX20 1TR

press.princeton.edu

Published on the occasion of the exhibition *Gorey's Worlds*, organized by the
Wadsworth Atheneum Museum of Art

Wadsworth Atheneum Museum of Art, Hartford, CT, February 10–May 6, 2018
Tacoma Art Museum, Tacoma, WA, June 23–September 30, 2018

Published with assistance from Connecticut Humanities, Clifford Ross, and James B. Lyon

Additional support provided by the National Endowment for the Arts

Cover illustrations: (front) Harry Benson, *Edward Gorey in His New York City Apartment,
at His Desk with Cats*, 1978 (detail). Gelatin silver print. Collection of the artist.
© Harry Benson; (back) Edward Gorey, "Without his clippings, Jasper now wrote
long letters to Ortenzia, which went unanswered." Illustration for *The Blue Aspic*,
1968. Pen and ink on paper. The Edward Gorey Charitable Trust.

ISBN 978-0-691-17704-5

Library of Congress Cataloging-in-Publication Data

Names: Wadsworth Atheneum Museum of Art, author, organizer, host institution. |
Monroe, Erin. | Greskovic, Robert. | Arluke, Arnold. | Shortsleeve, Kevin. | Tacoma
Art Museum, host institution.
Title: Gorey's worlds / Erin Monroe ; with contributions by Robert Greskovic, Arnold
Arluke, and Kevin Shortsleeve.
Description: Hartford, Connecticut : Wadsworth Atheneum Museum of Art in
association with Princeton University Press, 2018. | "Published on the occasion of the
exhibition Gorey's Worlds, organized by the Wadsworth Atheneum Museum of Art." |
Includes bibliographical references and index.
Identifiers: LCCN 2017026343 | ISBN 9780691177045 (hardcover : alk. paper)
Subjects: LCSH: Gorey, Edward, 1925-2000—Exhibitions. | Gorey, Edward,
1925-2000—Art collections—Exhibitions. | Art—Private
collections—Connecticut—Hartford—Exhibitions. | Wadsworth Atheneum Museum
of Art—Exhibitions.
Classification: LCC NX512.G67 A4 2018 | DDC 741.973—dc23 LC record available
at https://lccn.loc.gov/2017026343

British Library Cataloging-in-Publication Data is available

Designed by Roy Brooks, Fold Four, Inc.

This book has been composed in Amasis and Champion Gothic

Printed on acid-free paper. ∞

Printed in China

10 9 8 7 6 5 4 3 2 1

Contents

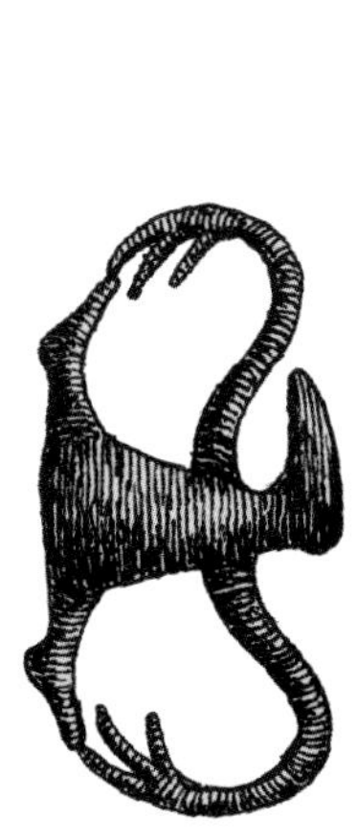
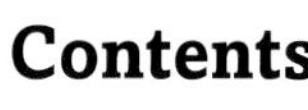

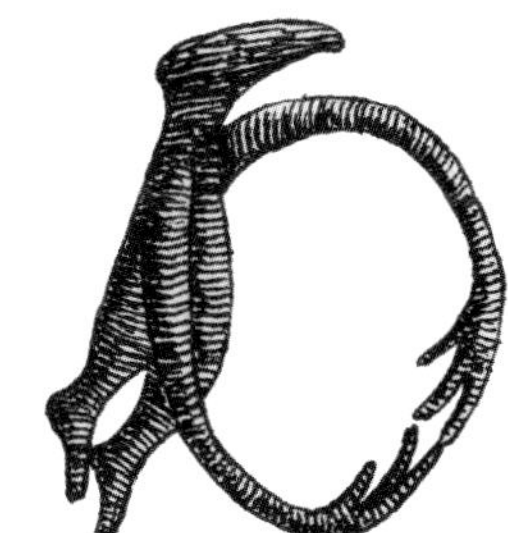

Foreword

The generosity of American collectors is the bedrock of our nation's art museums. Many an American institution has a story to share of its leading citizens banding together to create a place for art or of philanthropists opening their collecting accomplishments and personal visual environments to public view. And even more intimate are the opportunities to see collections formed by artists alongside their own work and the spaces in which they worked. It is an example of this last category that this exhibition and this book bring to life.

The celebrated American illustrator and author Edward Gorey (1925–2000) bequeathed his personal art collection of nineteenth- and twentieth-century art, primarily small-scale works on paper, to the Wadsworth Atheneum in 2001. This collection is defined by its subtleties and nuances rather than ego or grandeur. Words such as "peculiar," "absurd," "mystical," and "unforgettable" provide apt description of both Gorey's eclectic taste in art and his own oeuvre. And it is through such an exhibition and book—uniting Gorey's art collection with his work and his *personalia*—that we see these worlds referred to in the project's title, *Gorey's Worlds*.

Gorey's work has long delighted and amused audiences with his pen and ink drawings that illustrate tales of hapless children, kohl-eyed swooning maidens, and whimsical creatures. His gothic sensibility also extends to his theatrical work—not least of which is the opening sequence to PBS's *Mystery!*—which blends the bizarre and the comic with eloquence, ultimately creating fictions that have endured. Gorey's illustrations, book cover designs, and prints have been the subject of numerous exhibitions, but *Gorey's Worlds* is the first to take an in-depth look at his artistic inspiration by uniting the contents of his bequest with examples of his artistry borrowed from both public and private collections.

Gorey's outsized enthusiasm for the ballet and George Balanchine (the great modern choreographer of the New York City Ballet) may have drawn him to consider the Atheneum for his gift; Balanchine was invited in 1933 by our pioneering director A. Everett "Chick" Austin Jr. and his Harvard University classmate Lincoln Kirstein (a dance impresario and cultural tastemaker) to establish a school for ballet in Hartford, Connecticut. Two decades later, as Gorey moved to New York City to launch his career as an artist and author, he became a devoted balletomane and attended nearly every performance during Balanchine's tenure in New York (1953–83). Perhaps it was inevitable that Gorey's love for the bizarre in art and his passion for Balanchine would lead him to the Wadsworth Atheneum. He also became familiar with the museum collections firsthand, visiting regularly while traveling between New York and his house on Cape Cod each summer.

The seventy-three objects in his bequest range from nineteenth-century European prints and modernist American drawings to folk art and offbeat paintings from the 1980s—a taste spanning Eugène Atget to Albert York. As the four essayists discuss in this volume, the art Gorey collected is just one lens through which to view his rich aesthetic heritage and contributions. The inspiration for Gorey's distinctive visual syntax and fantastic beasts can be traced in this exhibition and publication through myriad sources, including film, surrealist painting, esoterica, and even the ordinary stuff of life. But, in contrast to the profusion of images from social media in our present-day lives, Gorey's image hoarding and appropriation are revealed by this project to be deeply intentional, personal, and purposeful.

Every project requires a thoughtful champion. Ours is associate curator Erin Monroe, who elegantly explores in her essay the salient characteristics of the artwork Gorey collected and how that collection resonated with his own work. I am deeply appreciative of her research on the Gorey bequest, her interpretation of this material, and her efforts in bringing *Gorey's Worlds* to fruition. She and the three additional essay contributors have helped unlock Gorey's artistic mind-set and provide a fresh perspective on this cultural icon. To be sure, what was once Edward Gorey's private pursuit and delight is now part of a larger, public discourse in large part because of this finely wrought project.

The Wadsworth Atheneum is delighted to share this exhibition with the Tacoma Art Museum. We are grateful to Mark Holcomb, Interim Executive Director, and Rock Hushka, Chief Curator and Curator of Contemporary and Northwest Art, for their enthusiasm and commitment to this project. The exhibition would not have been possible without the invaluable assistance provided by Andreas Brown and Andrew Boose, co-trustees for the Edward Gorey Charitable Trust; Rick Jones, Director, and Gregory Hischak, Curator, at the Edward Gorey House. Critical support for the catalogue and the exhibition, including a two-day colloquium convened in 2016, was provided by Connecticut Humanities, a nonprofit affiliate of the National Endowment for the Humanities, the generosity of Clifford Ross, an award from the National Endowment for the Arts, and James B. Lyon.

Edward Gorey orchestrated, through his work and collecting, a visual world rich in textures and ultimately whimsical in effect. There is great promise in spending time in *Gorey's Worlds*; it is our hope and the hope of our funders that we have built a critical bridge—from enthusiasm to understanding, from the visual to the soulful—by putting these ideas and great objects thoughtfully together. May this project bring us closer to his visual feast, and may we be fortunate enough to feel the joy his work and collecting created and continue to engender.

Thomas J. Loughman
Director and CEO

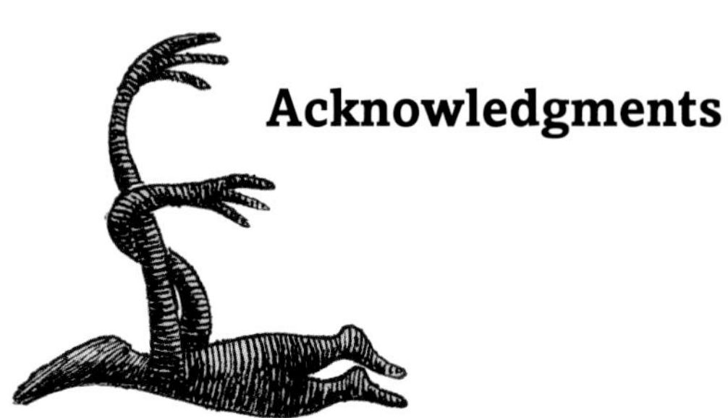

Acknowledgments

This publication and exhibition would not have been possible without the support of the Edward Gorey Charitable Trust and the co-trustees, Andrew Boose and Andreas Brown. They graciously shared many of Edward Gorey's drawings, preliminary sketches, and archival materials that aided the study and interpretation of his bequest to the Wadsworth Atheneum. I am particularly grateful to Andreas for his tireless efforts to locate archival material and other curiosities relevant to the artwork Gorey collected, and for sharing his knowledge of Gorey's body of work. I gained an understanding of Gorey as an artist and collector on my research visits to the Edward Gorey House and conversations with Rick Jones, Director, and Greg Hischak, Curator.

I am indebted to the incredibly talented and dedicated staff at the Wadsworth Atheneum, including my former curatorial colleagues Betsy Kornhauser and Eric Zafran, who championed this project more than a decade ago, and more recently to Robin Jaffee Frank, who helped me launch this exhibition. To my current colleagues who have assisted in bringing this catalogue and the exhibition to fruition, I am immensely grateful: Cecil Adams, Ulrich Birkmaier, Taryn Bunger, Mary

Busick, Jon Eastman, Mark Giuliano, Marci King, Allen Kosanovich, Adria Patterson, Allen Phillips, Julie Portfolio, Anne Rice, Linda Roth, Edd Russo, Nick Shifrin, Grant Smith, Stacey Stachow, John Teahan, and Steve Winot. My most sincere thanks goes to Lauren Cross, a fellow Gorey enthusiast, who was an inspired partner at the museum and whose editorial suggestions helped strengthen my essay. I have been fortunate to have had exceptional and enthusiastic curatorial interns without whom this project would not have been completed on time: Emily Devoe, Karolina Hac, Allie Kyff, and Beth Barbeau in particular for her careful edits and supreme organizational skills.

This book was truly a collaborative effort, in terms of the essays and the design. It was my great pleasure to work with three exceptional authors, Arnie Arluke, Robert Greskovic, and Kevin Shortsleeve, whose insightful essays on Gorey and his collections will be valuable and enjoyable to all who read them. At Princeton University Press we had the support of Michelle Komie and an anonymous reader. For the seamless production of this publication and its inspired design, I am most indebted to Lauren Lepow, copyeditor; Steven Sears, art book production manager; David Luljak, indexer; and Roy Brooks, designer, Fold Four, Inc.

I am grateful to my peers who traveled to Hartford to attend a two-day brainstorming session that proved vital to the conceptualization of this project: Lynn Garafola, Professor of Dance, Barnard College; Katherine Grier, Director of the Program in American Civilization at the University of Delaware; Shelley R. Langdale, Associate Curator of Prints and Drawings, Philadelphia Museum of Art; Thomas Michalak, Trustee of the Edward Gorey House; and Gilbert Gaytan, a Gorey admirer. More recently, I have benefited from the advice and good counsel of Jim Ballinger, Director Emeritus, Phoenix Art Museum, and Assistant to the Director for Planning and Program at the Wadsworth Atheneum, who helped champion new ideas, big and small, for this exhibition.

The variety of artists in Gorey's bequest gave me the opportunity to connect with new colleagues who in turn supported the project in many ways, from providing archival information to assisting with loans. They are: Andrew Arnot, Tibor de Nagy Gallery; Gigi and Harry Benson; George Booth, Sara Booth; James Edwards, Professor, University of Massachusetts (Dartmouth); Cecily Langdale, Director, Davis and Langdale Company; Jennifer B. Lee, Curator, Performing Arts Collections, Rare Book and Manuscript Library, Butler Library, Columbia University; Frank Maresca, Ricco/Maresca; Asma Naeem, Associate Curator of Prints, Drawings and Media Arts, National Portrait Gallery, Smithsonian Institution; Nina Nielsen and John Baker; Mark Pascale, Janet and Craig Duchossois Curator of Prints and Drawings, The Art Institute of Chicago; the Clifford Ross Studio and its dedicated staff, especially Amelia Maffin and Carly Sacher; Linda Salem, Librarian, Edward Gorey's Personal Library, San Diego State University; Jane Siegel, Rare Book Librarian, Rare Book and Manuscript Library, Butler Library, Columbia University; and Christine von der Linn, Senior Specialist, Art, Architecture, Fine Press and Illustrated Books, Swann Auction Galleries.

In addition, I am grateful to those individuals who knew Gorey personally and readily shared their recollections of him with me, including Glen Baxter, Gigi and Harry Benson, Robert Greskovic, Cecily Langdale, Kevin McDermott, Ken Morton, Skee Morton, Clifford Ross, and Carol Verburg. I thoroughly enjoyed our frequent discussions about this exceptionally talented artist and passionate collector.

My deepest gratitude goes to my family, Mark, Abigail, and Milly, with whom I share a love of silly words and nonsense rhymes, and to my parents and my sister, who instilled in me the quirky sense of humor required for this project. For your patience and support throughout this project, I thank you.

Erin Monroe
Robert H. Schutz Jr. Associate Curator of American Paintings and Sculpture

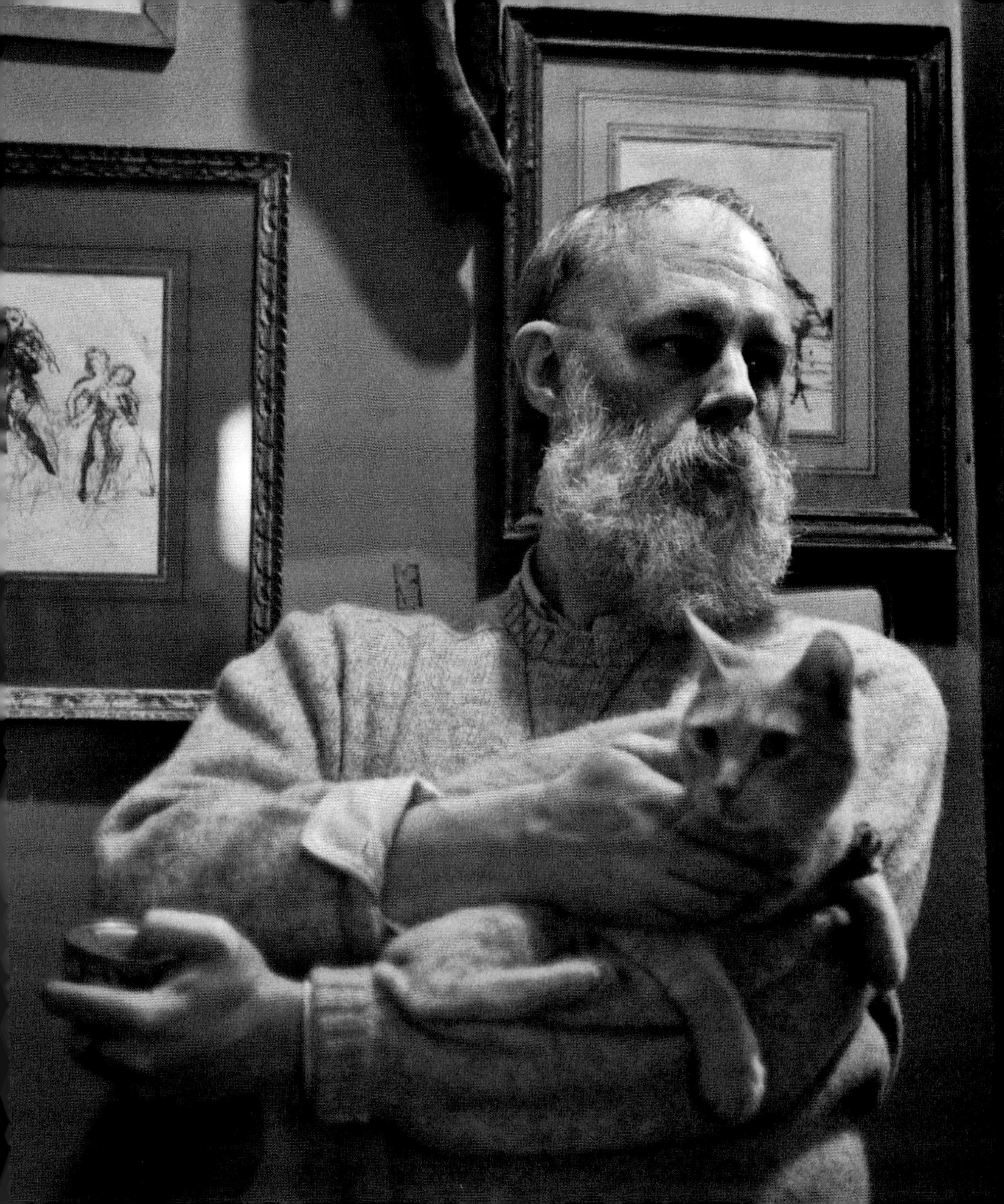

Erin Monroe

Gorey's Worlds

Edward Gorey may have thought of it as "The Doubtful Bequest," because its arrival was unannounced, like the peculiar visitor in one of his stories. Whereas Gorey's uninvited guest proved to be nothing but a nuisance to the family he descended upon, his bequest was a welcome addition to the Wadsworth Atheneum Museum of Art's holdings. Nevertheless, word of Gorey's intention to leave his collection of fine art to the museum was received without warning. The news was met with excitement and curiosity but also prompted another reaction: *What does it mean? Why us?* Gorey was notoriously evasive in conversations and in interviews, habitually avoiding directness and clarity. Therefore, the reason *why* he chose the Wadsworth Atheneum to be the sole recipient of his fine art collection was not explicitly stated in his will. The answer requires a degree of inference. First, that he chose to leave a bequest to a *public* institution suggests that he meant to share it widely. In essence, it became an invitation to step into his artistic mind-set and to consider the relationship between Gorey's artistry and the artists he admired.[1] The collection manifests many attributes characterizing Gorey's aesthetic: the compositions are primarily black-and-white, there is a potent gothic sensibility, and animals are prevalent. However, there are surprising distinctions too. Two noteworthy examples are the scarcity of images of children, and while much of Gorey's own art recalls a distant past, he also actively collected art of the present.

Second, the museum held great personal significance to him because of a shared history with the two *b*'s: Balanchine and the ballet. Gorey deeply admired the work of George Balanchine, the preeminent choreographer of the New York City Ballet during Gorey's lifetime, who was briefly involved with the Wadsworth Atheneum.[2] Prior to establishing himself in New York City, Balanchine, who was Russian, was first invited to Hartford, Connecticut, to establish a school for ballet. This plan was formulated by the museum's pioneering director A. Everett "Chick" Austin Jr. and his Harvard classmate Lincoln Kirstein, a dance impresario. Within days of his arrival, Balanchine found Hartford too small for his magnificent creative vision. He and Kirstein redirected their energies to New York City, where they established the School of American Ballet (SAB), in 1934, and the New York City Ballet (NYCB) in 1948.[3] By 1953, when a young Harvard graduate named Edward Gorey moved from Cambridge to Manhattan, the NYCB was thriving under Balanchine's direction. For nearly thirty years, Gorey habitually attended the NYCB, to drink in Balanchine's masterful choreography and modern costuming. Gorey described him as "the ballet equivalent of Mozart" and gleaned from his mastery how figures move across the stage and the page.[4]

Third, Gorey also spent time in the galleries at the Wadsworth Atheneum, on his seasonal journeys to and from Cape Cod, Hartford being more or less a halfway point on his car trip.[5] Documentation of his interest in a wide array of objects in the collection includes the nearly two dozen postcards he collected of notable artworks in the museum's holdings, ranging from antiquities to Hudson River School landscape paintings.[6] After he took up full-time residence on the Cape, Gorey continued to make occasional city visits—to Boston and New York, as well as Hartford—for a worthwhile exhibition or performance. For example, in 1997, he returned to Hartford to see the exhibition *Design, Dance and Music of the Ballets Russes, 1909–1929* featuring the museum's storied collection of ballet costumes and scenery designs.[7]

ACCUMULATING

Gorey loved collecting, which he preferred to call "accumulating." To better understand the Gorey bequest and his motivation as a collector, it is helpful to observe how he lived *with* his collections. From flea market finds to fine art purchased from Manhattan dealers, he filled his New York City apartment and then his home on Cape Cod with his collections. Gorey's relationship to these

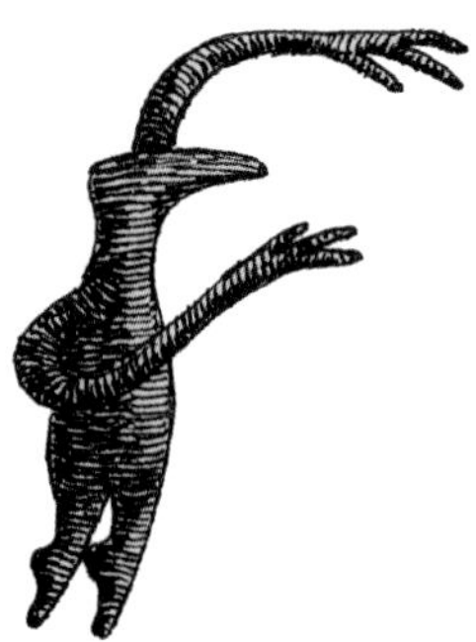

physical objects crossed into the emotional realm and is best understood in the context of the philosophy of the twentieth-century cultural critic Walter Benjamin. Benjamin observed the evolving relationship between one's private living space and its contents. He claimed, "For the private individual the private environment represents the universe."[8] He further described the significance of interiors and their contents to the collector, who "dreams that he is not only in a distant or past world but also, at the same time, in a better one."[9] Benjamin's philosophy is a logical jumping-off point for our interpretation of Gorey's interiors as an extension of himself, and, conversely, of how these interior spaces were Gorey's creative laboratories.

From 1953 to 1983, Gorey lived with as many as six cats in an apartment in Manhattan's Murray Hill neighborhood. In 1978, photojournalist Harry Benson photographed Gorey in his apartment for a feature in *People* magazine. Benson's portraits of Gorey are possibly the only surviving images that offer a glimpse of his collections at this address (fig. 1.1).[10] Holding one of his beloved cats, a plainly dressed Gorey stands in front of one of his quintessentially eclectic arrangements. Hanging in proximity to a weathered crucifix and a needlepoint of a skull is a print by Edvard Munch and drawings by Balthus, two artists known for their macabre, creepy imagery.[11] The flaking paint at the top of the wall transposes the imagery of decay from art to life. This snapshot of one wall in Gorey's apartment shows an example of his catholic taste in art and his idiosyncratic display methods.

In 1979, Gorey bought a nineteenth-century sea captain's house on Cape Cod. He went on to accumulate art, objects, and a vast library of twenty-six thousand volumes, creating what one journalist later described as "cloistered clutter."[12] Number 8, Strawberry Lane, Yarmouth Port, now a designated historic property, is open to the public and has preserved a few of Gorey's peculiar arrangements. The house during Gorey's lifetime is far better documented than is his city apartment. The actor-photographer Kevin McDermott created a beautiful visual record of this sanctum. Published in 2003, *Elephant House: or, The Home of Edward Gorey* is not only a tribute to an artist McDermott deeply admired and respected; it also informs our understanding of Gorey's obsession with physical objects, both natural and man-made, large and small (figs. 1.2a,b).[13] The photographs of Gorey's second-floor studio reveal a tiny room no larger than a walk-in closet. When it came time to translate his conceptual ideas into artworks, Gorey crammed his six-foot-four-inch frame into this intimate space, since he admitted he "[didn't] need much room" to do his drawings.[14] To channel these imaginary worlds onto the page, Gorey plucked props, plots, and patterns from his vast mental inventory and from his accumulated objects.

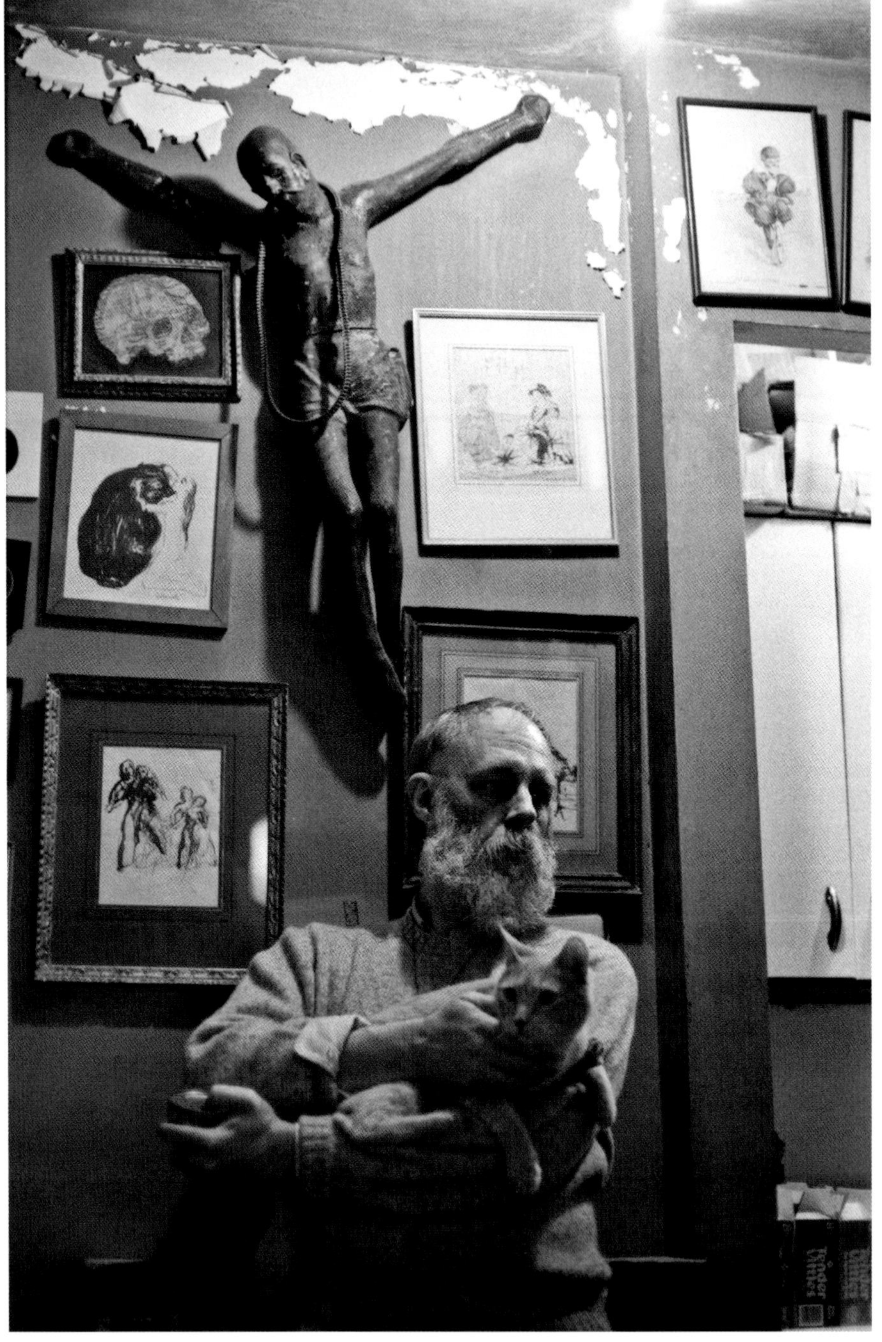

Fig. 1.1

Harry Benson (Scottish,
b. 1929), *Edward Gorey in His
New York City Apartment with
Cat*, 1978. Gelatin silver print,
30 × 24 in. (76.2 × 61 cm).
Collection of the artist.
© Harry Benson.

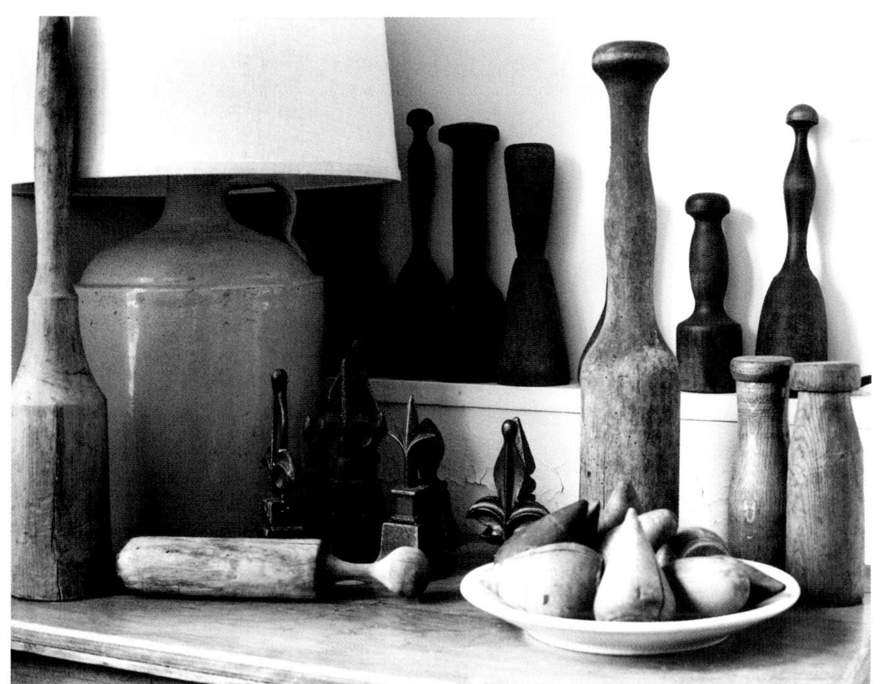

Fig. 1.2a

Kevin McDermott (American, b. 1964), *Detail of Edward Gorey's Living Room*, from *Elephant House*, 2000. Gelatin silver print. Collection of the artist.

Fig. 1.2b

Kevin McDermott, *The Studio*, from *Elephant House*, 2000. Gelatin silver print. Collection of the artist.

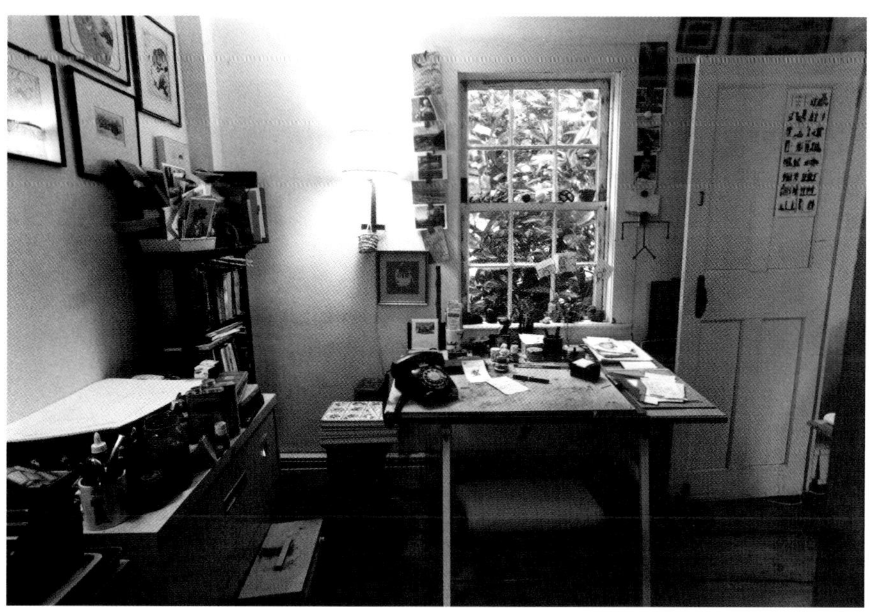

THE COLLECTIONS

The French Art

Gorey's studies as a French major at Harvard University laid the groundwork for a lifetime of Francophile interests. This may seem surprising since scholars and critics frequently note the Edwardian flavor of Gorey's aesthetic, evidenced by the formal interiors and gloomy Dickensian conditions. These English influences are altogether absent from the art he collected. He owned a single watercolor by the English artist Edward Lear—a drawing given to him by a friend—but he *purchased* nearly thirty prints and drawings by French artists such as Balthus, Pierre Bonnard, Eugène Delacroix, Jean Dubuffet, Édouard Manet, Charles Meryon, Odilon Redon, Georges Rouault, Félix Vallotton, and Édouard Vuillard, and photographs by Eugène Atget. Gorey wrote books in French and frequently interwove French phrases in his English texts.[15] His collections confirm his deep admiration for and close study of French artists and views of France.

Gorey's earliest purchases were three drawings by Balthus. This purchase was likely spurred by new financial stability. Gorey typically published one book a year, beginning in 1953 with *The Unstrung Harp*, until 1963 when he published three major works including *The Vinegar Works: Three Volumes of Moral Instruction*, a suite of cautionary tales that included the now-iconic *Gashlycrumb Tinies*, the tragic alphabet of twenty-six children who die untimely deaths; *The West Wing*, a Zen-like series of textless illustrations of menacing objects and ominous rooms; and *The Insect God*, the story of a toddler sacrificed to insects. Gorey also published *The Wuggly Ump*, about a fantastic creature that devours small children.

This success enabled him to buy "fine" art; in 1963 he bought three "minor but good" figure drawings by Balthus, one of his favorite artists.[16] They marked his appreciation for Balthus's larger body of work, which he knew firsthand from major exhibitions in New York. Gorey's vast library included every monograph on the artist and the first comprehensive catalogue raisonné of Balthus's work.[17] Similar to Gorey's own stories, Balthus's pictures featured recurring motifs of cats and children as harbingers of strange, ominous acts. (A notable difference, though, was that while Gorey's children might be threatening, they seemed virginal as contrasted with Balthus's young girls in their explicit poses.) Both artists drew on the literary tradition of nineteenth-century illustrated cautionary tales of Heinrich Hoffmann such as *Slovenly Peter* (*Der Struwwelpeter*). In the twentieth-century context, Gorey's and Balthus's works were often associated with surrealism and the prevailing interest in dreams.[18]

Balthus was particularly interested in dreaming and made a series of paintings about dreaming figures. One of the drawings Gorey owned, *Étude de Personnages*, is a preparatory study for one of these pictures (fig. 1.3). The figures in the sketch closely resemble the two people in *La Rêve II* (1956–57; Private Collection), where a standing female figure with flowing hair reaches toward a sleeping figure — also female — whose head is resting on the arm of a couch. In the drawing owned by Gorey, however, the sleeping figure appears to be male. His darkened eyes are in a trancelike state, and his body is slumped, passive. The figures' bodies fade into the blank page, suggesting an apparition. Their haunted appearance brings to mind Gorey's characters that are preoccupied by seen and unseen forces, such as the Throbblefoot Spectre in *The Object-Lesson* or the shadowy "phantom" in *The Listing Attic* (fig. 1.4).

Balthus's pen and ink drawing of a Spahi is of a more worldly subject (fig. 1.5). The artist created portraits of these cavalry soldiers during his service in Morocco for the French military from 1930 to 1932. The Spahis were recruited from French colonies in North Africa. Balthus sketched the soldiers carrying out their daily activities and resting during downtime in the barracks, as with the reclining figure in the drawing Gorey owned.[19] This drawing de-emphasizes the soldier's uniform and instead focuses on his shirtless torso and reclining pose. This posture creates an undercurrent of sexual tension. Balthus's image making was profoundly influenced by his military experience. Traveling to a new environment far from France opened his mind and expanded his worldview. Balthus said it liberated him from the aesthetics of the postimpressionists and the concern for light.[20] Focusing on the figure reaffirmed Balthus's interest in drawing people, an interest to which he remained committed for the rest of his career. By 1963, when Gorey was collecting Balthus's work, the French painter had a reputation for paintings filled with sexual tension. His figures, notably young girls, appeared in provocative poses with fixed gazes suggesting that they were suspended in a permanent daydream and slightly vulnerable.

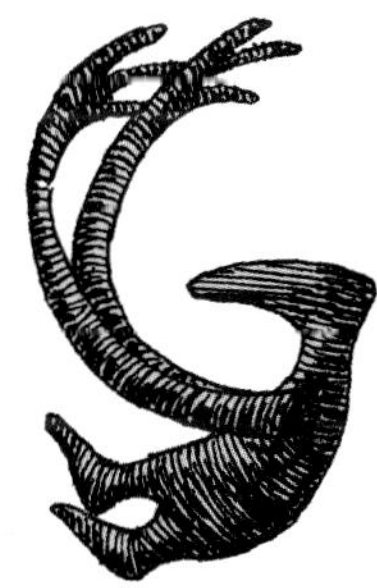

Gorey's early work from the 1960s resonates with the moods, motives, and characters in Balthus's paintings and drawings. There are notable affinities between two of his stories he wrote around the time he bought the Balthus drawings. In 1961, he published *The Curious Sofa: A Pornographic Work* and *The Fatal Lozenge*. In *The Curious Sofa*, sexual tension abounds in the form of

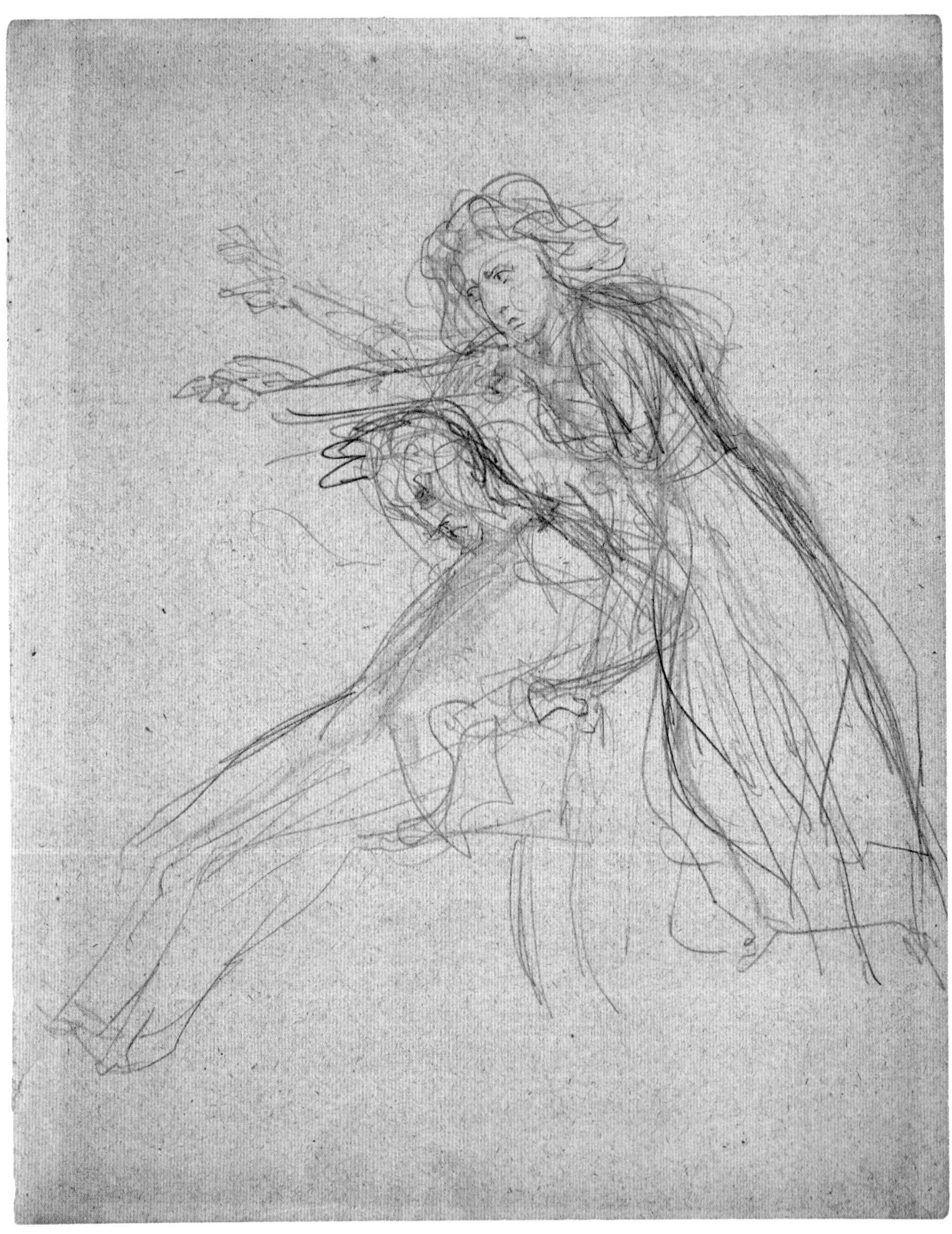

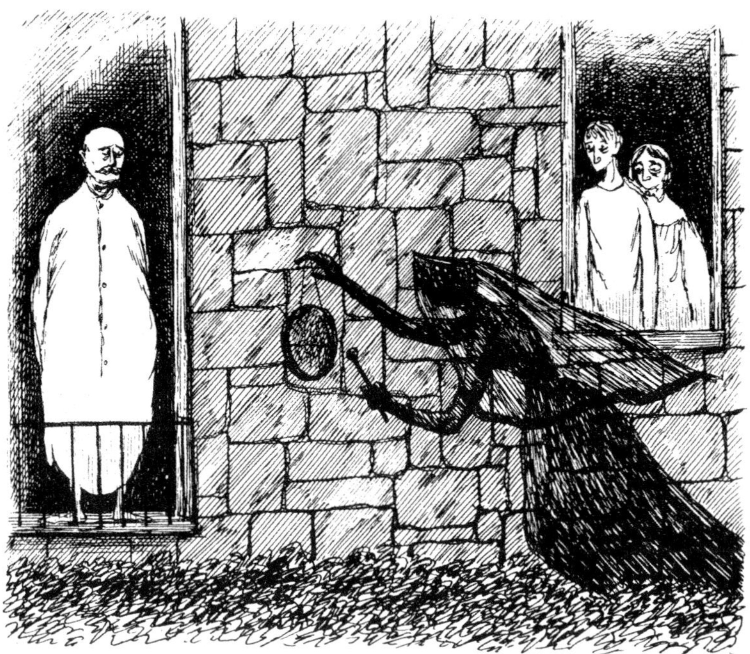

innuendos and playful words, such as the naughty game of "Thumbfumble," and references to objects placed in suggestive places. In *The Fatal Lozenge*, Gorey's first of many clever alphabet primers, *Z* is illustrated by a Zouave, an infantry soldier often recruited from the same region as the Spahi (fig. 1.6). Gorey's merciless soldier impales a baby; the soldier wears loose pants in the North African fashion and open jacket similar to the uniform worn by the Spahi.[21] Like Balthus, Gorey seems to have been inspired by the exoticism or foreignness of these soldiers.

In addition to the Balthus drawings, Gorey later purchased two depictions of interior spaces by Pierre Bonnard and Édouard Vuillard, two nineteenth-century French artists who were core members of Les Nabis, a group of avant-garde artists centered in Paris (figs. 1.7, 1.8). Their pictorial aims were more expressive than realistic, and even after the group disbanded in 1899, Bonnard and Vuillard worked together and continued exploring the depiction of interior spaces.[22] These intimate compositions were also very

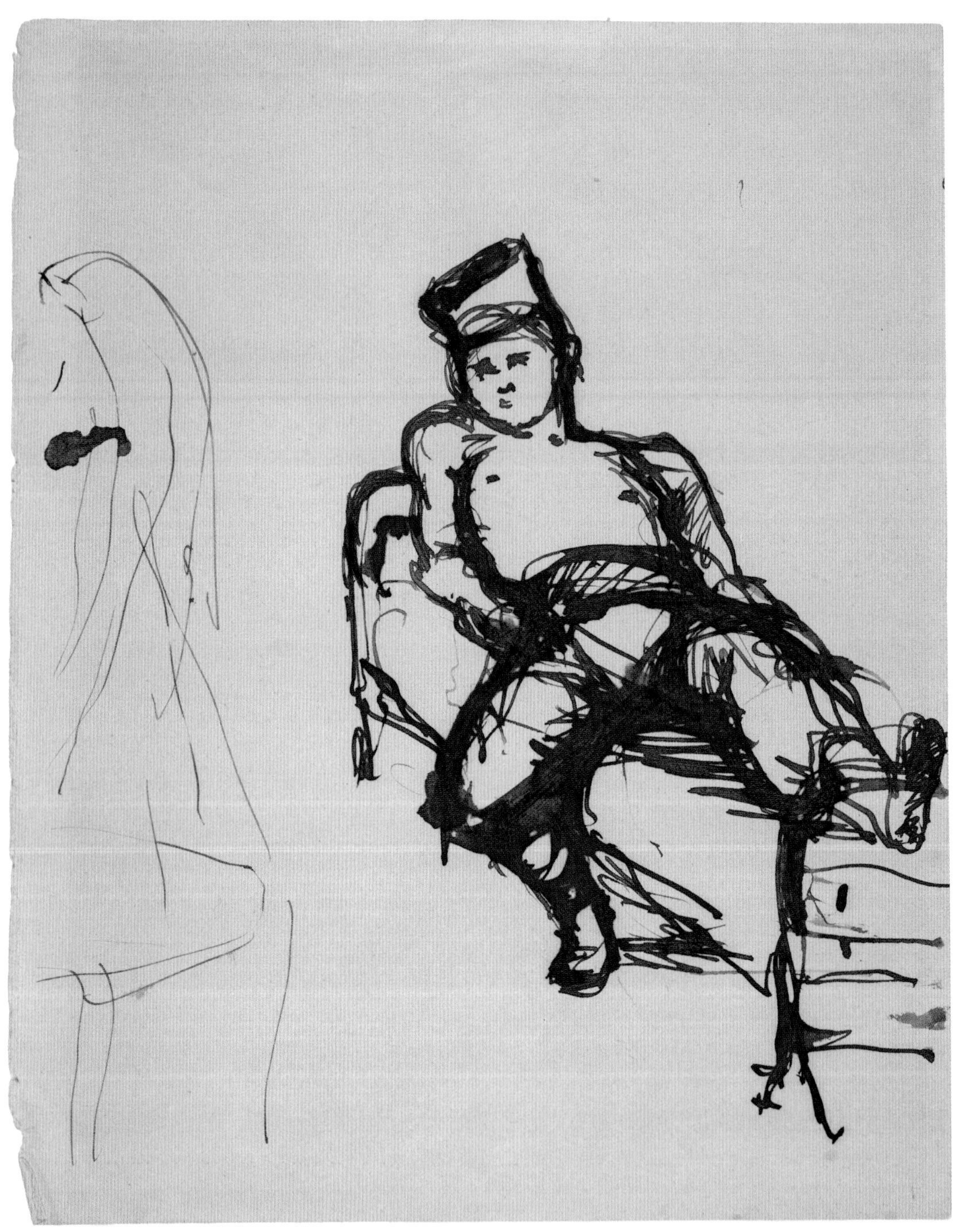

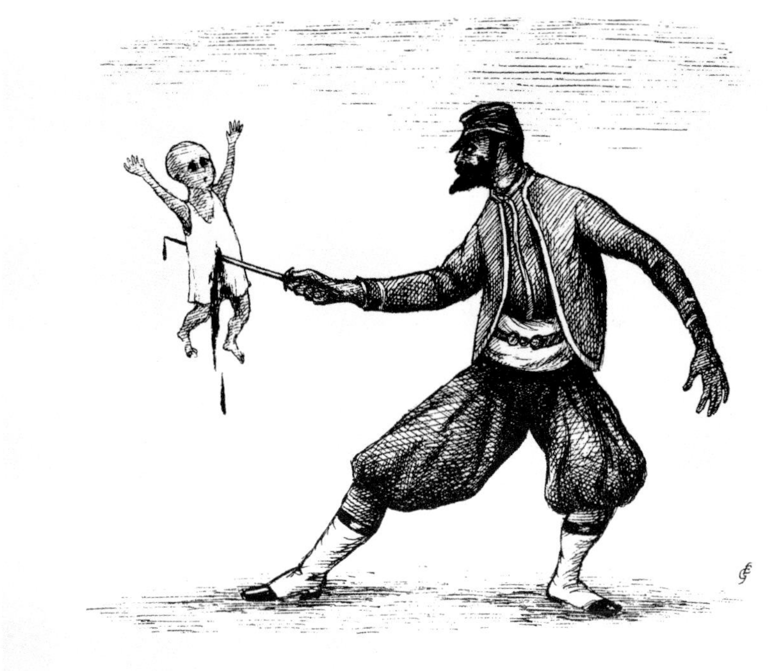

Fig. 1.5

Balthus (Balthasar Klossowski de Rola), *Spahi*, 1930–31. Ink on paper, 8 ⅜ × 6 ⅜ in. (21.3 × 16.2 cm). Wadsworth Atheneum Museum of Art, Hartford, Conn. Bequest of Edward Gorey, 2001.13.21.

Fig. 1.6

Edward Gorey, "The Zouave used to war and battle / Would sooner take a life than not: / It scarcely has begun to prattle / When he impales the hapless tot." Illustration in *The Fatal Lozenge*. New York: Ivan Obolensky, Inc., 1960.

similar in scale to Gorey's artwork and resonated with his tendency to use private spaces as backdrops to his stories.

Gorey purchased an untitled sketch by Bonnard in 1977 after seeing it in an exhibition at the Acquavella Galleries.[23] The remnants of a meal or tea are set on a table with a view of a large window framed by curtains decorated with a curlicue pattern. The window is prominent and serves as a wide portal to an unseen world. Windows have a venerable history as symbolic motifs for artists and writers, including Gorey. In his Cape Cod house, the desk in his studio faced toward the window with a view of a magnificent magnolia tree. There, he transcended the tiny studio space by embarking on his favorite journey, "looking out the window," which went hand in hand with his favorite occupation, "drifting."[24] Gorey's love for windows and for Bonnard is further evidenced by a postcard he sent to his friend Robert Greskovic. It was a reproduction of Bonnard's painting *The Window* (Tate Gallery, London), accompanied by a message that simply read: "Why can't life be like this?"[25]

Fig. 1.7

Pierre Bonnard (French, 1867–1947). *Interior*, c. 1927. Charcoal and graphite on paper, 6⅜ × 4⅞ in. (16.2 × 12.4 cm). Wadsworth Atheneum Museum of Art, Hartford, Conn. Bequest of Edward Gorey, 2001.13.28.

Fig. 1.8

Édouard Vuillard (French, 1868–1940). *Interior*, c. 1890. Graphite on paper, 6⅛ × 4 in. (15.6 × 10.2 cm). Wadsworth Atheneum Museum of Art, Hartford, Conn. Bequest of Edward Gorey, 2001.13.72.

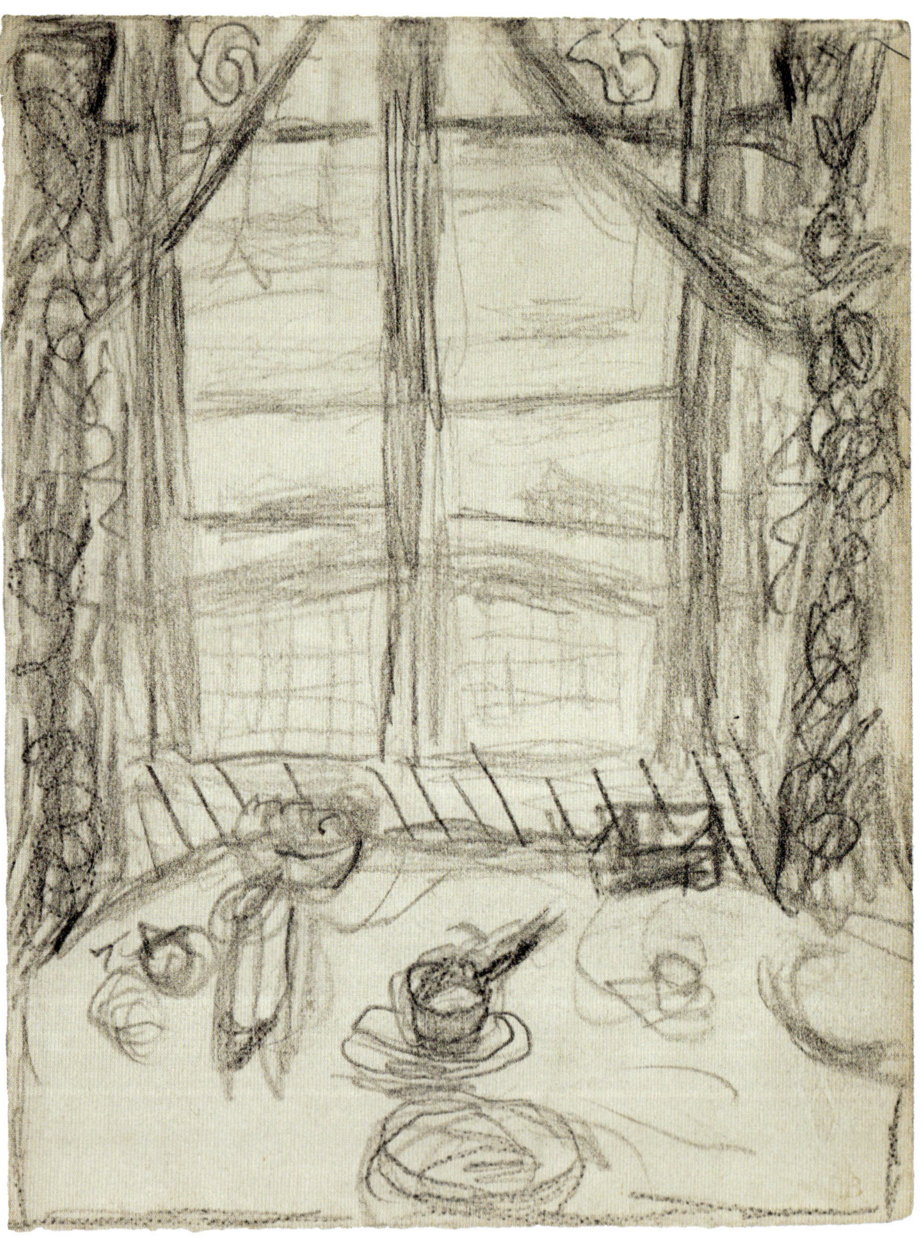

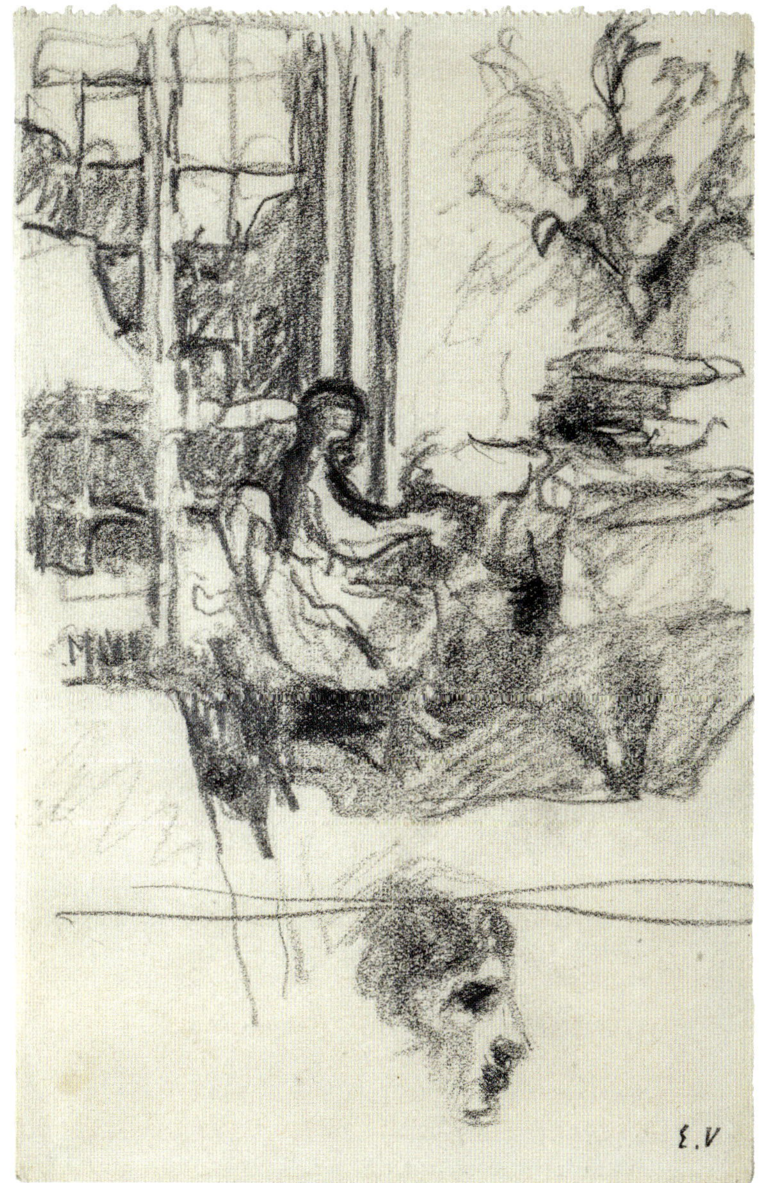

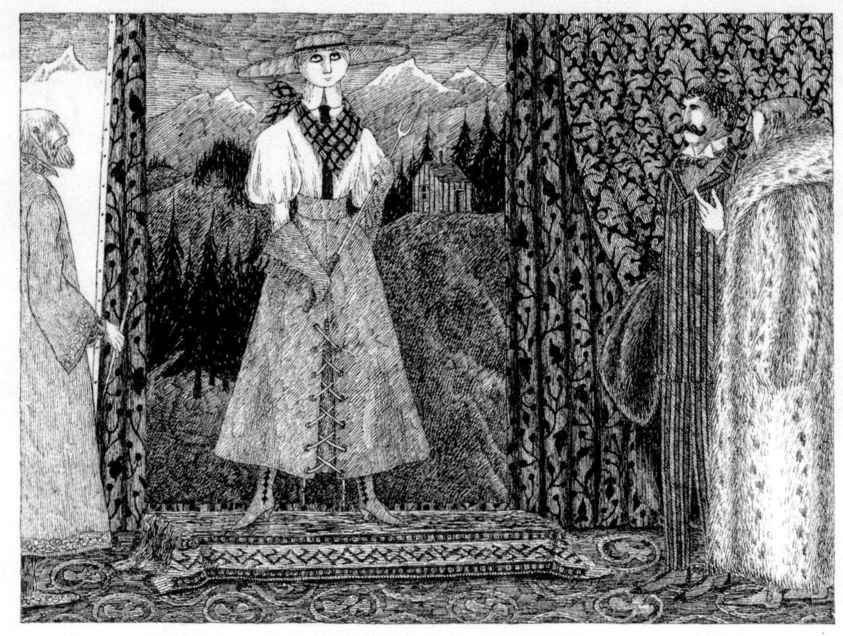

The contents that appear in Vuillard's drawn interior—the seated figure, the furnishings, and so forth—are roughly articulated and unfinished, reinforcing the scene's evocative mood. The seated figure's sketched legs appear to dissolve into her chair below. Gorey similarly blended his characters into their immediate physical surroundings, emphasizing flatness and texture over depth and perspective. In *The Blue Aspic*, for example, Gorey seems to mock his love of decoration by literally framing the opera singer Ortenzia Caviglia within the actual painted landscape scene behind her (fig. 1.9). In another scene from the same story, the texture of Jasper Ankle's hound's-tooth suit, the wood grain of the furniture, and the geometric wall tiles are painstakingly delineated as if in the same plane (fig. 1.10).

Gorey's extensive collection of French artists included more than twelve different architectural views of Paris, ranging from nineteenth-century prints to modern photographs. He owned seven prints by Charles Meryon, five of which were from the artist's well-known portfolio of etchings of the city, published in the mid-nineteenth century.[26] Meryon's dense cross-hatched prints prefigure Gorey's labor-intensive line work (figs. 1.11, 1.12). In addition

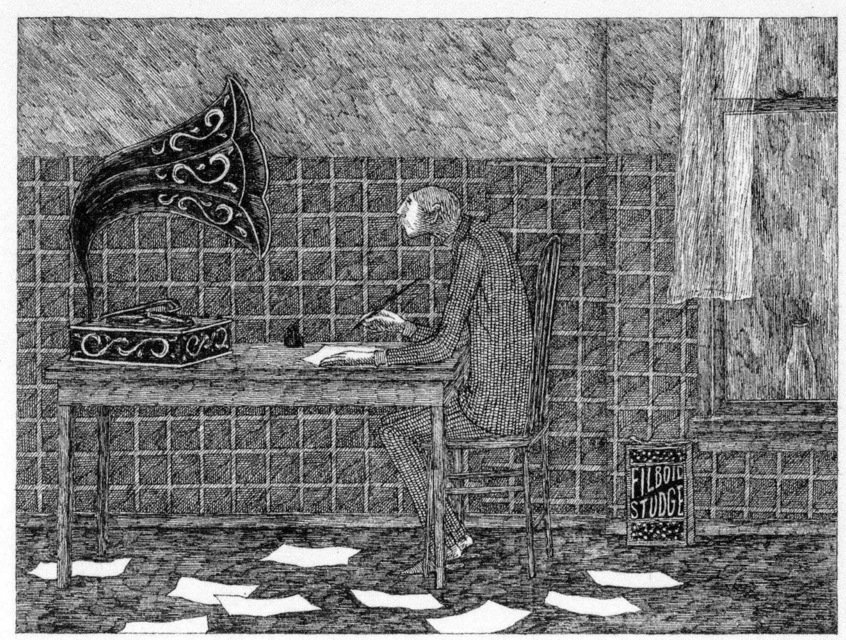

Fig. 1.10
Edward Gorey, "Without his clippings, Jasper now wrote long letters to Ortenzia, which went unanswered." Illustration for *The Blue Aspic*. New York: Meredith Press, 1968. Pen and ink on paper, 7 ¼ × 8 ⁹⁄₁₆ in. (18.4 × 21.7 cm). The Edward Gorey Charitable Trust.

to their technical appeal, Meryon harnessed the moodier qualities of Paris. In some instances, Meryon added fantastic phenomena to his otherwise "real" views, which Gorey likely appreciated. In *Le Ministère de la Marine* (*The Admiralty, Paris*), for example, the official building is under attack by a fantastic horde of flying horsemen and airborne sea creatures.[27] The scene resembles a weird, dystopian nightmare akin to science fiction. Meryon's images were at times puzzling and bizarre, and, as one scholar noted, they suggested a "long and lonely meditation on life and nature, on time and space, and the bewildering abysses of his imagination."[28] One explanation for these disquieting compositions may be that the visions arising in the "abysses of his imagination" were realities for him. He suffered from *folie* (madness) and was ultimately committed to the asylum.[29] Whatever the impetus, Meryon's combination of varied objects and levels of reality resulted in compositions closely related to surrealist collage.[30]

The nightmarish quality of Meryon's Paris also extended to Gorey's unnamed worlds where otherwise innocuous settings turn dangerous or deadly. A similar group of menacing flying perpetrators threaten society in Gorey's dystopian tragedy *The Evil Garden*. Seduced by the "free" admission, a group of

Fig. 1.11

Charles Meryon (French,
1821–1868). *Le Petit Pont, Paris*,
1858. Etching on paper,
12¼ × 8¾ in. (31.1 × 22.2 cm).
Wadsworth Atheneum
Museum of Art, Hartford,
Conn. Bequest of Edward
Gorey, 2001.13.57.

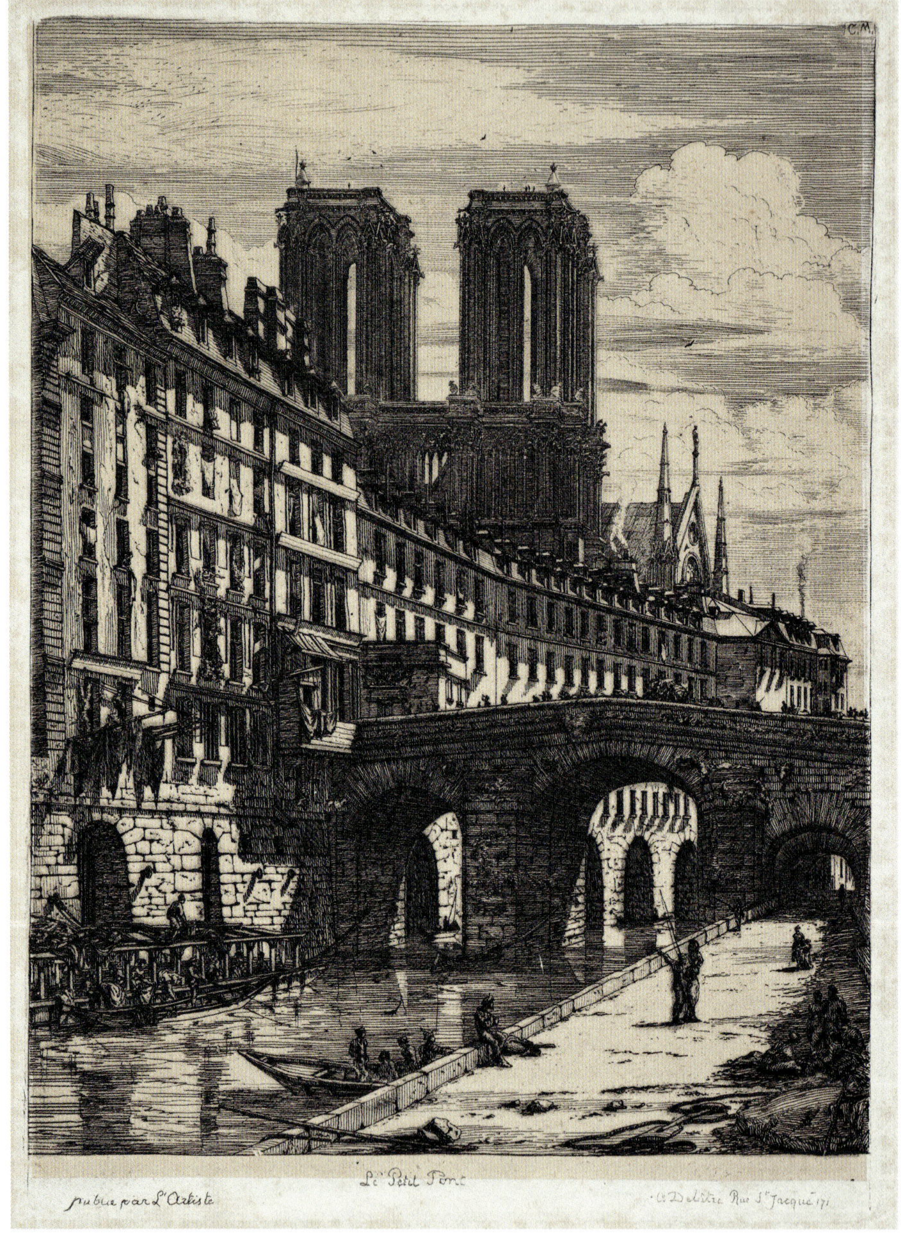

16

people innocently enter a public garden where, within moments of entering, they encounter threats large and small. The flowers smell putrid, moths are the size of peacocks, and the plants are carnivorous. A swarm of hairy bugs carries off an infant in a scene resembling a Meryon fantasy (fig. 1.13).

Similarly, the theme of madness also extends to the characters Gorey invented. Numerous characters, young and old, are troubled and display erratic behavior, suffer from fits—like poor Susan in *The Gashlycrumb Tinies*—or are driven to madness by their obsessions. Such is the case of Jasper in *The Blue Aspic*, whose unrequited love for Ortenzia Caviglia escalates to impel his creepy stalker-esque pursuit. Committed to an asylum, like Meryon the artist, the bereft Jasper stares at his records ("no gramophone was available to the inmates"); released, he ends up murdering Ortenzia (fig. 1.14).

Gorey's collection of dreamlike imagery included Odilon Redon's lithograph of floating eyeballs, an enigmatic composition inspired by Gustave Flaubert's prose poem *The Temptation of Saint Anthony* (fig. 1.15). This image recalls Meryon's fantasy worlds and his Vuillard sketch with a disembodied head beneath the more finished interior (see fig. 1.8). The mystical and grotesque reappear in Gorey's haunted worlds, where similar implausible, nonsensical happenings feel dreamlike and surreal.

The largest body of work by a single artist in Gorey's art collection is a group of ten photographs by Eugène Atget.[31] Gorey owned all the important monographs and the definitive catalogue raisonné of Atget's work to feed his voracious appetite for his "haunting" photographs.[32] In contrast to Meryon's invented fantasies, Atget's camera lens captured the bizarreness of reality. The American photographer and champion of Atget's work Berenice Abbott described this effect as "the shock of realism unadorned."[33] The sparseness of Atget's aesthetic made them ideal backdrops to Gorey's doom-laden tales.

In fact, many of Gorey's characters appear to have wandered into one of Atget's unpeopled Parisian scenes. Such is the case for the lead character—an author—who wanders the streets aimlessly in Gorey's alphabet book *The Chinese Obelisks*. The letter *P* was for "a Place he did not know at all." In the illustration, a (suspiciously familiar) fur-coated man stands between two wrought iron gates that echo the stone walls in Atget's *Passageway* (figs. 1.16, 1.17). In *The Gashlycrumb Tinies,* "I is for Ida," who falls from a rowboat and drowns in a lake, without a soul present to save her. Atget's mesmerizing photograph of Rambouillet Park, located just outside of Paris, features an empty rowboat floating in a barren lake (figs. 1.18, 1.19). Even Atget's floral

Fig. 1.12

Charles Meryon, *Le Ministère
de la Marine (The Admiralty,
Paris)*, 1866. Etching on paper,
9 × 7⅞ in. (22.9 × 20 cm).
Wadsworth Atheneum
Museum of Art, Hartford,
Conn. Bequest of Edward
Gorey, 2001.13.53.

Fig. 1.13

Edward Gorey, "A hissing
swarm of hairy bugs / Has got
the baby and its rugs."
Illustration for *The Evil Garden*.
New York: Fantod Press, 1966.
Pen and ink on paper, 4 × 5 in.
(10.2 × 12.7 cm) (image), 7 ×
8 in. (17.8 × 20.3 cm) (sheet).
The Edward Gorey Charitable
Trust.

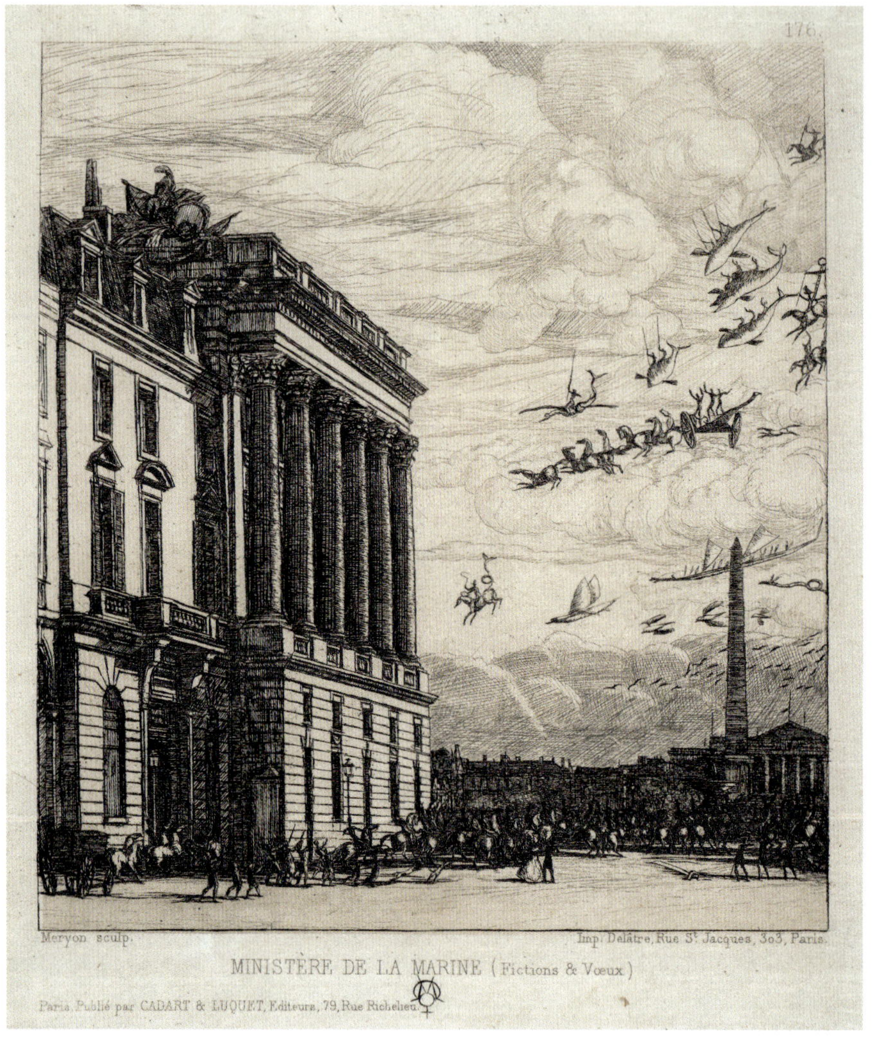
Meryon sculp.
Imp. Delâtre, Rue St Jacques, 3o3, Paris.
MINISTÈRE DE LA MARINE (Fictions & Vœux)
Paris, Publié par CADART & LUQUET, Editeurs, 79, Rue Richelieu.

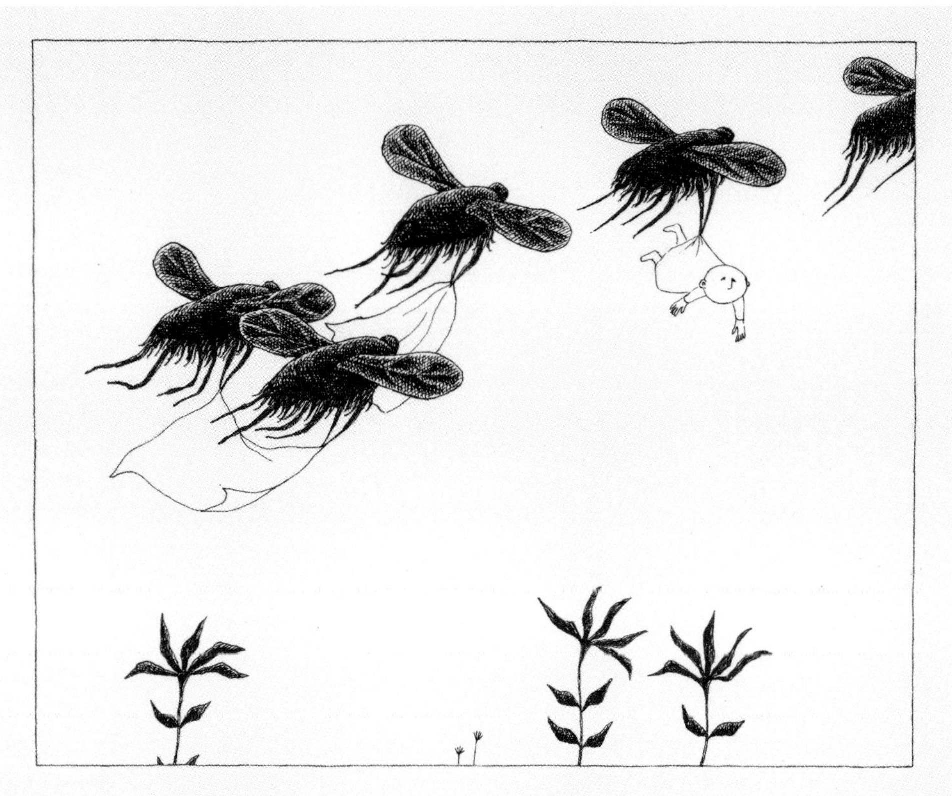

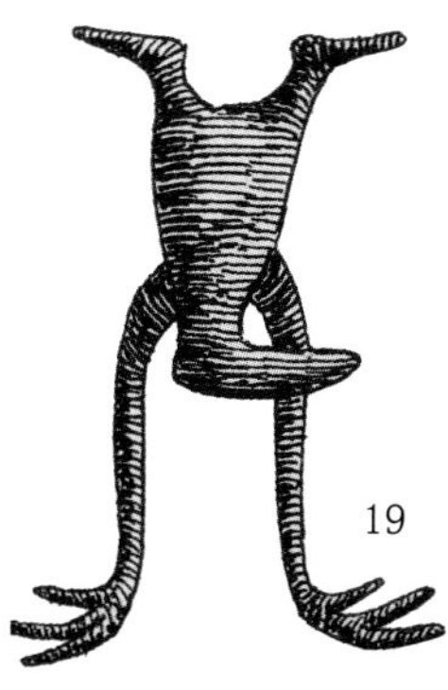

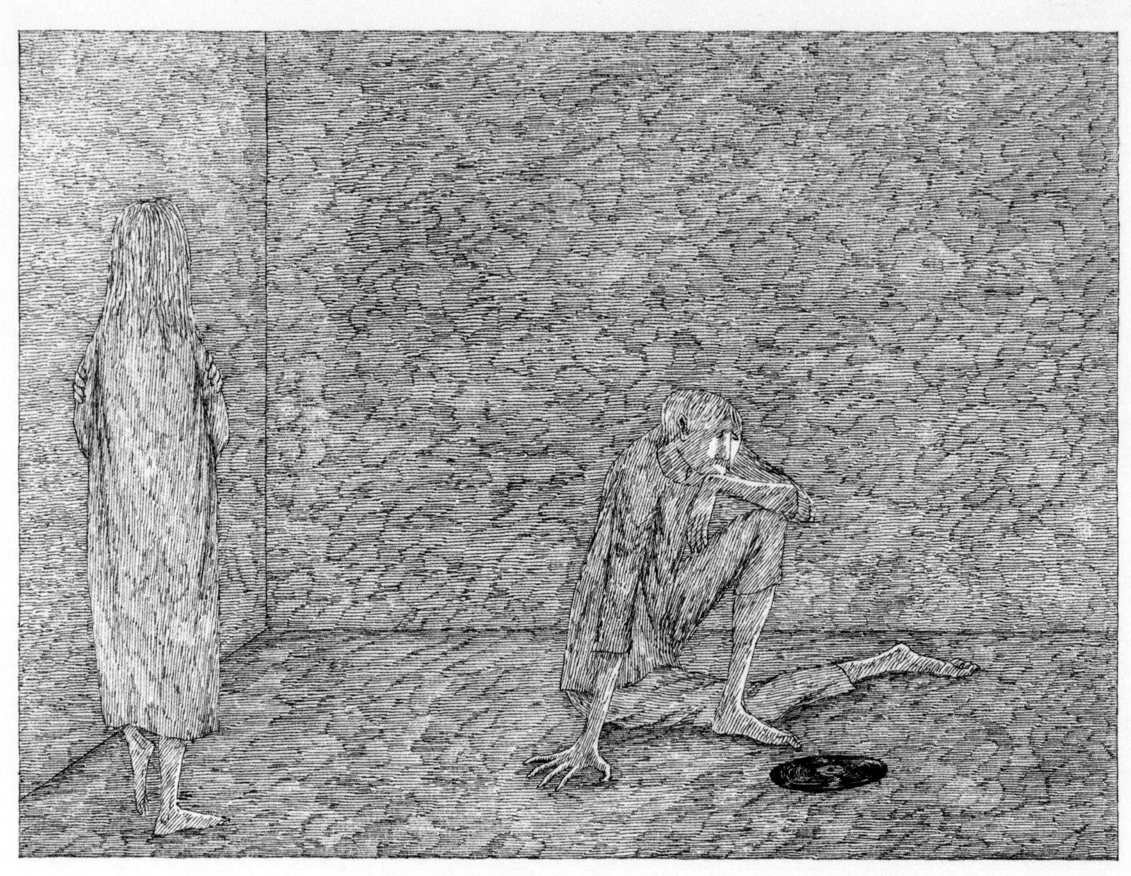

Fig. 1.14

Edward Gorey, "Jasper was
committed to an asylum where
no gramophone was available
to the inmates." Illustration for
The Blue Aspic. New York:
Meredith Press, 1968. Pen and
ink on paper, 7 ¼ × 8 ⁹⁄₁₆ in.
(18.4 × 21.7 cm). The Edward
Gorey Charitable Trust.

Fig. 1.15

Odilon Redon (French,
1840–1916), *Et que des yeux
sans tête flottaient comme des
mollusques (And the eyes without
heads were floating like
mollusks)*, 1896. Lithograph
on paper, 12 ⅛ × 8 ¾ in.
(30.8 × 22.3 cm). Wadsworth
Atheneum Museum of Art,
Hartford, Conn. Bequest of
Edward Gorey, 2001.13.63.

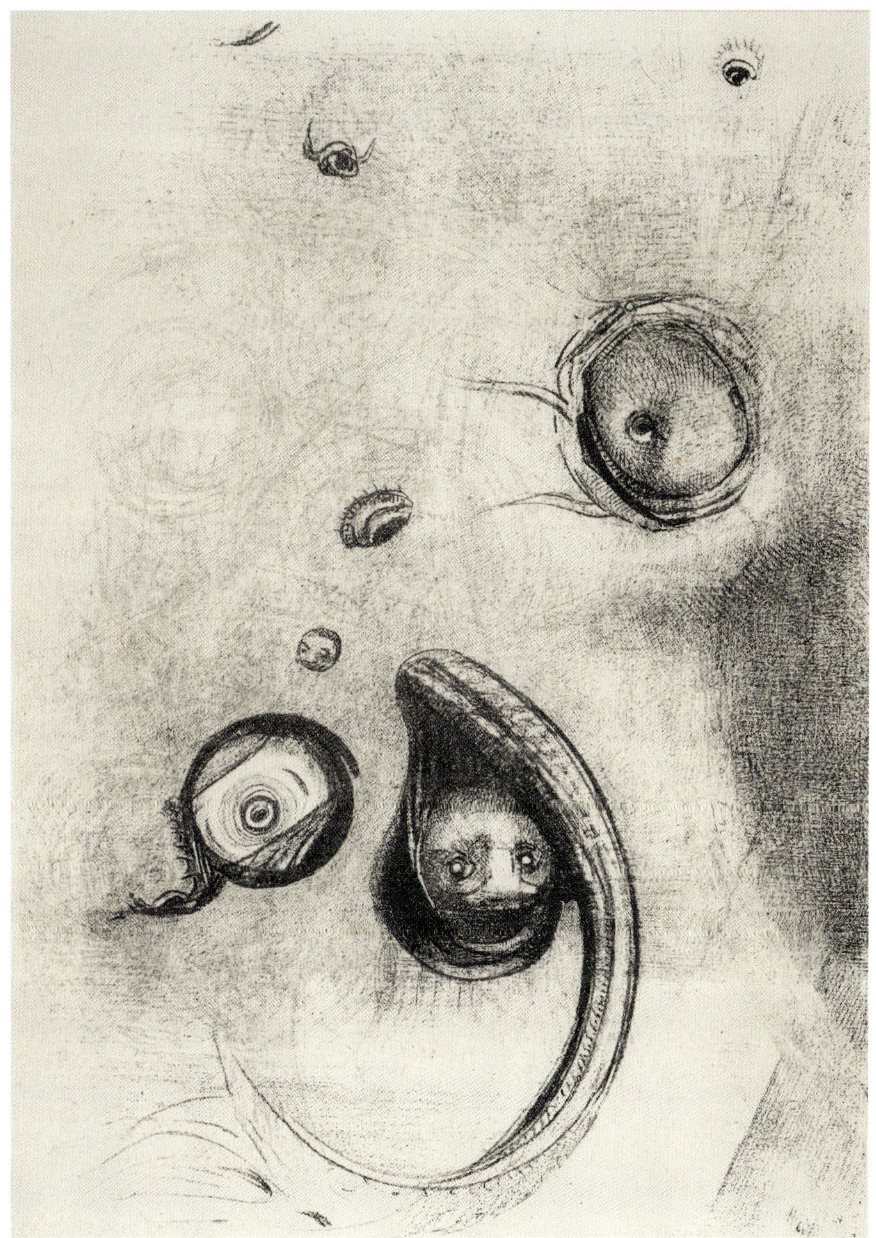

studies, such as *Ombelles*, resonate with Gorey's flora and fauna. In *Ombelles*, the flowers resemble giant hogweed, a highly toxic plant whose sap can burn the skin and eyes, making it a plausible muse for Gorey's *The Evil Garden*, or for "The Plant" in his parody of Tarot cards *The Fantod Pack* (fig. 1.20). "The Plant" symbolized "*July / tics / sexual indecision / impetigo / loss of intellect / misplaced confidence / writhing sickness / loose ends / palsy / assailed credit / dissolution / scandal / worms.*"[34]

In *Naturaliste, rue de l'École de Médecine*, Atget captures the eerie juxtapositions in a macabre window display (fig. 1.21). A dopey-eyed skeleton is surrounded by skulls and other curiosities housed like specimens in clear jars. In the upper portion of the window, a reflection distorts the items on display. Abbott considered the effect of reflections in Atget's works and posed the question "Is there anything more mysterious than reality?" which hints at Gorey's interest in sourcing ideas from current events and the evening news.[35] The skeletons in Atget's street view are echoed by other graphic images Gorey collected (figs. 1.22a,b, 1.23). He owned two anatomical engravings of a skeleton whose posture seems remarkably "alive." Many of Gorey's leading ladies strike a similarly expressive pose, with one arm outstretched and wrist slightly cocked downward.[36] In his collection was a print titled *Life and Death*, a double-picture illusion depicting two children whose heads form the eye sockets of a skull, originally published by Currier and Ives and popularized by a morbid Victorian preoccupation with death.

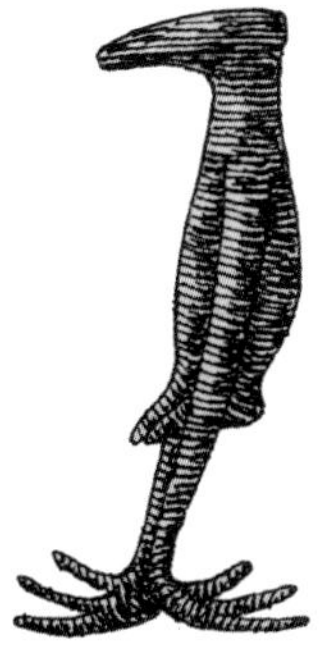

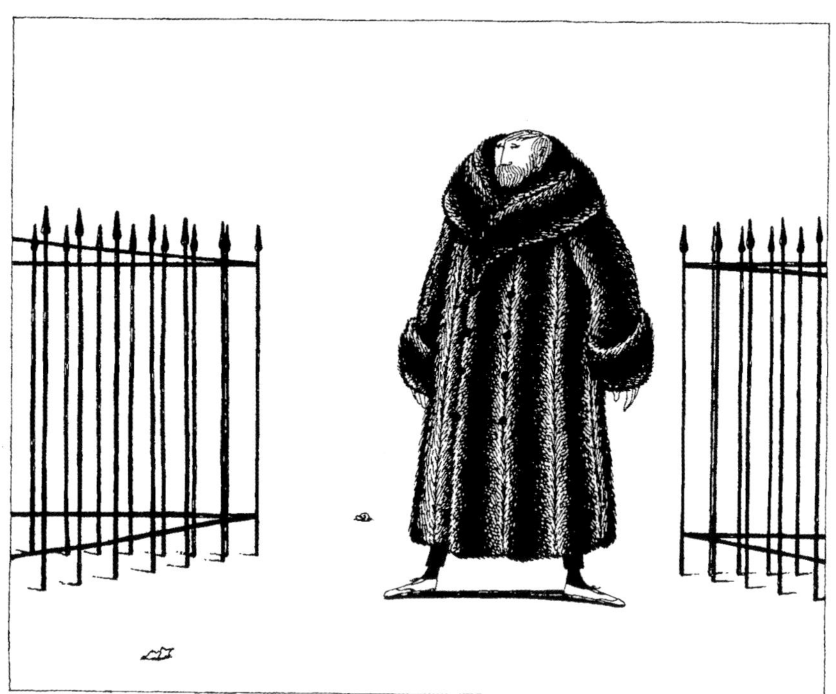

Fig. 1.16

Edward Gorey, "P was a Place he did not know at all." Illustration in *The Chinese Obelisks*. New York: Fantod Press, 1970.

Fig. 1.17

Eugène Atget (French, 1856–1927), printed by Berenice Abbott (American, 1898–1991), *Passageway*, n.d. Gelatin silver print, 6⅝ × 9⅛ in. (16.4 × 22.7 cm). Wadsworth Atheneum Museum of Art, Hartford, Conn. Bequest of Edward Gorey, 2001.13.17.

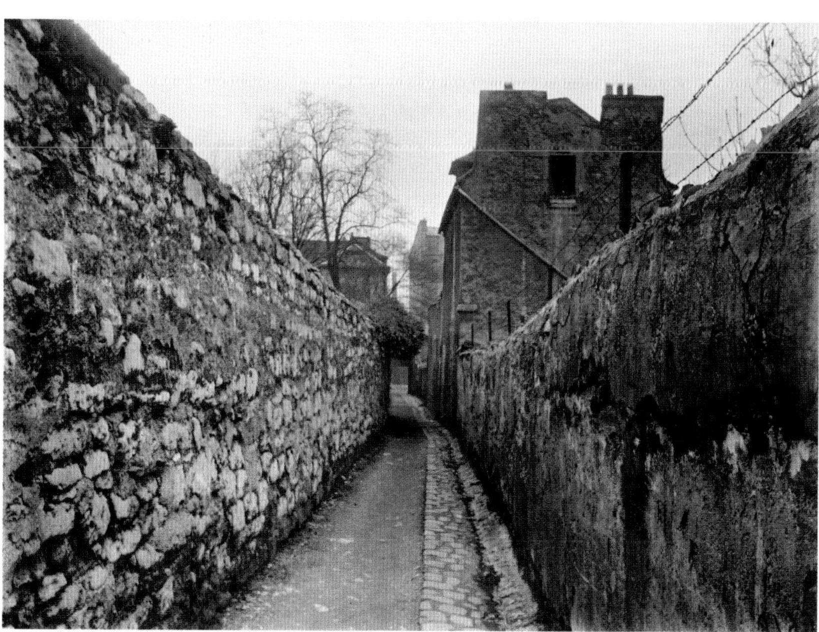

Fig. 1.18

Edward Gorey, "I is for Ida
who drowned in a lake."
Illustration in *The Gashlycrumb
Tinies: Or, After the Outing*.
New York: Simon and
Schuster, 1963.

Fig. 1.19

Eugène Atget, printed by
Berenice Abbott, *Parc de
Rambouillet: (S. ne et Oise)*, n.d.
Gelatin silver print, 6⅝ ×
9³⁄₁₆ in. (16.6 × 22.9 cm).
Wadsworth Atheneum
Museum of Art, Hartford,
Conn. Bequest of Edward
Gorey, 2001.13.15.

Fig. 1.20

Eugène Atget, printed by
Berenice Abbott, *Ombelles*,
before 1900 (original). Gelatin
silver print, 8¹⁵⁄₁₆ × 6¹³⁄₁₆ in.
(22.7 × 17.3 cm). Wadsworth
Atheneum Museum of Art,
Hartford, Conn. Bequest of
Edward Gorey, 2001.13.11.

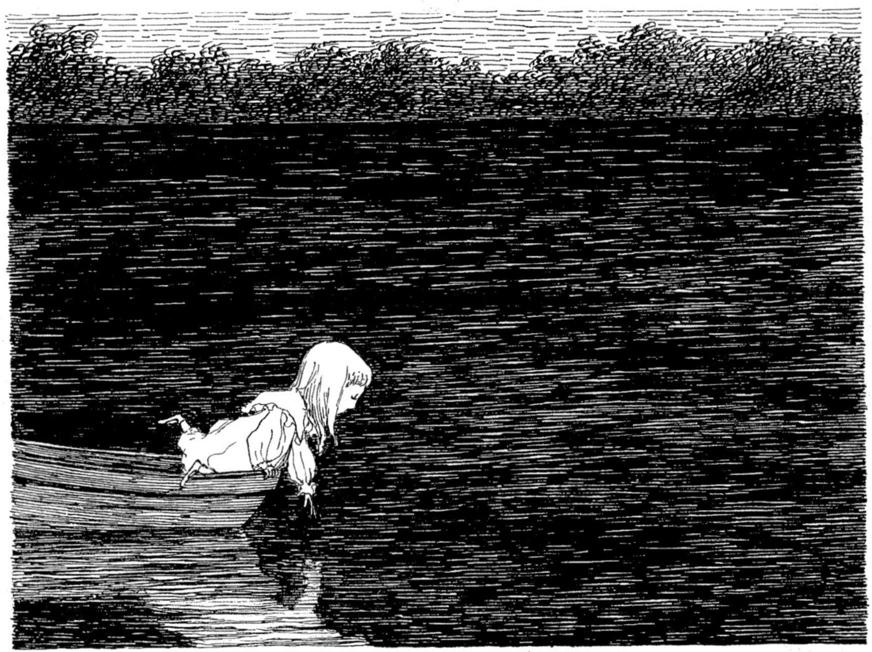

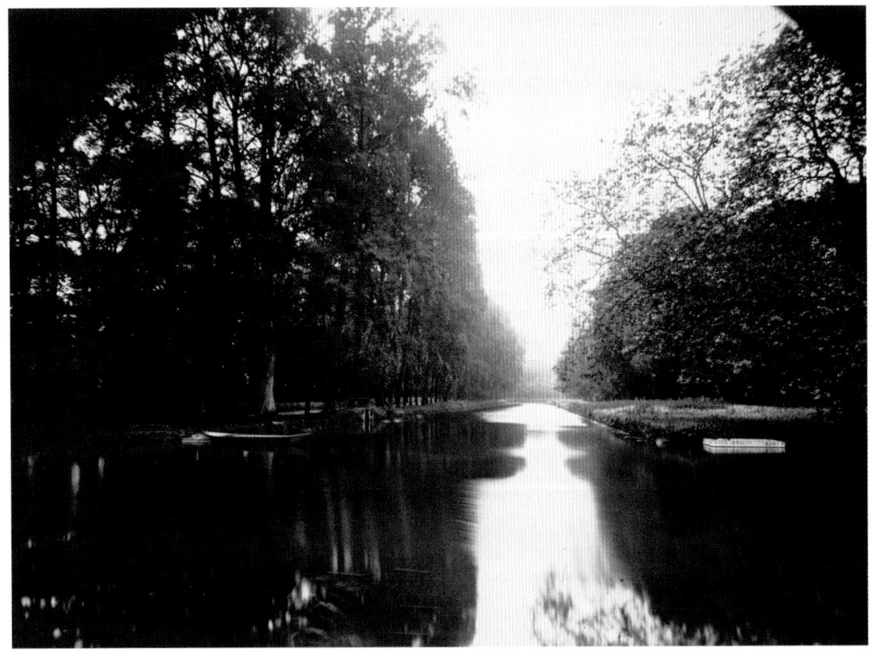

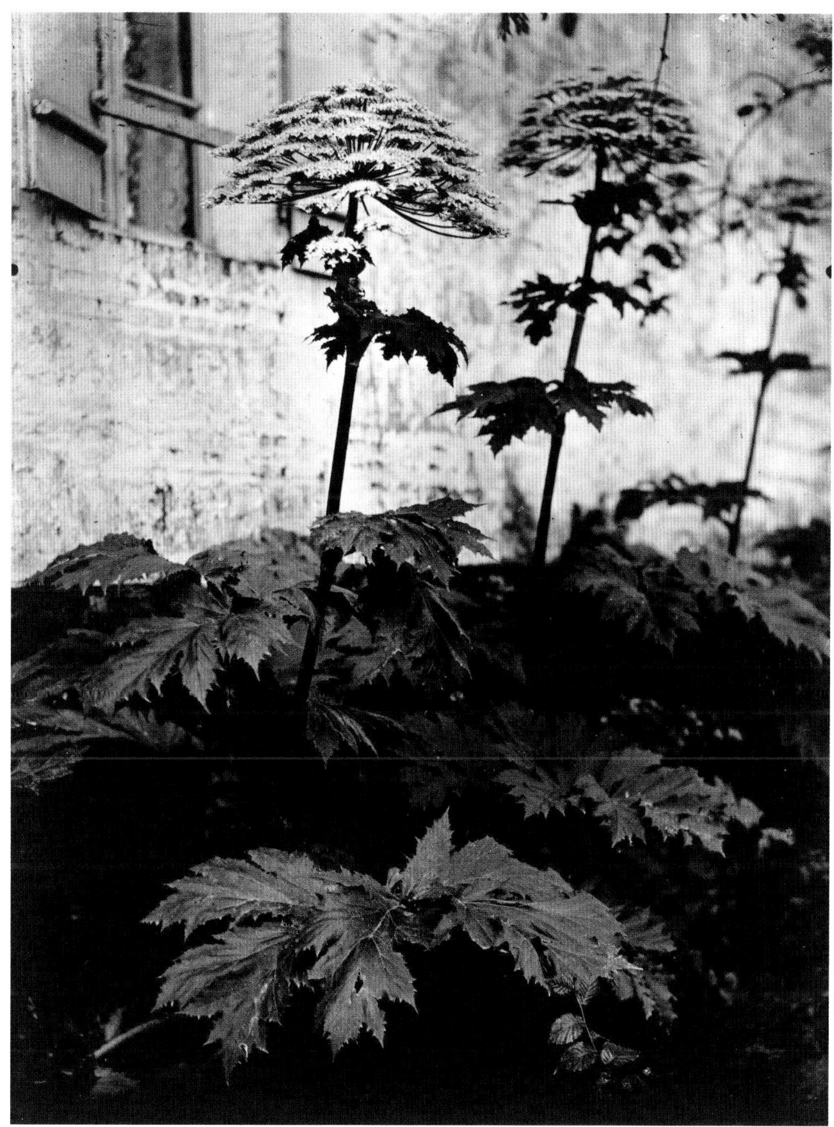

Fig. 1.21

Eugène Atget, printed by
Berenice Abbott, *Naturaliste,
rue de l'École de Médecine*,
1926–27 (original). Gelatin
silver print, 8 ½ × 6 ¾ in.
(21.6 × 17.2 cm). Wadsworth
Atheneum Museum of Art,
Hartford, Conn. Bequest of
Edward Gorey, 2001.13.12.

Fig. 1.22a

Unidentified Artist, *Study of
a Skeleton—Front View*, n.d.
Engraving on paper,
11 × 8 ⅛ in. (28 × 20.7 cm).
Wadsworth Atheneum
Museum of Art, Hartford,
Conn. Bequest of Edward
Gorey, 2001.13.36.

Fig. 1.22b

Unidentified Artist, *Study of a
Skeleton—Rear View*, n.d.
Engraving on paper,
11 × 8 ⅛ in. (28 × 20.7 cm).
Wadsworth Atheneum
Museum of Art, Hartford,
Conn. Bequest of Edward
Gorey, 2001.13.37.

Fig. 1.23

Unidentified Artist, after
Currier and Ives, *Life and
Death*, c. 1885.
Chromolithograph on paper,
10 ⁵⁄₁₆ × 8 ⁹⁄₁₆ in. (26.2 ×
21.8 cm). Wadsworth
Atheneum Museum of Art,
Hartford, Conn. Bequest of
Edward Gorey, 2001.13.41.

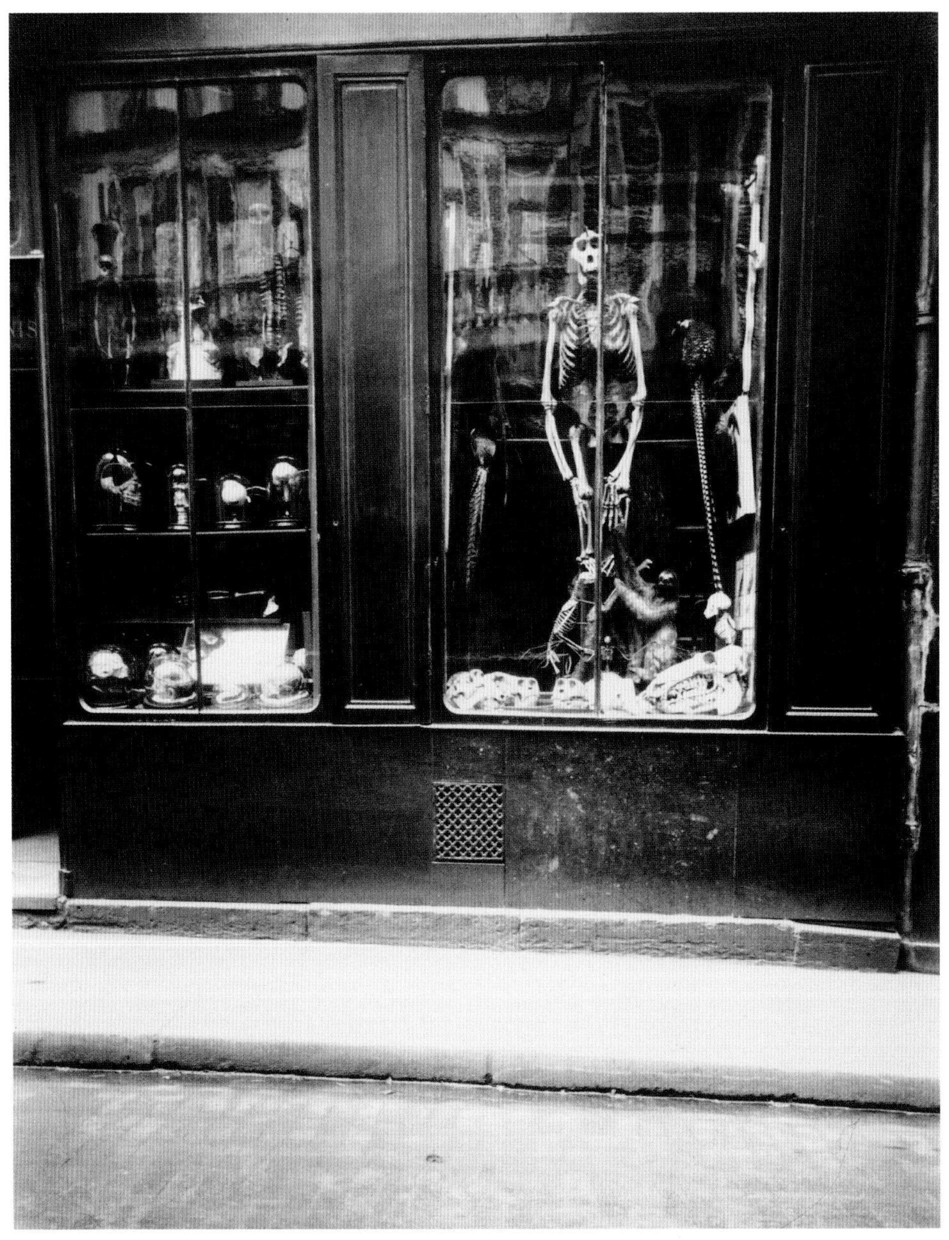

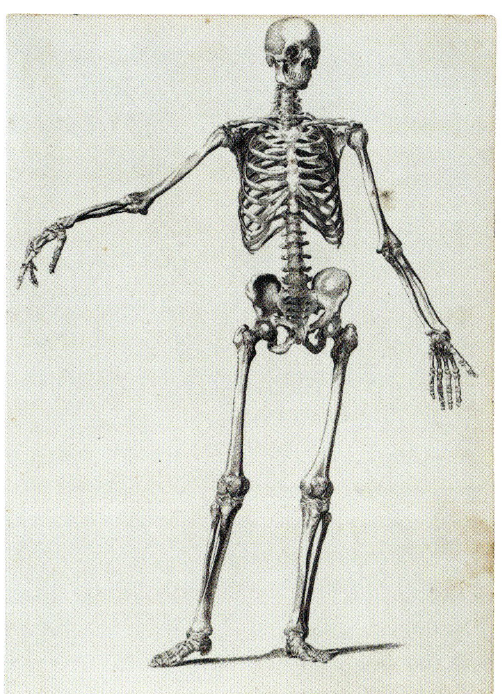 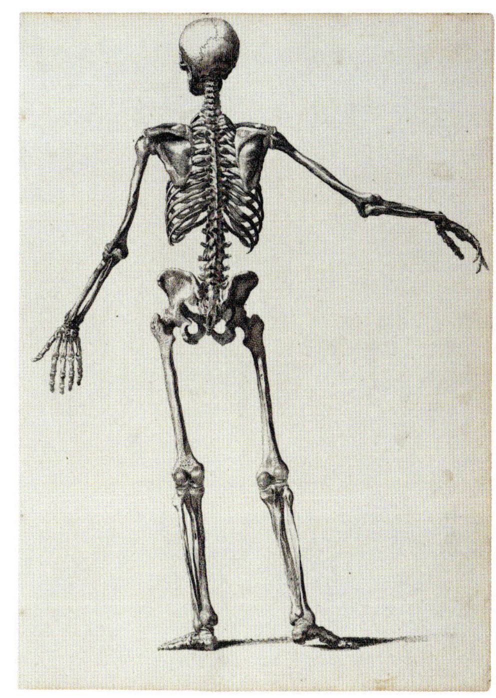

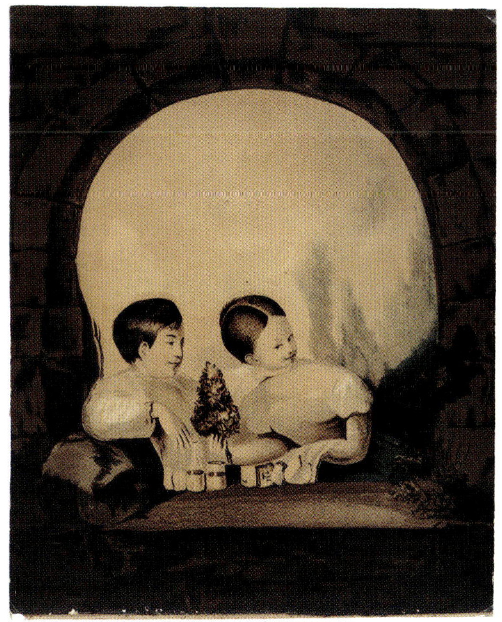

The American Art

As a collector of modest means, Gorey initially spent a few hundred dollars on a single work of art.[37] This changed in 1977 when Gorey became involved in the revival of Bram Stoker's *Dracula* on Broadway. The show won the Tony Award for Most Innovative Production of a Revival, and Gorey won a Tony for Best Costume Design. The production's multiyear run afforded Gorey the money for a down payment on his Cape Cod home, earning it the moniker "the house that 'Drac' built." This success also enabled Gorey to purchase more expensive works of art, which he did almost immediately. Within months of the *Dracula* premiere, Gorey acquired four drawings by his favorite American artist, Charles Burchfield, spending nearly ten times what he was accustomed to laying out. Gorey admired the modernist's "pulsating nature" and "ghostliness."[38] In Burchfield's playful *Study of Bats in Flight*, the two bats at the center of the page are prominent and distinct; they have expressive faces that give them an oddly human expression. Burchfield's drawing bears comparison with Gorey's *Dracula* set designs (figs. 1.24, 1.25). In Gorey's bat-embellished drop curtain set design, for example, everything is batty: the clouds, the railings, the creatures scaling the curtains; and a similar playfulness informs Burchfield's drawing. Gorey's admiration for the nocturnal creatures also extended to his stories—see, for example, *The Gilded Bat*— and the countless hand-sewn stuffed bats he made.[39] In his life and in death, Gorey was concerned for animals and specifically bats. Another part of his legacy was to create a charitable trust whose sole purpose was to support various animal welfare groups including the Bat Conservation International Foundation in Austin, Texas.

The haunted landscapes in Burchfield's *Nature's Mystic Spiral* and *September Mood* appealed to Gorey's gothic taste (figs. 1.26, 1.27). In *Nature's Mystic Spiral*, a radiating orb with hazy, hypnotic rings hovers above a mysterious form. Burchfield's journals regularly described his unusual sensory reactions to trees, birds, and clouds, often referred to as synesthesia, which sometimes bordered on hallucination, and in this condition he created a rich visual vocabulary of semiabstract forms.[40] This included the flame-like shapes coming off a house in *September Mood*. A similarly ominous scene is echoed in Gorey's *The Willowdale Handcar*. The story follows three friends who discover an unattended handcar at the railroad station, and their ill-fated journey down the tracks. They become distant observers of life as they pass by strange and tragic events, including a burning house that appears as if borrowed from a Burchfield landscape (fig. 1.28).

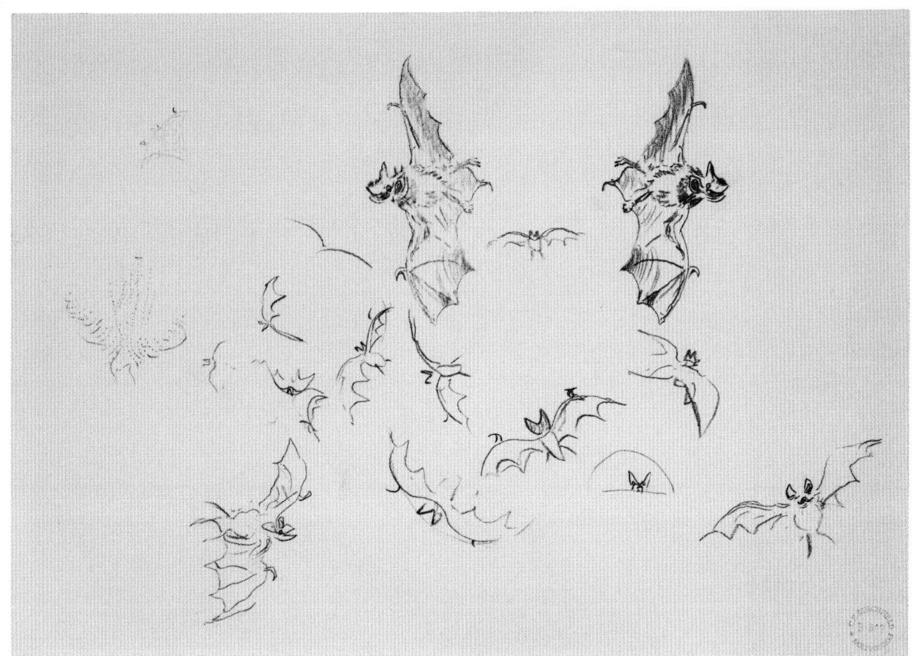

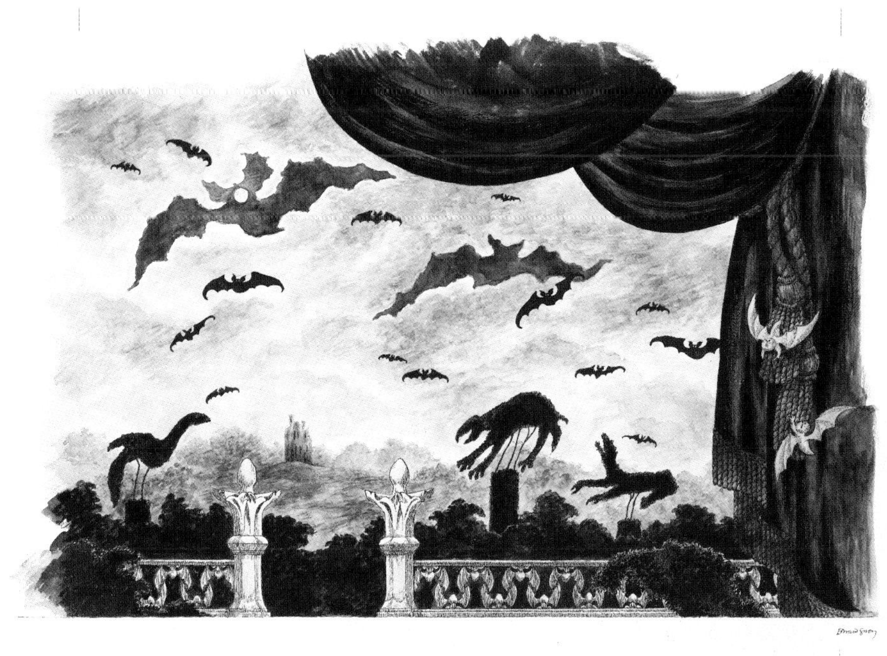

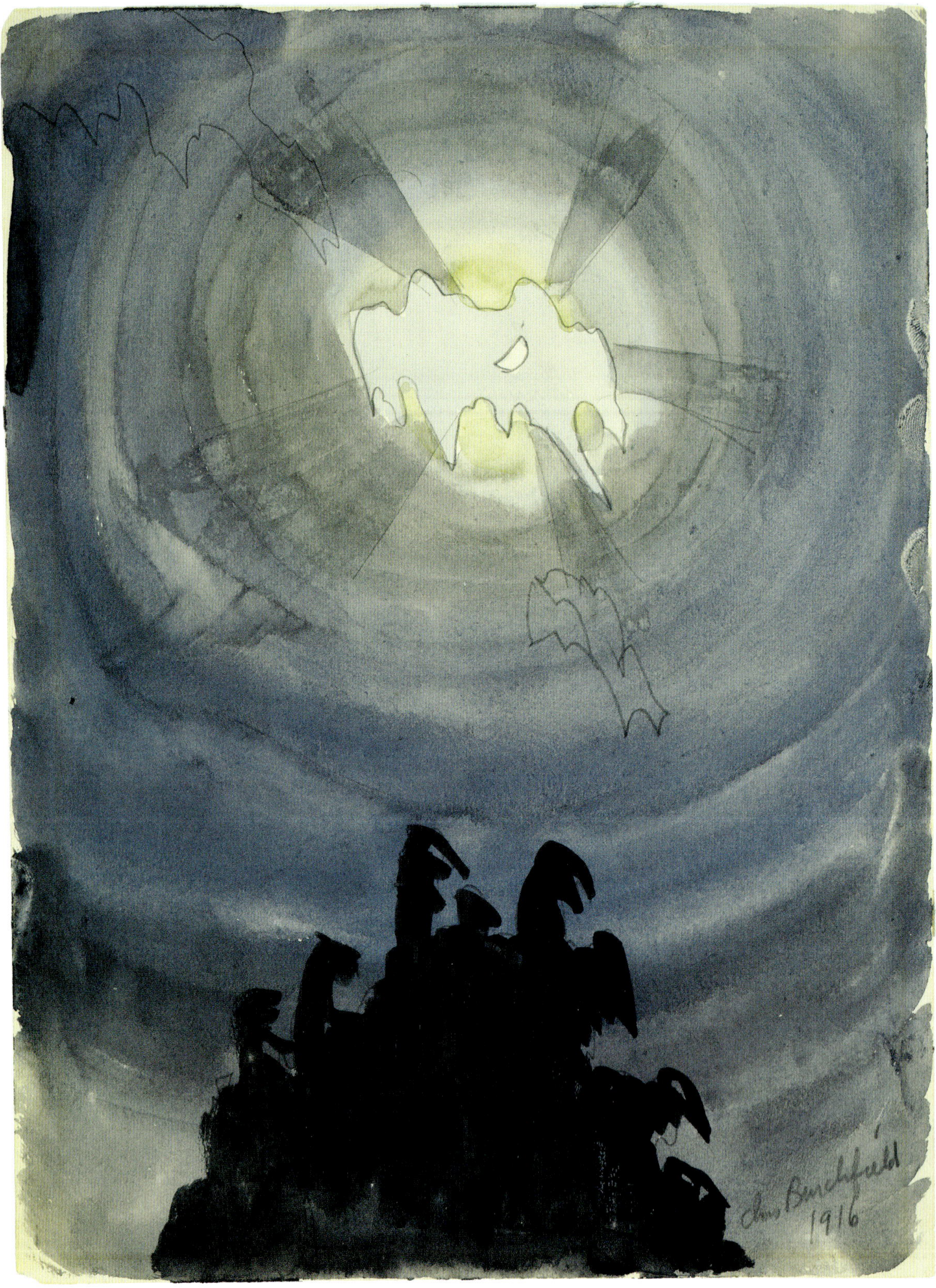
Chas Burchfield
1916

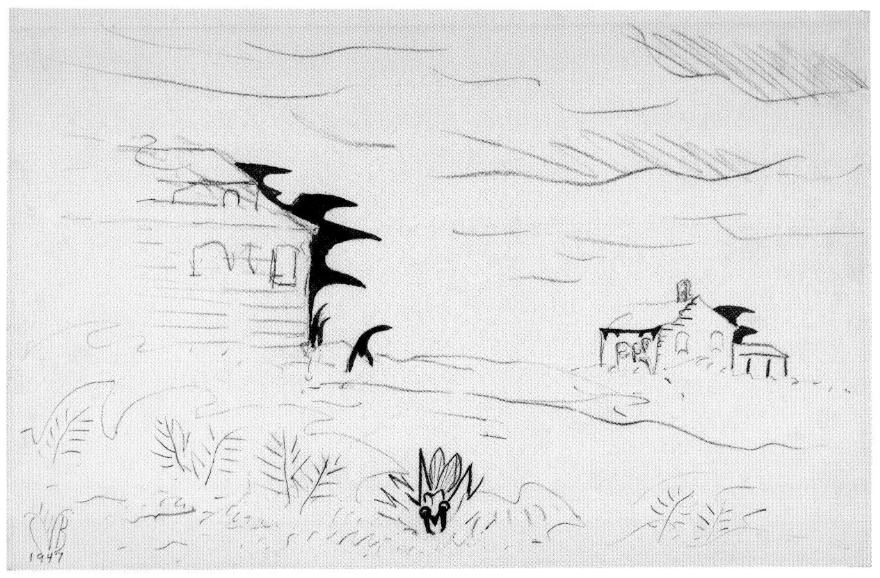

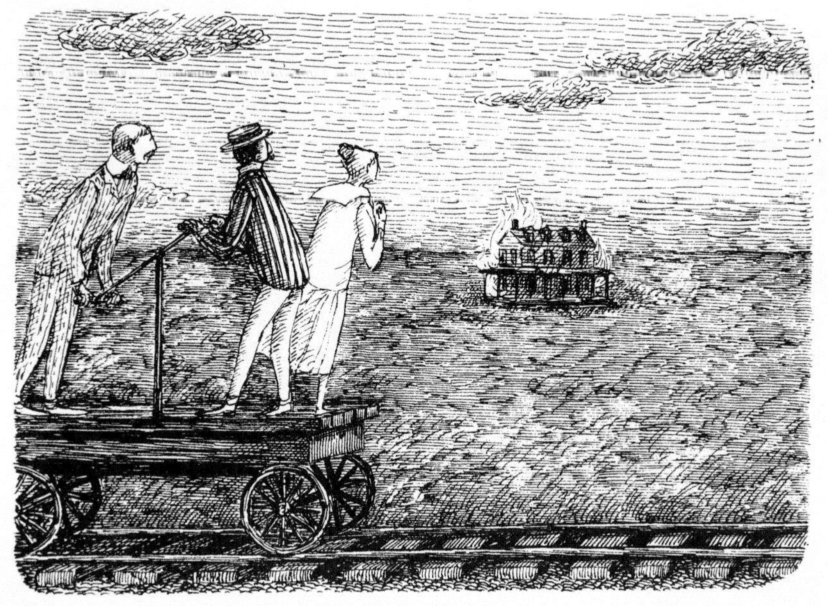

Fig. 1.26

Charles Ephraim Burchfield, *Nature's Mystic Spiral*, 1916. Watercolor and graphite on paper, 12 × 9 in. (30.5 × 22.9 cm). Wadsworth Atheneum Museum of Art, Hartford, Conn. Bequest of Edward Gorey, 2001.13.32.

Fig. 1.27

Charles Ephraim Burchfield, *September Mood*, 1947. Conté crayon and ink on paper, 10 7/16 × 16 7/8 in. (26.6 × 42.9 cm). Wadsworth Atheneum Museum of Art, Hartford, Conn. Bequest of Edward Gorey, 2001.13.35.

Fig. 1.28

Edward Gorey, "A few minutes after they were on their way again, / they saw a house burning down in a field. / 'Whooee!' said Sam. 'The engines will never be in time to save it.'" Illustration in *The Willowdale Handcar; Or the Return of the Black Doll*. Indianapolis: The Bobbs-Merrill Company, Inc.: 1962.

Kevin McDermott, *Entrance Room*, from *Elephant House*, 2000. Gelatin silver print. Collection of the artist.

The Folk Art

Gorey collected almost as many works of art made by unknown or self-taught artists as by those formally or academically trained. Outnumbered only by his collection of ten prints by Atget, nine American landscapes commonly described as sandpaper drawings or sand paintings were among Gorey's acquisitions.[41] He displayed them together as a group above the fireplace mantel in his front room, lending them singular prominence (fig. 1.29). The sandpaper drawings were made by amateur artists, primarily women, who taught themselves the technique popularized in America by the 1835 publication of B. F. Gandee's *The Artist or, Young Ladies' Instructor in Ornamental Painting, etc.* A composition was drawn using black or white chalk on a prepared paper often treated with marble dust, to emphasize gradations of light and shadow, rather than line. Gorey was proud of his early recognition of this underappreciated genre.[42]

The subjects frequently depicted were popular tourist sites like Niagara Falls or Mount Vernon, or illustrations sourced from such magazines as *Sartain's* or *Currier & Ives*. Gorey owned one of the most popular images ever translated into the medium, *The Magic Lake,* based on a well-known illustration to Henry Beck Hirst's romantic poem "The Pilgrim of Love," published in 1852 (fig. 1.30). In the scene, Brunhilda is a girl plagued by dreams and awaits her mysterious king, who is actually a spirit of the night.[43] An illustration in Gorey's wordless tale *The Prune People* closely resembles the cave-like setting of *The Magic Lake*, and there is an uncanny resemblance between the two depictions of figures in a cave seen from behind (fig. 1.31). The idea to compose a story about prune-headed people was possibly inspired by other sources as well. He owned a valentine of a prune-headed older man — wearing a similar top hat — who seeks the attention of a young, beautiful girl.[44]

There are other striking motifs and settings in the folk art drawings that remind us of Gorey's gothic settings (figs. 1.32, 1.33). A landscape featuring a church surrounded by a graveyard offers a more general context for Gorey's stories, whereas *View of Ruins and Obelisk by a Lake* is a more specific precursor.[45] Obelisks appear with some frequency in his work. Ancient monoliths adorn the front and back covers of Gorey's *The Chinese Obelisks* — though they have no clear bearing on the plot — and cats have chance encounters with the structures, as in number eight in *Category*, Gorey's wordless series of fifty dancing cats. In *The Epiplectic Bicycle*, Embley and Yewbert return home from their adventures only to discover an ancient obelisk "raised to their memory 173 years ago" (fig. 1.34).

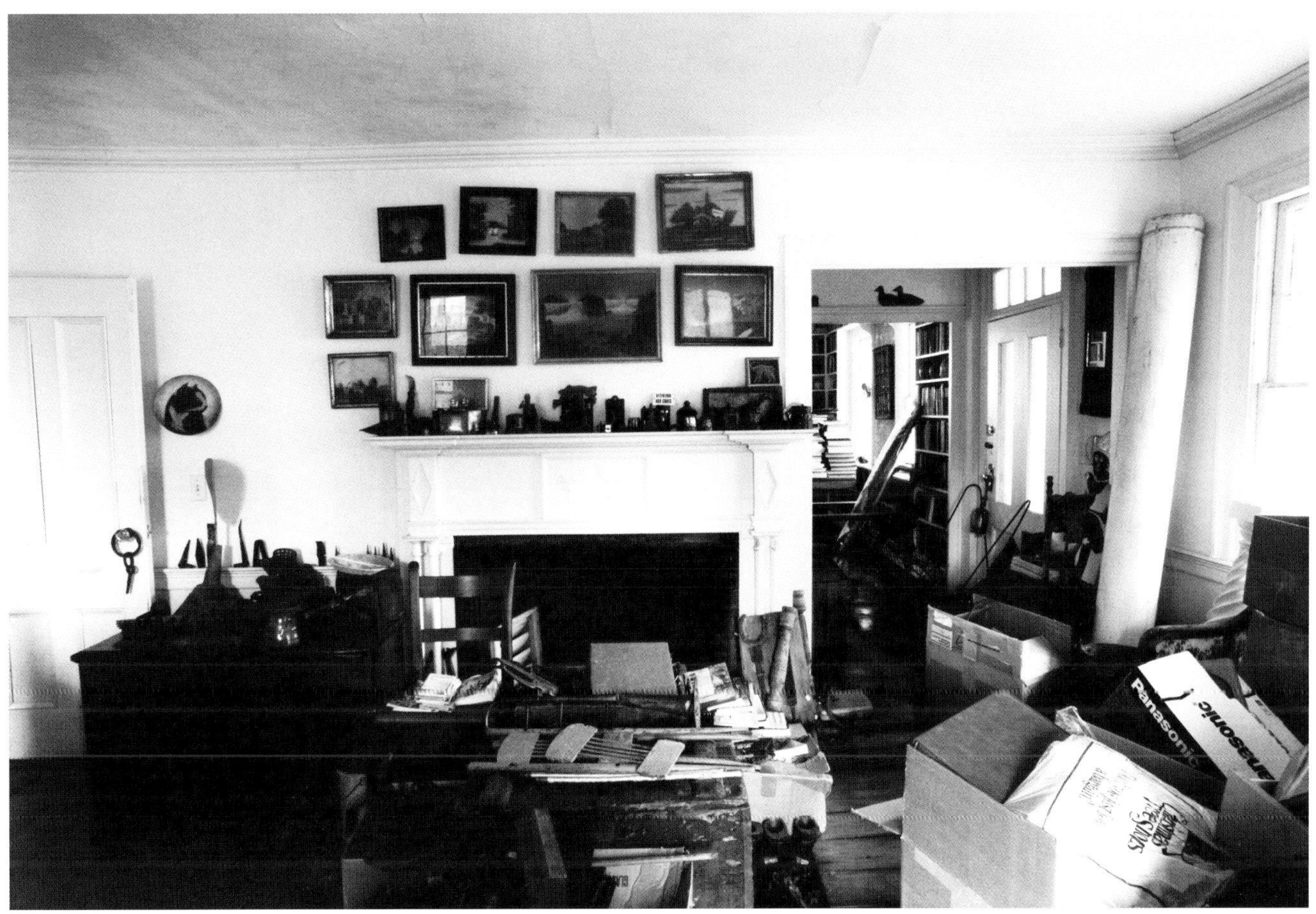

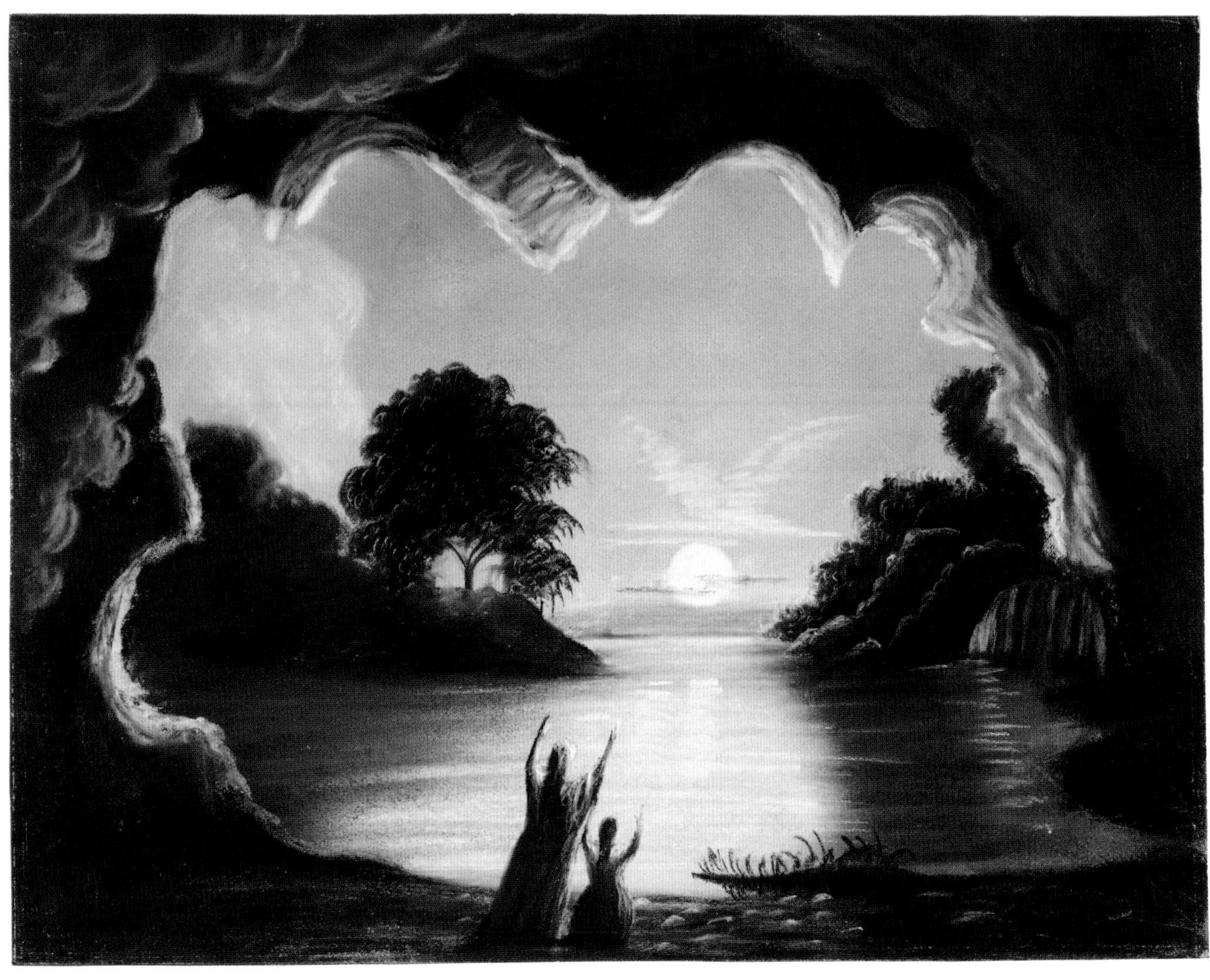

Fig. 1.30

Unidentified Artist (American), *The Magic Lake*, c. 1850. Chalk or charcoal on marble-dusted paper, 7 ¼ × 9 ½ in. (18.5 × 24.2 cm). Wadsworth Atheneum Museum of Art, Hartford, Conn. Bequest of Edward Gorey, 2001.13.2.

Fig. 1.31

Edward Gorey. Illustration in *The Prune People*. New York: Albondocani Press, 1983.

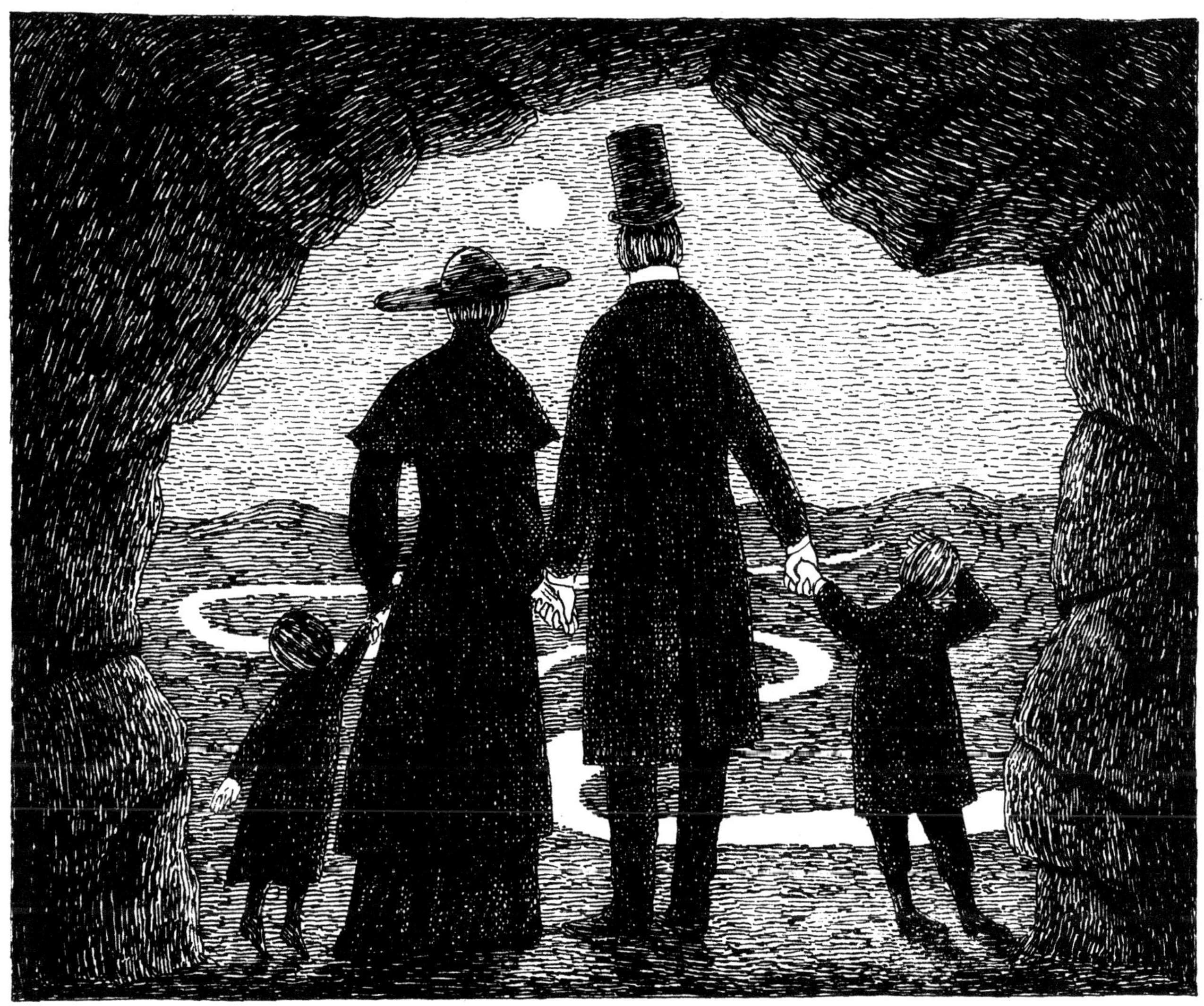

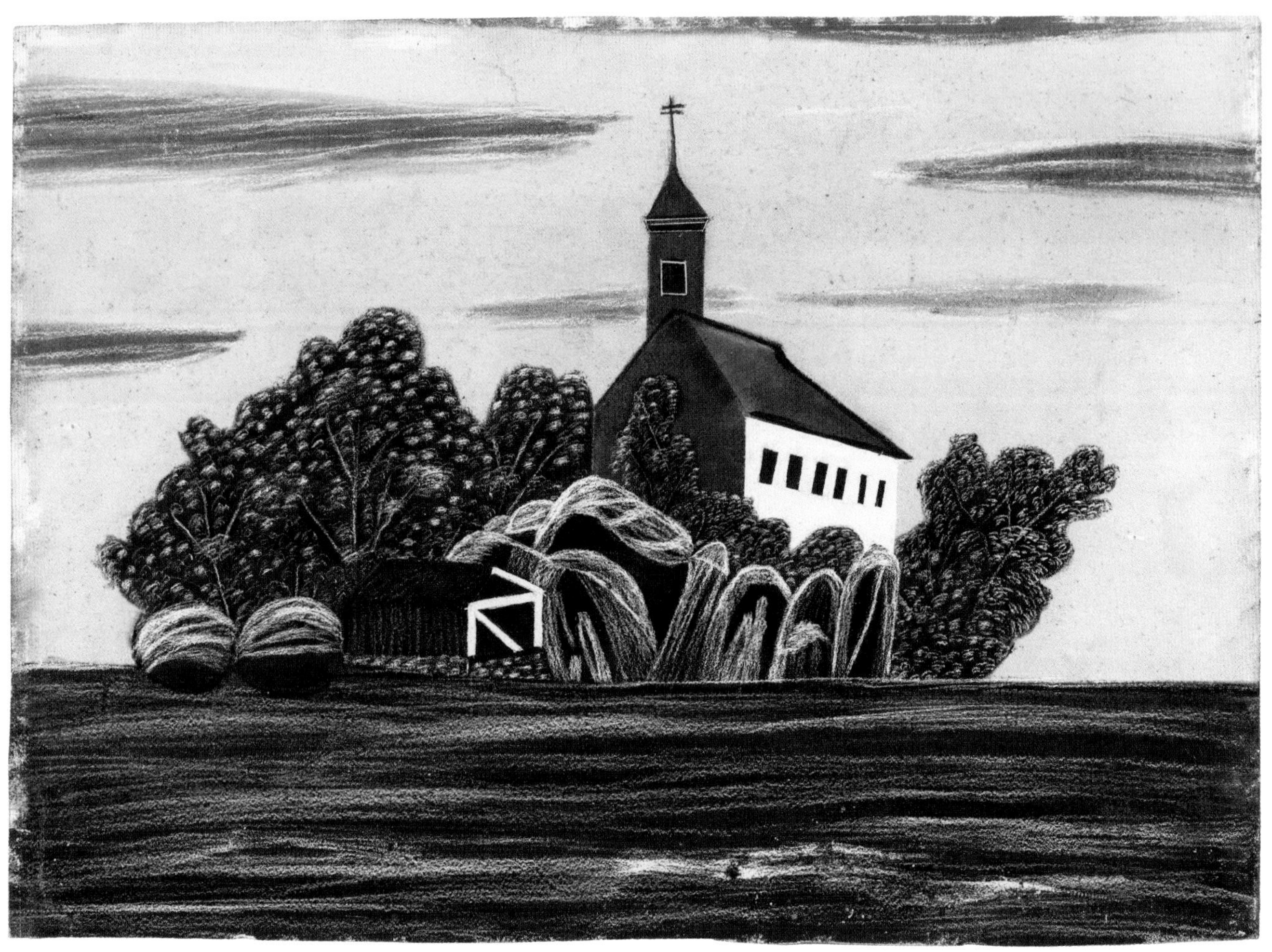

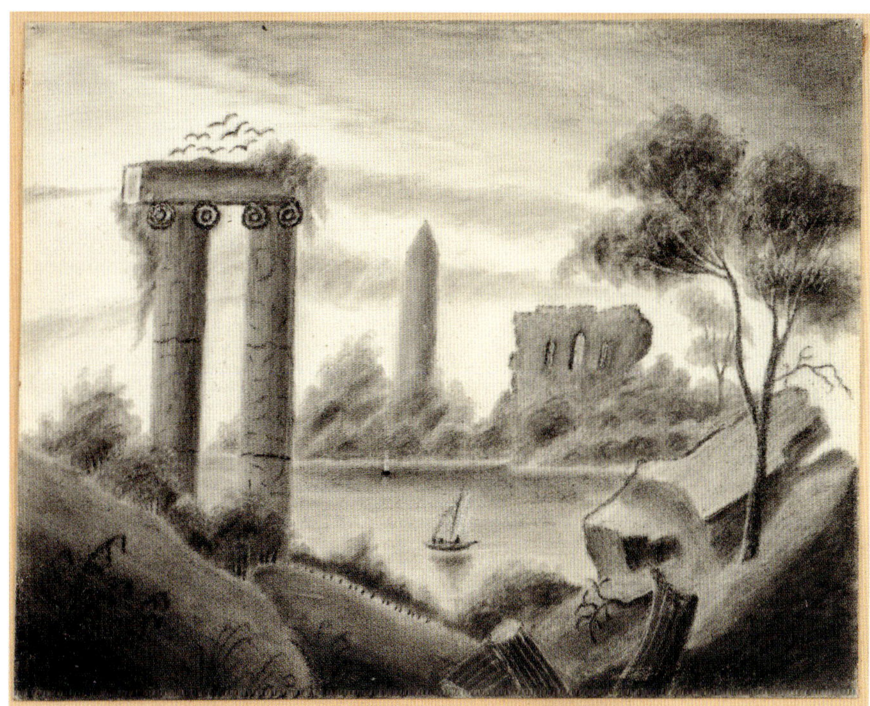

Fig. 1.32

Unidentified Artist (American), *Church and Graveyard*, c. 1850. Chalk or charcoal on marble-dusted paper, 9⅝ × 13⁵⁄₁₆ in. (24.5 × 35.4 cm). Wadsworth Atheneum Museum of Art, Hartford, Conn. Bequest of Edward Gorey, 2001.13.5.

Fig. 1.33

Unidentified Artist (American), *View of Ruins and Obelisk by a Lake*, c. 1850. Chalk or charcoal on marble-dusted paper, 8 × 10¹⁵⁄₁₆ in. (20.4 × 27.8 cm). Wadsworth Atheneum Museum of Art, Hartford, Conn. Bequest of Edward Gorey, 2001.13.1.

Fig. 1.34

Edward Gorey, "To discover there was nothing to be seen but an obelisk." Illustration in *The Epiplectic Bicycle*. New York: Dodd, Mead & Company, 1969.

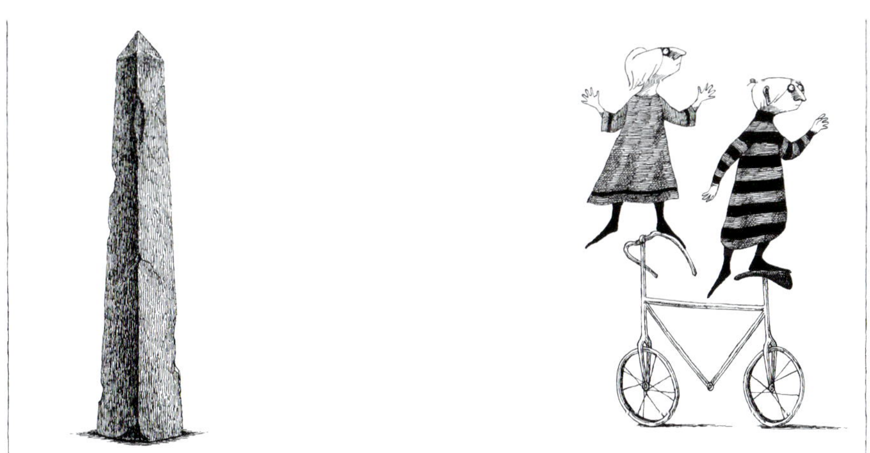

to discover there was nothing to be seen but an obelisk

If the genre of folk art has a spectrum—ranging from entirely unknown or decidedly anonymous artists to those who were "known" and thoroughly researched—Gorey embraced both extremes. In addition to the sandpaper drawings, Gorey owned three small hooked rugs made by women in Labrador and Newfoundland, Canada, for the Grenfell Company, and a pencil drawing by Bill Traylor, one of the most important self-taught African American artists of the twentieth century: Gorey purchased *Camel*, a double-sided drawing on cardboard with a horse on the verso, in 1988 (fig. 1.35). Born into slavery in Benton, Alabama, in 1854, Traylor worked on a cotton plantation, first as an enslaved worker and then as a sharecropper. At the age of eighty-four, he moved to the segregated capital city of Montgomery. Elderly and homeless, Traylor began to draw captivating images of people and animals on discarded cardboard in a bold, graphic style. In the late 1970s, Traylor's work was discovered by the art world and exhibited in galleries and museums. His increased exposure, especially in the New York galleries, coincided with Gorey's remaining few years in the city. In Gorey's archive are exhibition announcements, articles, and reviews pertaining to Traylor's work that he carefully filed over the years.

Traylor's camel hovers at the center of the sheet without any background design or contextualization, like a cartoon waiting for a caption. Gorey's work shares certain formal qualities with Traylor's. The strange shapes of Traylor's animal are mirrored in the long legs and oversized features of Gorey's fantastic beings, such as the Wuggly Ump (fig. 1.36, see also fig. 3.8). Like Gorey's drawings, Traylor's line work is economical, but his forms are full of imagination. Both artists' images are so powerful that they seem to tell a story, encouraging readers/viewers to imagine a plot on their own.

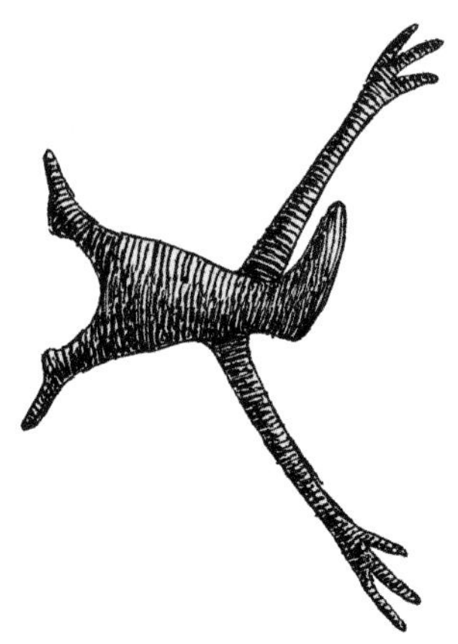

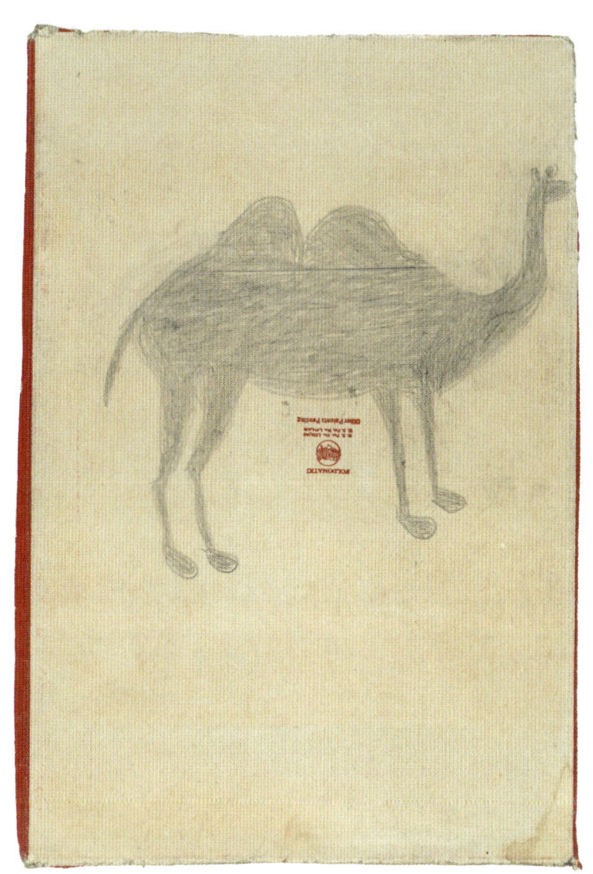

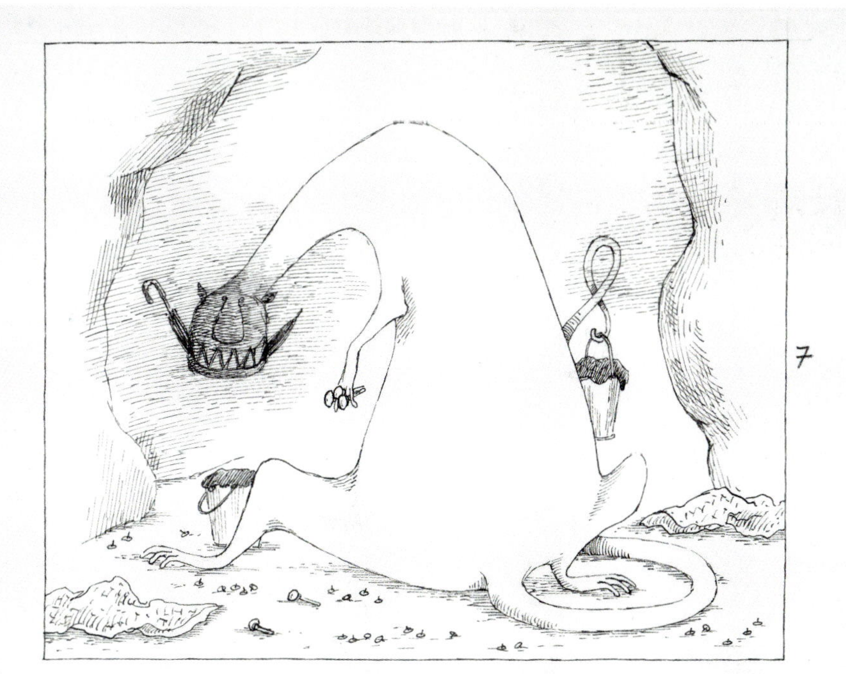

7

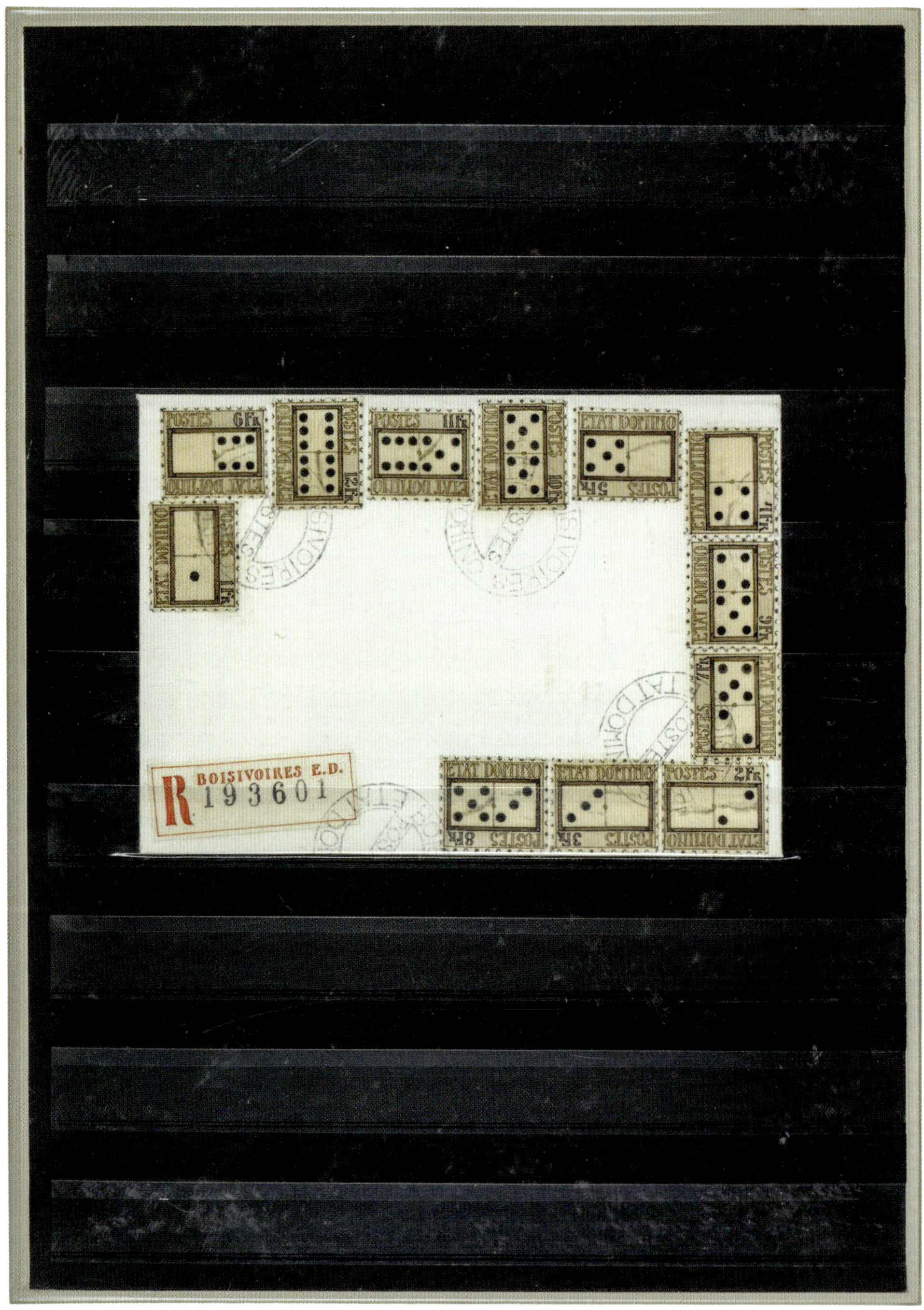

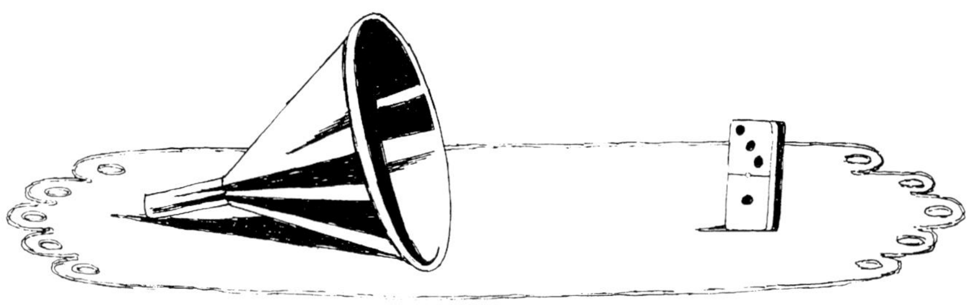

The Contemporary Art

Much of the artwork Gorey collected was created a century earlier and, when
it was topographical, depicted places he would never visit in person. Yet he
also actively acquired artwork of his own day and pictures made by artist
friends, including several paintings, drawings, and collages dating to the 1970s
and 1980s. Between 1974 and 1975, he purchased three works by Donald
Evans. Evans remains an obscure American artist, in part because of his tragic
death at age thirty-one in an apartment fire in Amsterdam; moreover, his
preferred artistic genre was by no means mainstream. He conceived of fictional
countries and hand-drew postage stamps for them, at their actual size.[16]
These small-scale works have an aesthetic and intellectual kinship with
Gorey's works. Evans, like Gorey, delighted in wordplay—in English and in
French—elements of the absurd, and meticulously handcrafted details.

One of Evans's collages, *Domino*, is in the Wadsworth's collection
(fig. 1.37).[47] The domino-shaped postage stamps are exquisitely drawn, and
their surface detail includes trompe l'oeil rivets and cracks, inspired by the
artist's own ebony and ivory set. The piece contains humorous allusions
using invented French words and phrases. The words "Etat Domino," literally
"Domino State," appear on each stamp. Evans created the circular postmark
for the invented country's post office in the capital of Boisivoires (translation:
Ivorywoods).[48] Every textural detail is rendered as convincing as possible,
from the hand-perforated edges to the cancellation marks. Gorey, too, enjoyed
games and created his own fortune-telling cards and playful interactive books
where the reader turns bisected or precut pages to create combinations of
different characters or creatures. Gorey also relied upon inanimate objects for
his humor. In his *Menaced Objects Series*, the "Domino Intimidated by a Funnel,"
he impossibly and absurdly attributes feeling to a domino (fig. 1.38). In real life,
we never encounter Gorey's menacing objects, just as we cannot visit Evans's

Edward Gorey, *Phantasmagorey*, 1974. Pen and ink with collage on paper, 8 × 10 in. (20.3 × 25.4 cm). Collection of Clifford Ross.

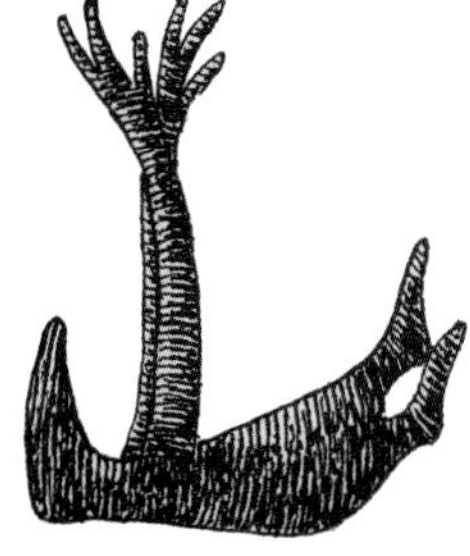

invented worlds. Nonetheless, we can appreciate how profoundly both artists, each in his own way, subversively threatened the ordinary in their art.

In Gorey's collection of contemporary art were works created by artists he knew personally, including drawings made by the English artist Glen Baxter, illustrations by George Booth, and a painting made by Clifford Ross.[49] As a high school senior interested in books of all kinds, with no knowledge of Gorey, he acquired *The Willowdale Handcar* in a secondhand book shop in the spring of 1970. Ross's curiosity was blessed by a bit of serendipity when he came across the Gotham Book Mart, a Manhattan cultural haven for bibliophiles and authors, during a walk later that same year. Serendipitously, Ross learned that "Mr. Gorey" was in fact present, holed up in the back office, and from that first meeting, the two developed a friendship. As Ross recalled, "He never positioned himself as a mentor, but became one in the form of a truly inspiring figure — the definition of an artist obsessively pursuing his vision — with absurdly wide-ranging interests fueling his vision."[50] For his senior thesis in the Art History Department at Yale University, Ross curated the first survey of Gorey's work, *Phantasmagorey*, at Sterling Memorial Library. The signature image created for the cover of Ross's catalogue for the exhibition, the *Phantasmagorey* drawing, remains a metaphorical self-portrait of Gorey (fig. 1.39). Each vignette is a facet of Gorey's creative worlds: femmes fatales, cats, books, a fur-coated self-portrait, bats and the night, children, and decorative urns. Ross prefaced the catalogue with the definition of "phantasmagoria": "a complex succession of things seen or imagined." No other single concept or word has come closer to defining Edward Gorey.

During a visit to Ross's studio in the mid-1980s, Gorey selected a small-scale landscape of a storm-filled sky over Long Island for his own collection (fig. 1.40). Ross sees the "free and loose oil painting" as "the antithesis of Gorey's style" but dark at the same time.[51] With its violent, unsettled sky, the painting sets a mood akin to the threatening atmosphere of many Gorey tales. At that time, Ross was an artist in transition; a year or two after that studio visit, he was experimenting with large-scale mixed-media paintings using papier-mâché. On a subsequent visit to Ross's studio Gorey's curiosity, and a quick push from Ross, led Gorey to sculpt tiny finger puppets in the studio (fig. 1.41). These playful objects fused Gorey's love of fantastic creatures with theatricality. He made these fragile, delicate puppets for many years, continually adding costumes and props for various staged performances.

Gorey also collected the work of Albert York, an artist so reclusive that Gorey is unlikely to have been able to meet him, even if he had tried. Between

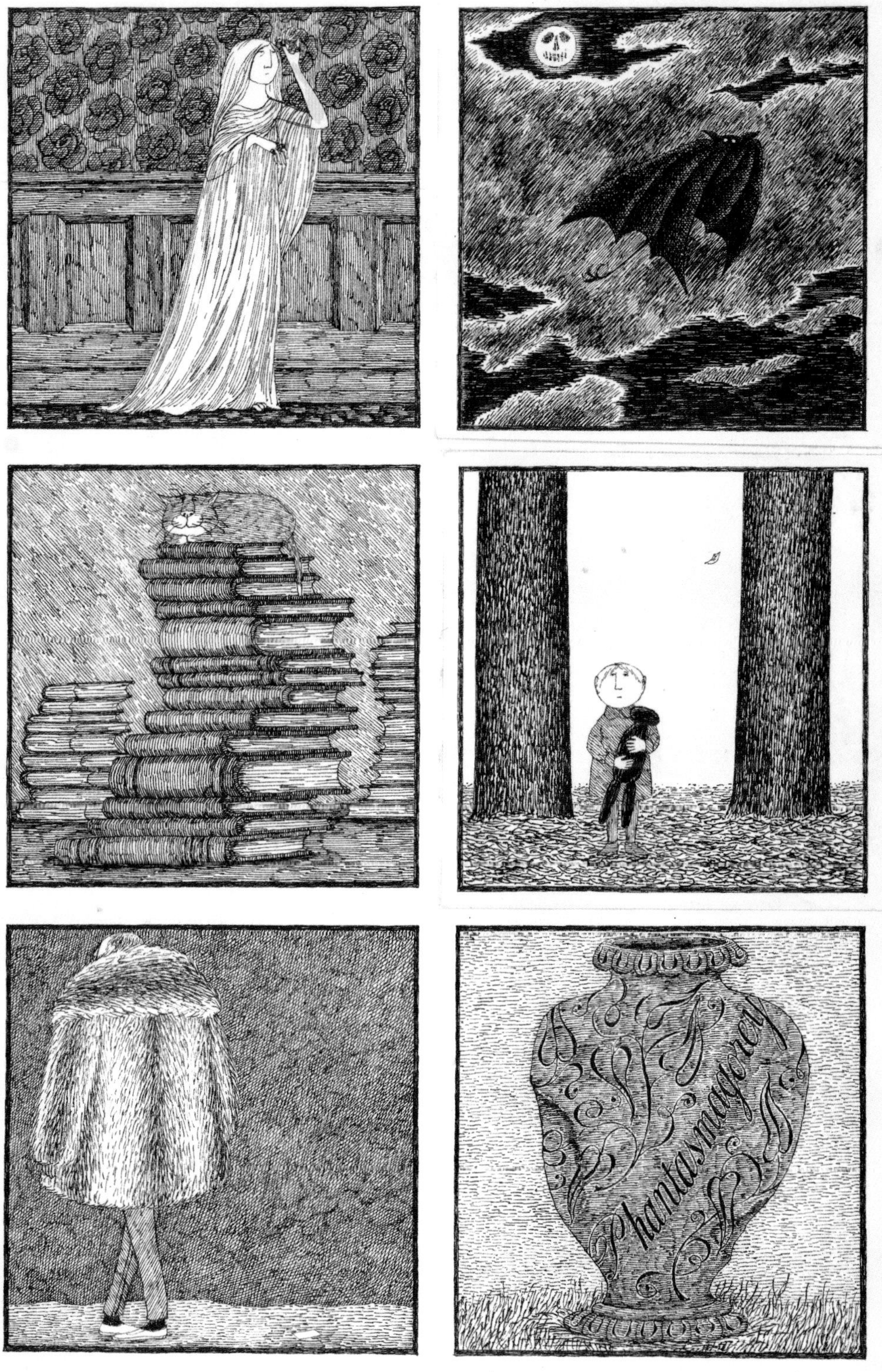
Phantasmagorey

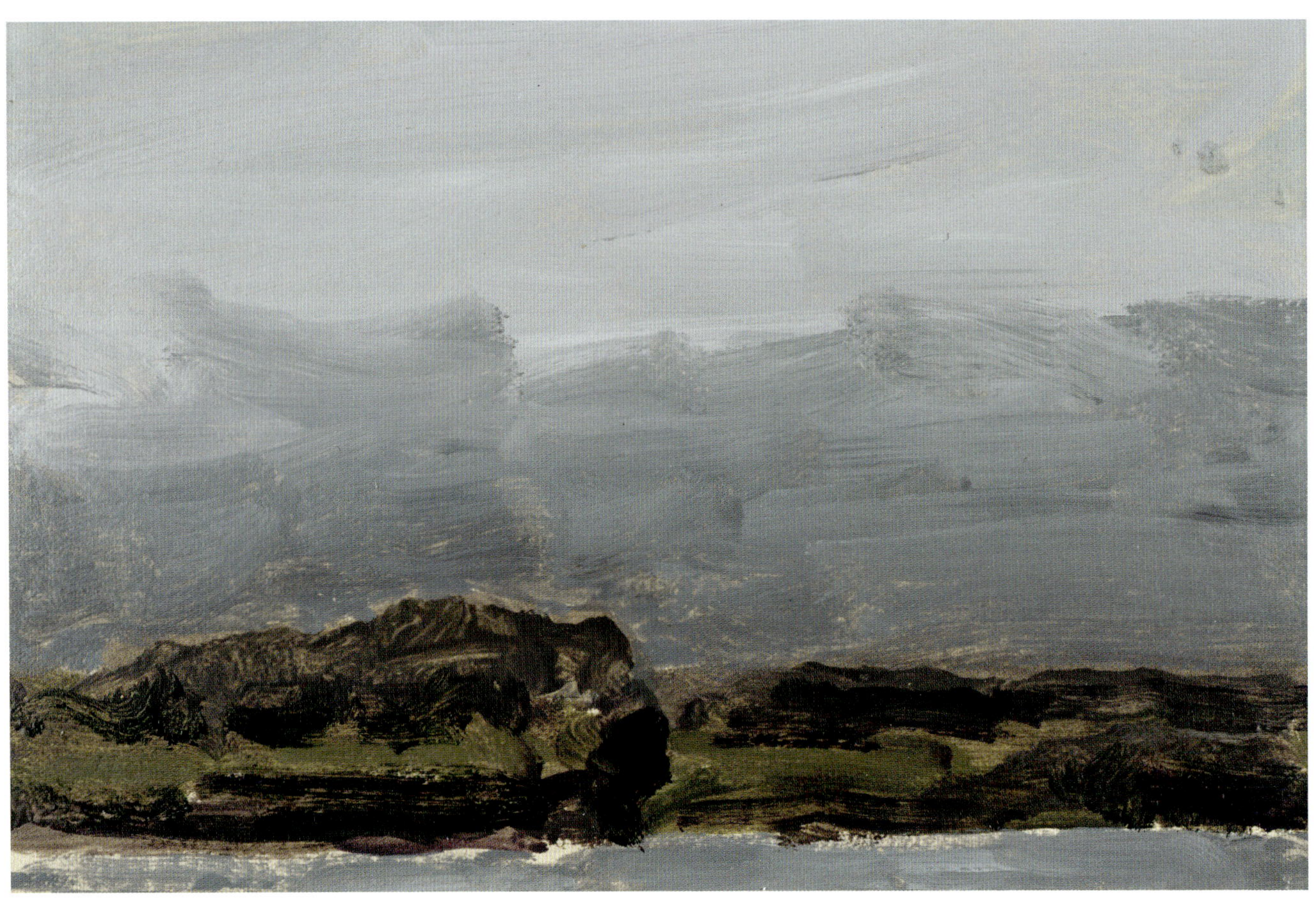

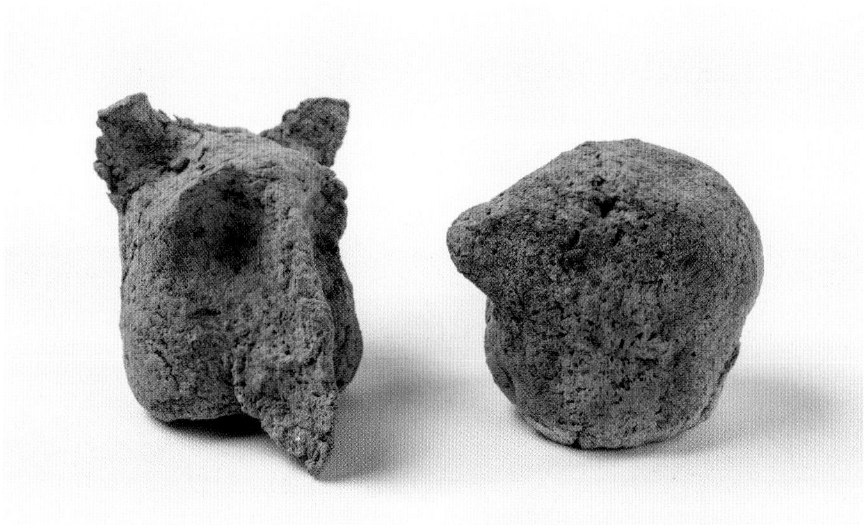

Fig. 1.40

Clifford Ross (American, b. 1952), *Storm Over Georgica Cove [East Hampton, New York]*, 1983. Oil on board, 5 × 7¾ in. (12.7 × 19.7 cm). Wadsworth Atheneum Museum of Art, Hartford, Conn. Bequest of Edward Gorey, 2001.13.64.

Fig. 1.41

Edward Gorey, *Finger Puppets*, c. 1986. Papier-mâché, 2½ × 2½ × 1½ in. (6.4 × 6.4 × 3.8 cm) (left); 2½ × 3 × 2 in. (6.4 × 7.6 × 5.1 cm) (right). Collection of Clifford Ross.

1984 and 1988, Gorey acquired eight of his pictures—five paintings and three drawings. Gorey was an early appreciator of the quiet modernity in York's unassuming still lifes and landscapes.[52] Like Ross's thick, colorful brushwork, York's painterliness was very different from Gorey's own style. Pictures such as *Dandelions in a Blue Tin*, now in the Wadsworth's collection, or *Brown Cow in a Wooded Landscape* (Private Collection) resonated with Gorey in other ways (figs. 1.42a,b). York's quietly subversive approach to ordinary subjects, such as dandelions or cows, seemed to mask something inclement. Similar to Gorey's work, bristling disturbance seems imminent.[53]

Gorey admired York's work so intensely that he dedicated a book to him: *The Prune People II* (1985), a sequel to his first book featuring prune-headed figures. Following his usual working methods, Gorey wrote text descriptions in his calligraphic penmanship before sketching the corresponding illustrations. The sheet of his preliminary ideas records his succinct descriptions of the fourteen character types, such as: "5/: two men dancing a tango in tails" (figs. 1.43, 1.44). Since Gorey meticulously dated his working drafts and sketches, we know that he began crafting *The Prune People II* in November 1982, just weeks after seeing York's fall exhibition, which opened at David & Langdale Company, Inc., October 12, 1982. Gorey continued to flesh out his ideas over the next two years. One might go so far as to say that the eloquent silence of York's paintings inspired Gorey's textless story.[54]

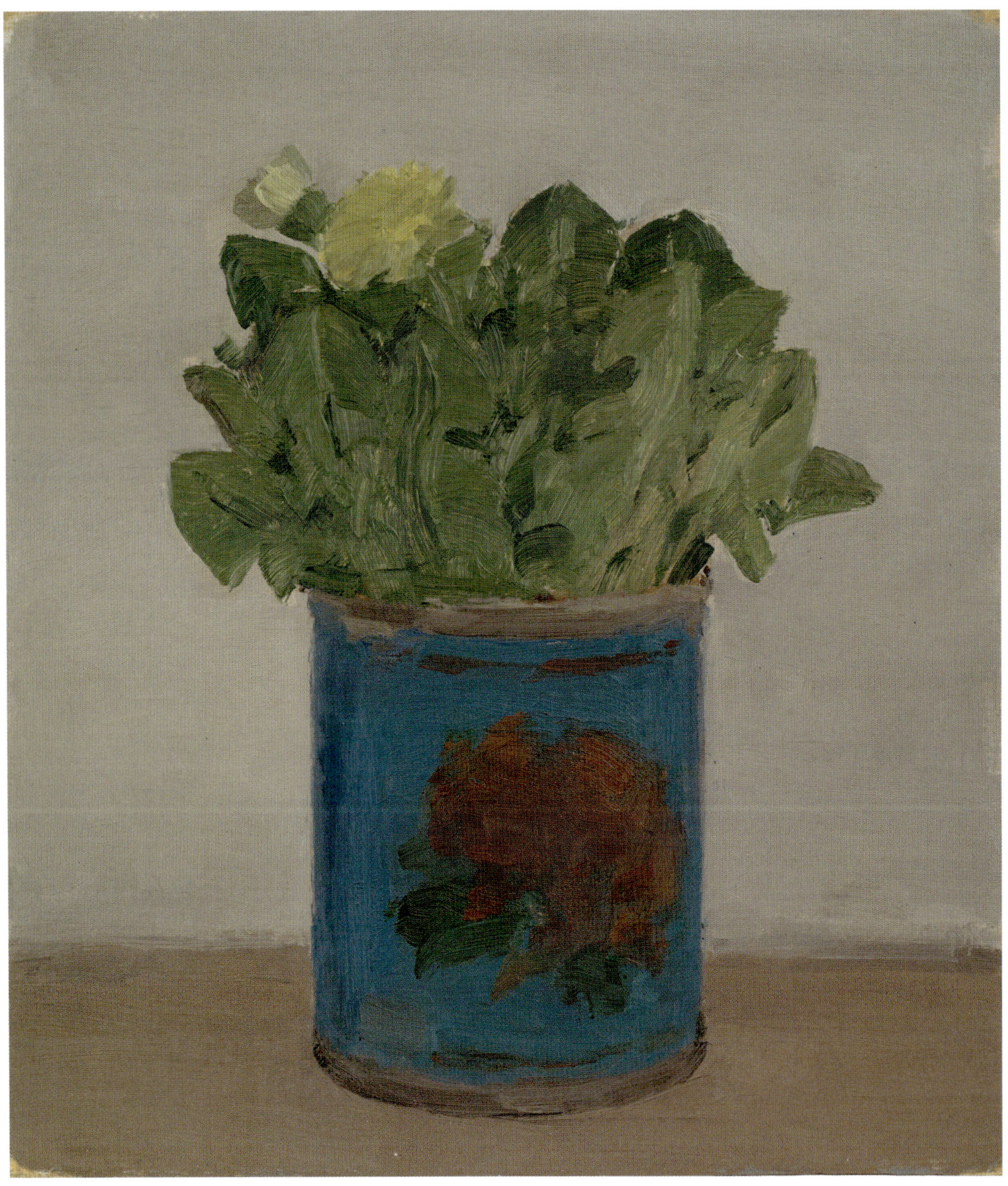

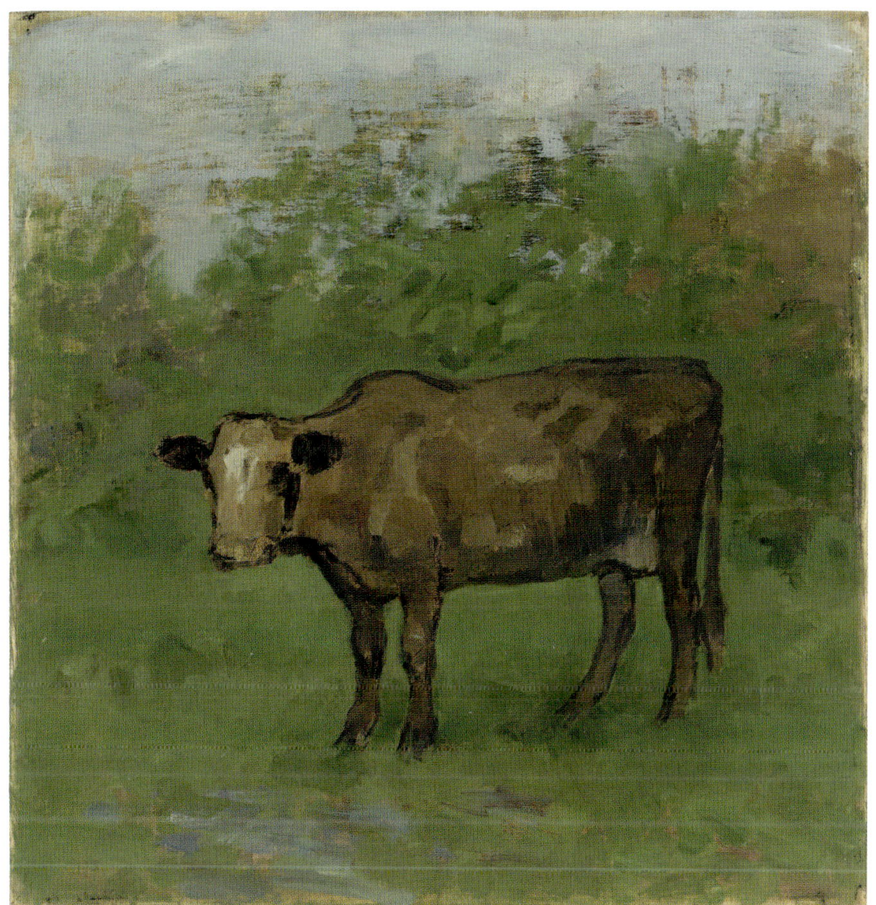

Fig. 1.42a

Albert York (American, 1928–2009), *Dandelions in a Blue Tin*, 1982. Oil on panel, 12 × 10¾ in. (30.5 × 27.3 cm). Wadsworth Atheneum Museum of Art, Hartford, Conn. Bequest of Edward Gorey, 2001.13.73.

Fig. 1.42b

Albert York, *Brown Cow in a Wooded Landscape,* 1984. Oil on panel, 14¼ × 14 in. (36.2 × 35.6 cm). Collection of Nina Nielsen and John Baker.

For Albert York –

6.xi.82 – 24.x.84

The Prune People – II 2

√1/ on mountainous rocks, fantastic — a picnic?
√2/ a fantômas figure — where?
√3/ nun or nuns   in crypt?
√4/ people with torches   on flat?
√5/ two men dancing a tango in tails
√6/ athletic group   in front of bldg/on steps
7/ chinese execution — kneeling figures, rolling heads   last?
8/ ~~spectre   on battlements w/ head under arm~~
√9/ victorian sofa in centre
√10/ office building corridor — card
√11/ bicycle picture — dark trees, shrubbery
√12/ derelicts amidst débris
√13/ inexplicable bed picture — one under
√14/ fireworks: heads at bottom   last?
15/ people in window — victorian high window
    w/ tree in front

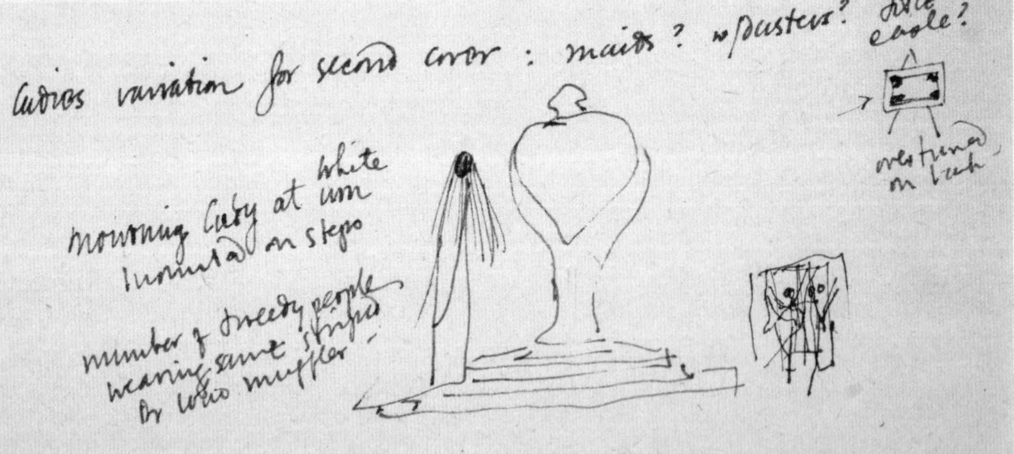

various variation for second cover : maids? w/posters?   title on eagle?

mourning lady at white urn   overturned on black
    hunched on steps

number of tweedy people
wearing scarves striped
or who muffler.

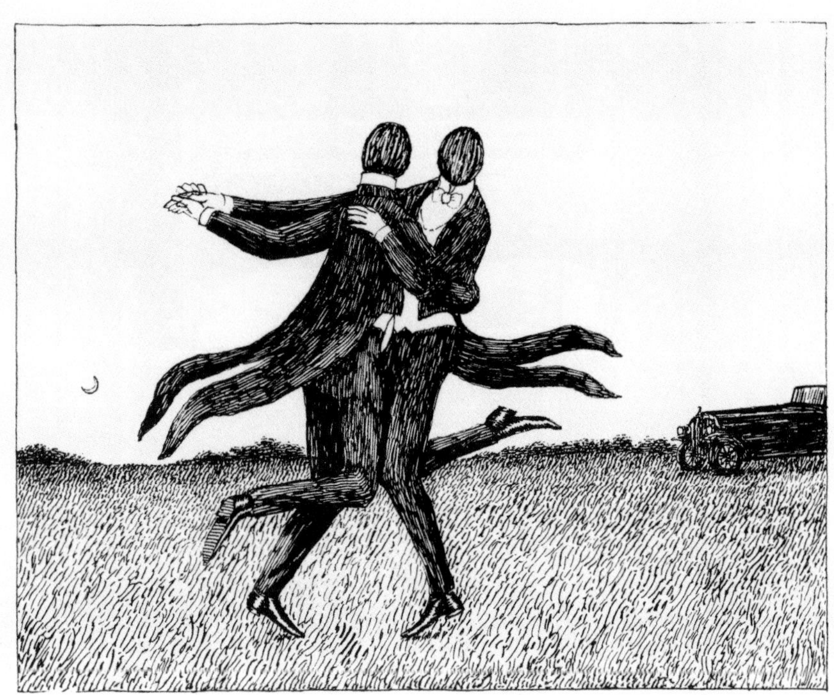

Fig. 1.43

Edward Gorey, Draft of illustration descriptions for *The Prune People II*, October 24, 1984. Pen and ink and graphite on paper, 11 × 8 ½ in. (27.9 × 21.6 cm). The Edward Gorey Charitable Trust.

Fig. 1.44

Edward Gorey, *Two men dancing a tango in tails*. Illustration in *The Prune People II*. New York: Albondocani Press, 1985. Columbia University Rare Book and Manuscript Library, Alpern Collection.

CONCLUSION

If one were to summarize Edward Gorey's wide-ranging creative talents, the short list might include artist, author, illustrator, costume and set designer, and puppeteer. In light of the bequest he made to the Wadsworth Atheneum, we can also add collector, or, in his words, "accumulator." This last passion was clearly very personal and fueled his creativity. Collecting allowed him to transcend reality, to "keep real life at bay." And while there are affinities between Gorey's aesthetic and the artists he admired, there are innumerable influences too imperceptible to trace. This element of mystery, something quietly seductive, is what pulls us into Gorey's worlds over and over.

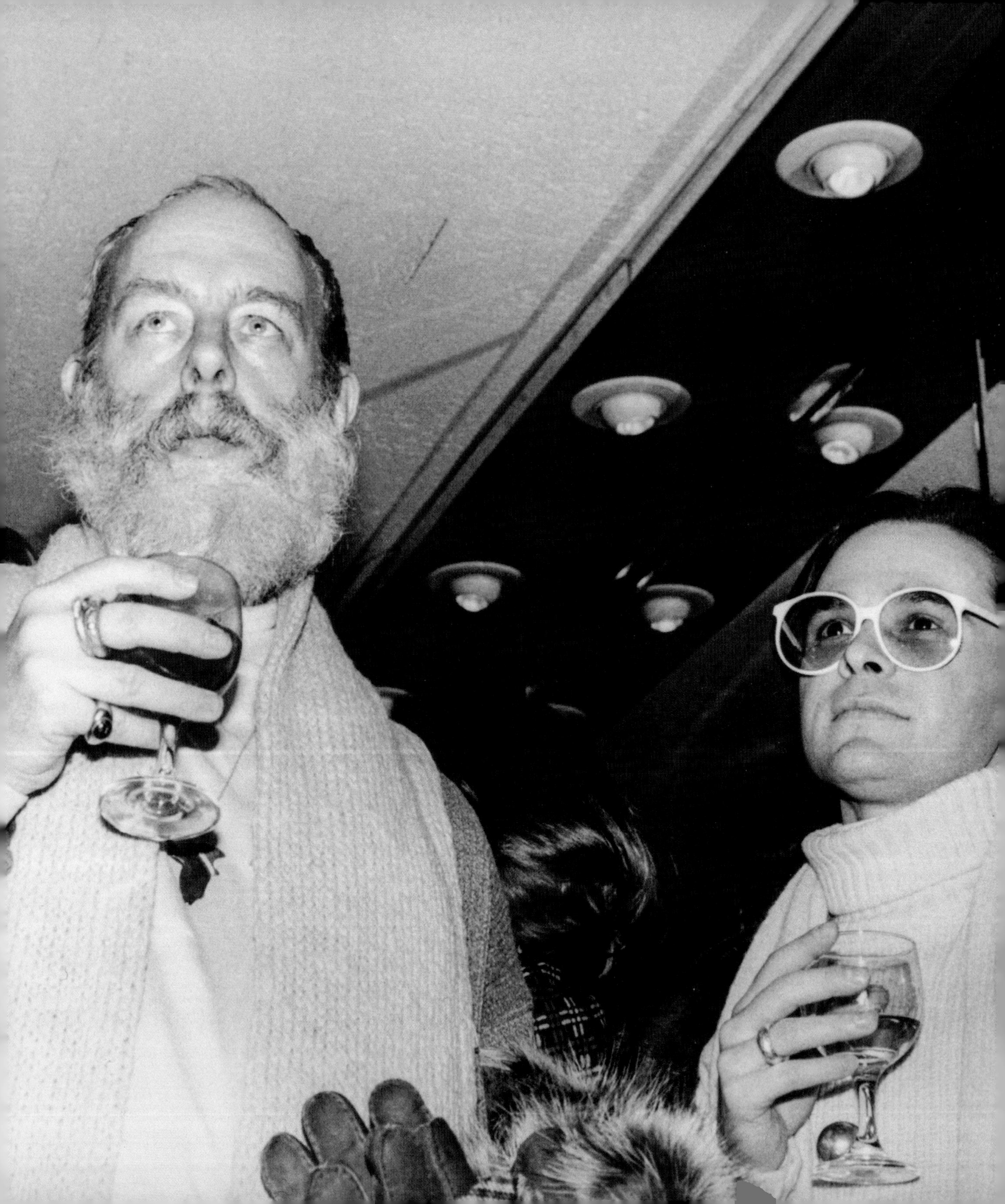

Robert Greskovic

The Man Who Wanted to Be Entertained

I want to be en-ter-TAINED!" was something I'd hear Edward Gorey exclaim in a tone intermixed with determination and exasperation. Sometimes it came after Ted—as he was known to those of us who had him for a friend, as I luckily did over the last three decades of his life—had seen a movie or a ballet or an opera or some other "little work," as he might say, that failed, shall we say, to entertain him particularly (fig. 2.1). Take, for example, a remark made as he left a late-afternoon showing by a New York creator of works that, under the "avant-garde" rubric, blended music, dance, and other modes of performance into a would-be original entity. Ted's point in this instance hinged on the fact that this showing was given late in the day and not in the evening— the usual time for him to be out at one event or another: "It's all well and good," he noted, recounting the lackluster showing, "to whoops off to see such things, but when you emerge into daylight, you're left asking yourself: 'Now what do I do with the rest of my blighted day?'"

When he was in New York City, Ted regularly spent evenings, and, on given days, matinee hours in various theaters. As has been often documented, Ted's time away from home in and around the city, where I hung out with him, was spent mostly at New York City Ballet (NYCB). It was after his 1953 move to New York that Ted succumbed to the charms of NYCB in its first, City Center home and to the "genius"—Ted's word—of George Balanchine,

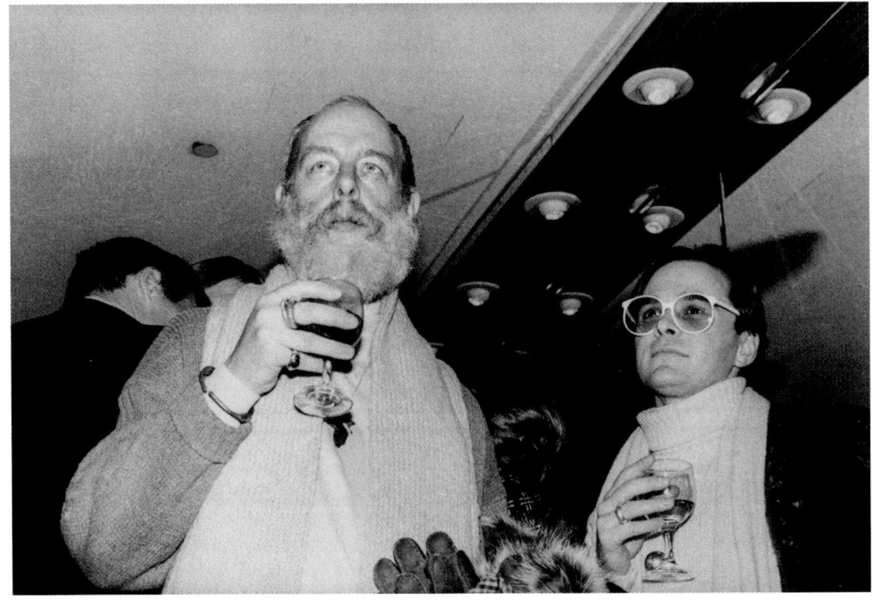

Fig. 2.1

Steven Caras, *Edward Gorey and Robert Greskovic at the New York City Ballet's Tchaikovsky Festival press conference, held at the Russian Tea Room in New York City on February 9, 1981.* Photograph. © Steven Caras, All rights reserved.

NYCB's founding artistic visionary. Ted kept an apartment in New York until 1983, before he decamped full-time to Cape Cod, where he lived when he wasn't in the city; thereafter he decided it was just easier to buy all the available subscription tickets to the company's seasons. These preseason, mail-order blocks of tickets were the ballet equivalent of season tickets.[1] Ted would also purchase tickets from the box office for additional performances not part of any subscription. In total, Ted committed to some 160 ballet performances per year. This tally, however, excluded the annual, monthlong run of *The Nutcracker*,[2] a ballet uppermost on Ted's list of favorite Balanchine works. It's this thirty-or-so-successive-performance run of *The Nutcracker* that makes it inaccurate to assert, as some have, that Ted went to every single NYCB performance during his stays in NYC. I know of only one year in which Ted decided that he'd attend every *Nutcracker*, meaning thirty-plus straight shows. In the end, "a lot" is closer to the truth than "every performance." Or, as the subtitle of his book *The Lavender Leotard* states in Ted's own words: "Going a Lot to the New York City Ballet."

In performances of NYCB, with Balanchine's work as his focus, Ted often found himself more than entertained. Balanchine was consistently on the record as plainspoken in ways that Ted welcomed; one of his favorite

Balanchine remarks was a little catchall piece of advice to a dancer or a choreographer: "Better don't do." Likewise, here and there the ballet master noted to interviewers that he and his dancers were simply "entertainers."[3] It's worth pointing out that Ted did not socialize, let alone schmooze, with Balanchine. His acquaintance with him was at best from afar, largely from sources that recorded the ballet master's comments, usually related by those who knew him personally. Ted didn't personally know many dancers; he was acquainted with a few, as well as a few of their mothers. The mother of one of his favorites, Patricia McBride, whom Ted would happily refer to as Patty, remarked memorably to him once, in a comeback he'd often repeat, that she'd had to miss her daughter in the leading part for the New York premiere of the Balanchine/Danilova staging of *Coppélia*,[4] which remained on Ted's short list of especial Balanchine works (figs. 2.2a,b). Why? Because it fell on her bowling night.

Ted deemed Balanchine the great theater artist as well as the great choreographer of his time; he also found Balanchine's ability as a performer to be striking and standard setting on those select occasions when the ballet master would take on pantomime roles with NYCB. Having seen some of the few performances when Balanchine enacted the role of the Don in his *Don Quixote*,[5] Ted noted to me that it was the finest bit of stage acting he'd ever seen (fig.2.3).

An ironic story dance critic Arlene Croce tells in her loving tribute to Ted[6] details an anecdote I'm not sure Ted ever fully heard. That is, that Balanchine once regaled a familiar waiter in a local coffee shop with his observations about a man, unmistakably Ted, who came regularly to the ballet but who only sat in the lobby. Balanchine's telling came from noting Ted in his favorite place to sit during intermission, on a bench in the theater's promenade area. There he'd make notes, doodle, correct his program, and chat with people he knew. As he'd sometimes nip into the lobby before curtain calls were over, he could be seen by Balanchine sitting outside the auditorium as he left his seat to go backstage. "There's this man," Balanchine is quoted as observing, "who comes all the time, but he never sees the ballet, only sits in the lobby to read and write." Nothing, of course, was further from the truth, even if Ted could be known, as were other NYCB regulars, to "sit out" individual ballets on a mixed bill when they were of little interest, but these were almost never works by Balanchine. So the irony here, one that would not likely have been lost on Ted, was that Balanchine's arguably biggest fan during this time was thought by the ballet master to be an eccentric who never cared to look at the ballets!

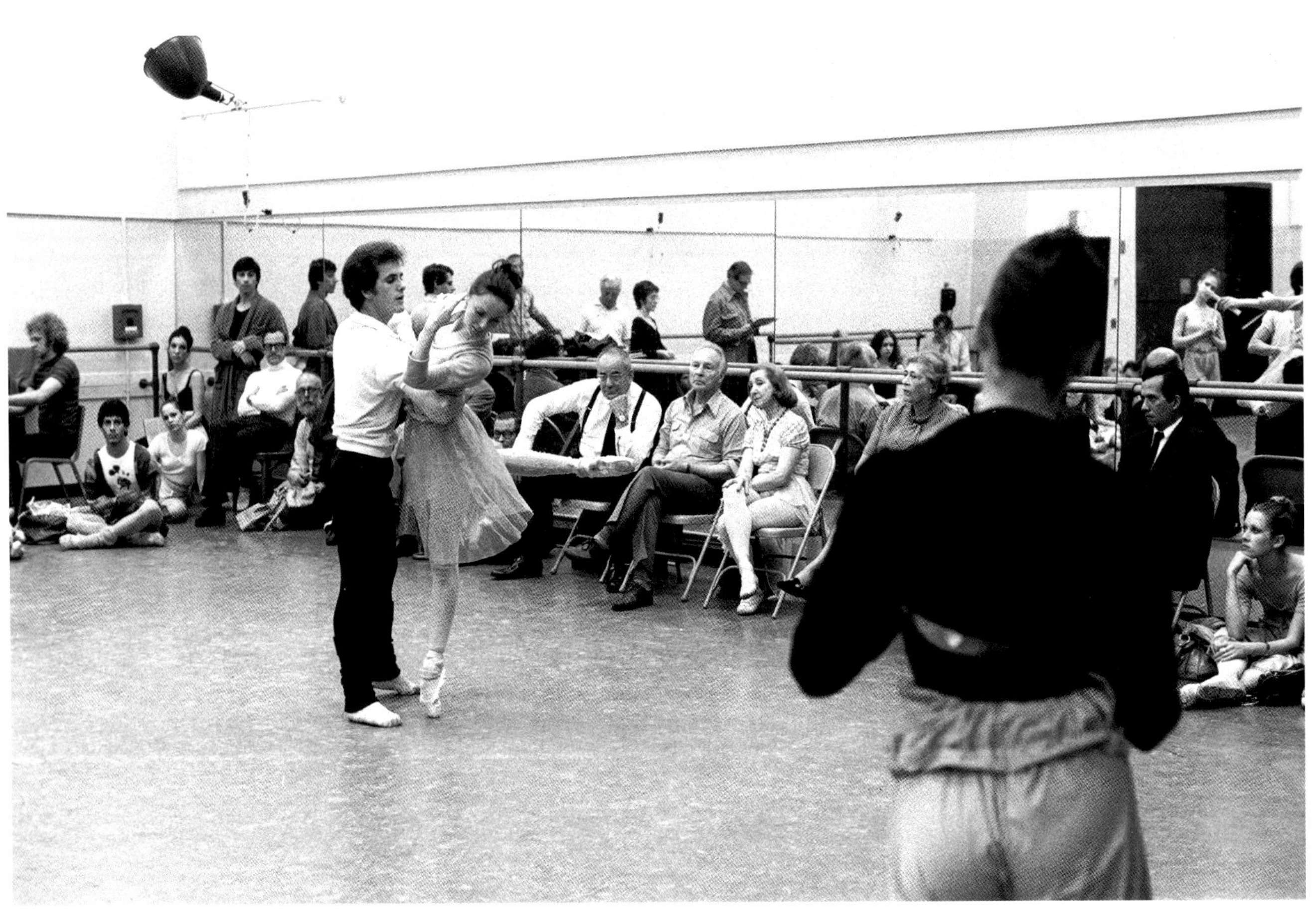

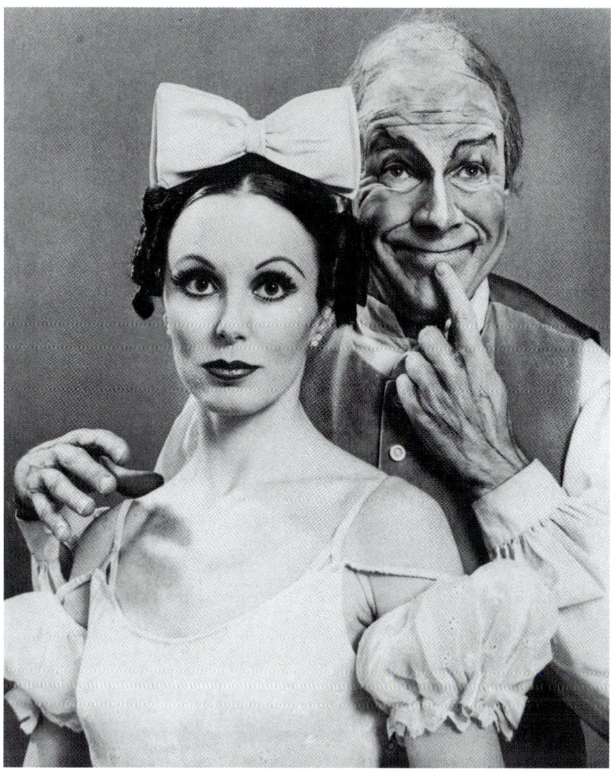

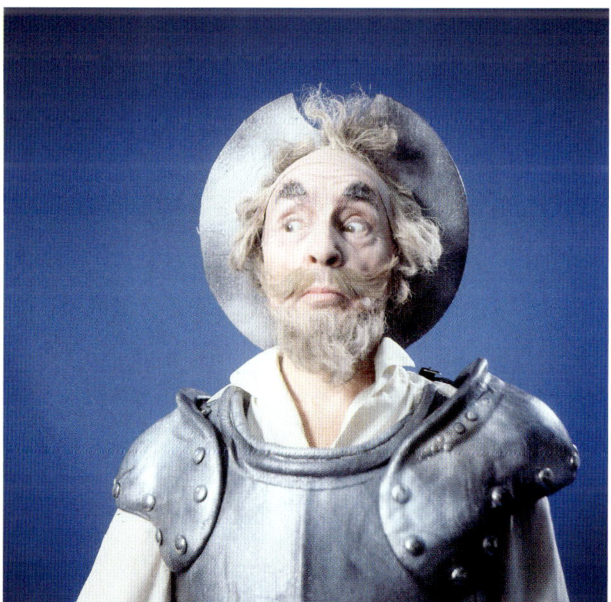

Fig. 2.2a

Martha Swope (American, 1928–2017), *Edward Gorey (seated on floor, seventh from left) watching New York City Ballet rehearsal of "Coppélia," Helgi Tomasson and Patricia McBride, (seated) Lincoln Kirstein, George Balanchine and Alexandra Danilova*, 1974. Photograph. New York Public Library for the Performing Arts, Billy Rose Theater Division.

Fig. 2.2b

Martha Swope, *New York City Ballet Studio portrait of Patricia McBride and Shaun O'Brien in "Coppélia,"* 1977. Publicity photo for *Live from Lincoln Center* telecast, Tuesday January 31, 1978. Collection of Robert Greskovic.

Fig. 2.3

Martha Swope, *New York City Ballet studio portrait of George Balanchine in "Don Quixote*," 1965. Photograph. New York Public Library for the Performing Arts, Billy Rose Theater Division.

Fig. 2.4

Edward Gorey, "Ballet in a Nutshell." Illustration for "Balletgorey" by Tobi Tobias, published in *Dance Magazine* (January 1974). Pen and ink on paper, 13 × 10 in. (33 × 25.4 cm). The Edward Gorey Charitable Trust.

Again, and Ted expressed it to me variously over the years as he'd come away from a performance of Balanchine's dances, he found Balanchine not merely the great choreographer of the age but really a great and nearly incomparable genius of theater. For example, he noted the special stroke of theatrical inspiration he found behind Balanchine's eventual recasting of the angels skimming about the stage, at the start of act 2 of *The Nutcracker*'s Land of Sweets scene, from adolescent girl ballet students, his initial choice, to today's little girl students. For Ted, seeing these "tinies," as he'd call them, at this time in this context, was enough to reduce one to tears.

Ted made light of intermission time at NYCB with "Ballet in a Nutshell," the illustration he did especially for a 1974 article[7] by Tobi Tobias in *Dance Magazine* (fig. 2.4). I was often present amid such exchanges, and can identify a number of the regulars depicted by their statements and in some cases by the silhouettes. My own presence and comment are indicated, third from the right, wherein Ted depicted me as if wearing the unplucked beaver coat he handed along to me once he started to acquire further, new fur coats. An observation of Ted's own is there, on the far right, even if the individual offering it isn't exactly a Gorey self-portrait. As for the dancer being assessed in his one-liner, "Her feet are like baked potatoes wrapped in foil," I'd rather not identify her by name today. Ted preferred at times like this to keep details vague "while," as he was wont to say, "we're all still alive." His illustration indicates site-specific motifs that reveal its setting to be decidedly the Philip Johnson–designed New York State Theater's Promenade. The little round stools and tables, as well as the outline of the large-scale sculptures by Elie Nadelman in the background, unmistakably place this gathering there (fig. 2.5).

Not that being entertained was easy. Among the many details Ted admired in *The Rocky Horror Picture Show*—especially the movie version, which he saw any number of times in raucous midnight showings at some Manhattan movie houses—was what seemed to him a key line. It's uttered by Tim Curry, whom Ted adored, as Frank-N-Furter, the "sweet transvestite, transsexual from Transylvania," with timing that Ted would happily approximate with sotto voce delivery: "It's not easy having a good time."[8] Likewise Ted would be in agreement with Croce, who once quoted James Agee in a 1971 article about Twyla Tharp, a dancer and choreographer whose efforts the dance critic then contrasted with those of would-be avant-garde practitioners. In making her case for Tharp's engaging works, which eschewed notably outré, avant-garde aims, Croce characterized her practice as "the difficult and considerable art of entertaining."[9] Croce and Tharp were two individuals

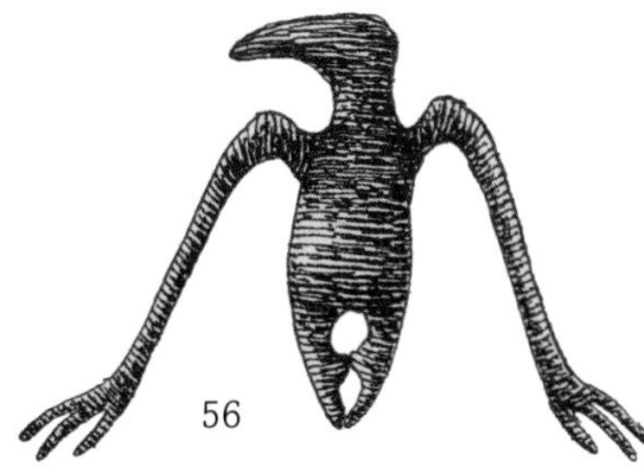

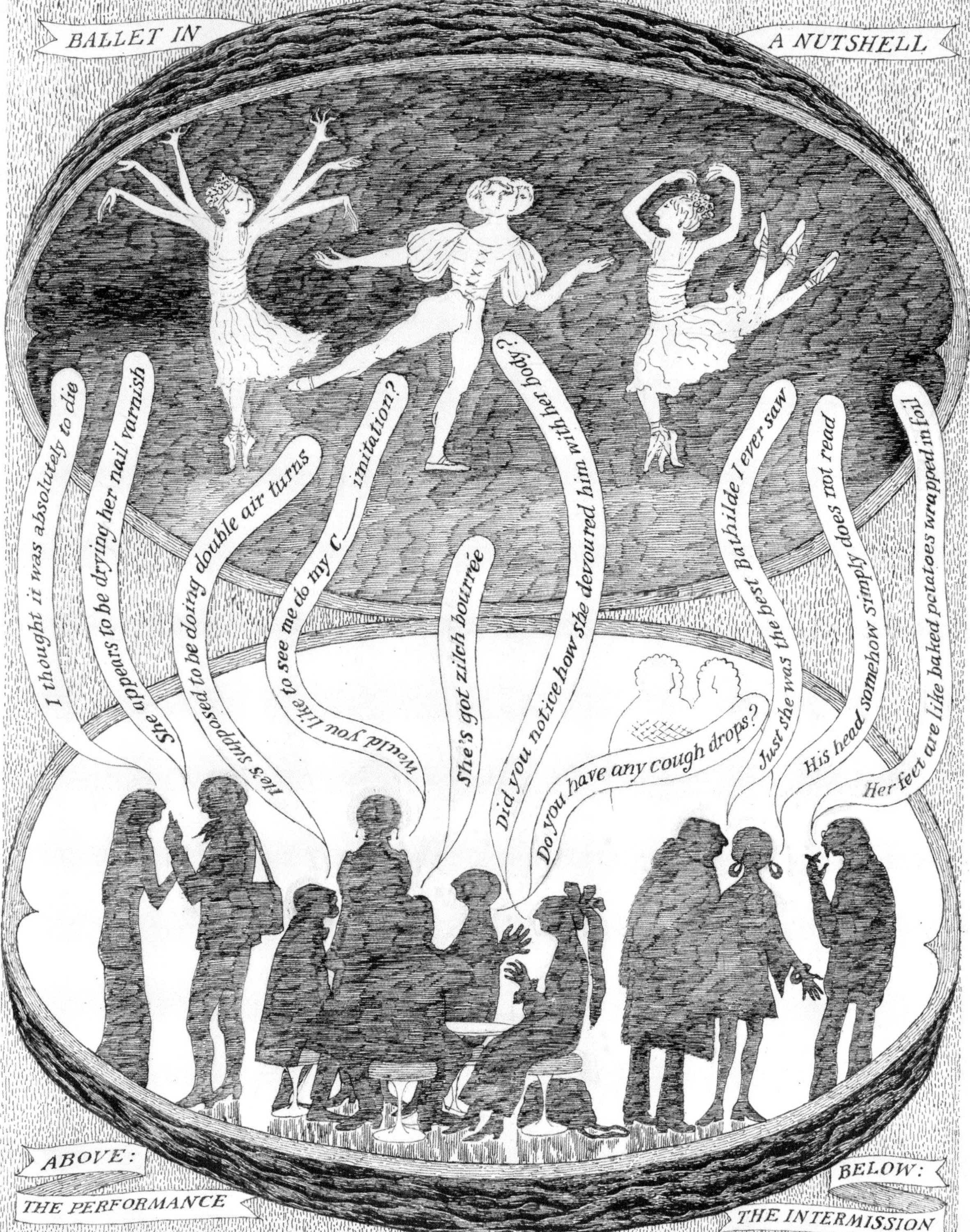

BALLET IN
A NUTSHELL
I thought it was absolutely to die
She appears to be drying her nail varnish
He's supposed to be doing double air turns
Would you like to see me do my c___ imitation?
She's got zilch bourrée
Did you notice how she devoured him with her body?
Do you have any cough drops?
Just she was the best Bathilde I ever saw
His head somehow simply does not read
Her feet are like baked potatoes wrapped in foil
ABOVE:
BELOW:
THE PERFORMANCE
THE INTERMISSION

Fig. 2.5
Bruce Chernin, *Edward Gorey, artist, author and regular attendant at the New York City Ballet*, 1973. Gelatin silver print, 10½ × 7½ in. (26.7 × 19.1 cm). Columbia University Rare Book and Manuscript Library, Alpern Collection.

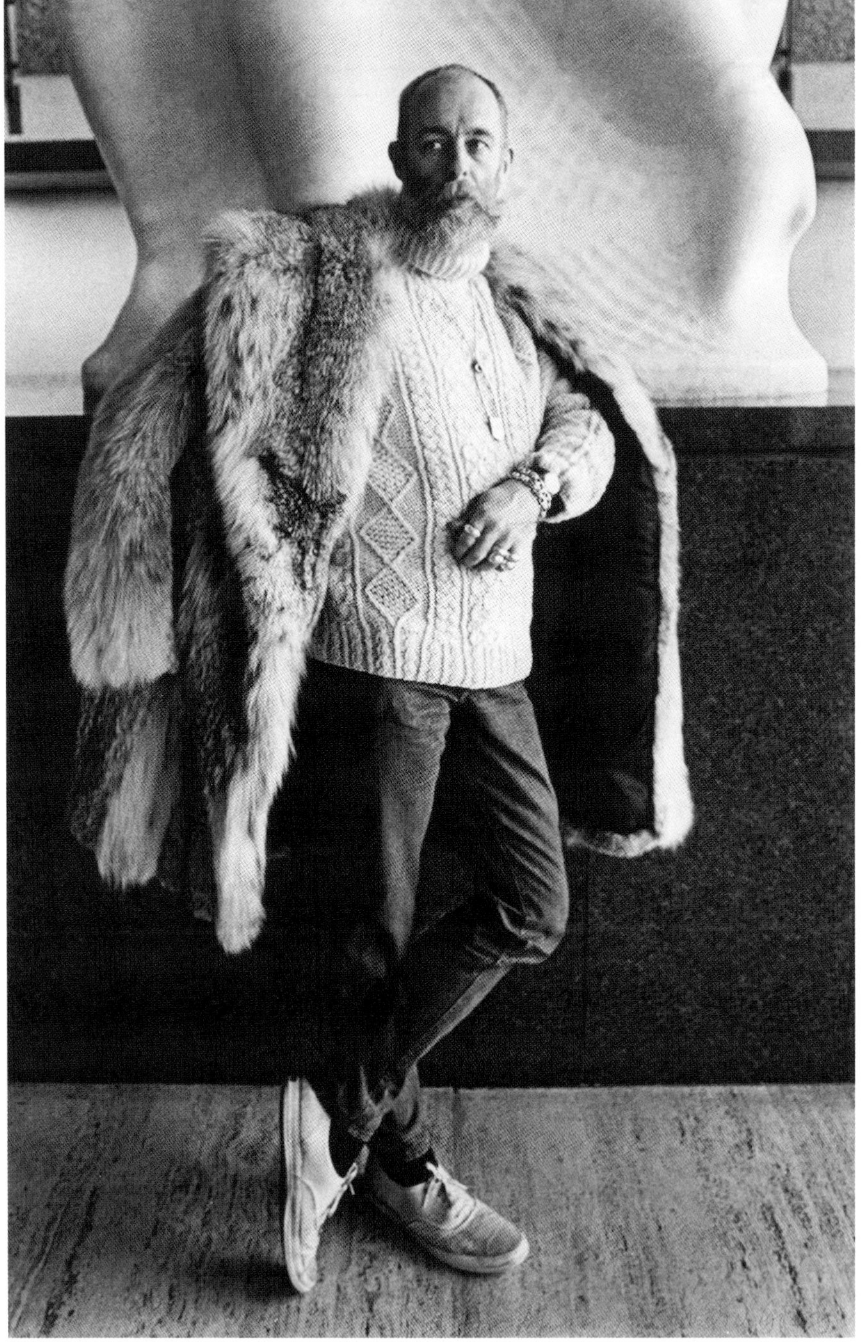

whom Ted found invaluable for their parts in the world of entertainment: Croce, as writer and thinker; Tharp, as performer and dancemaker.

At this point I'm put in mind of an ever-growing proposed text that Ted imagined over the years. The gist of it was pairings setting forth comparisons without spelling them out. A working title for the scheme as I understood it was *The Is, Isn't Book*. None ever got published, nor, to the best of my knowledge, was its content ever much written down, as such, by Ted. As I caught its drift over time, its entries went along the following lines:

> Entertaining is; earnest isn't.
> Balanchine is; Robbins isn't.
> Jane Fonda is; Nicole Kidman isn't.
> Croce is; Sontag isn't.
> Anthony Trollope is; Henry James isn't.
> Madame Grès is; Oscar de la Renta isn't.
> Matisse is; Picasso isn't.
> Satie is; Stravinsky isn't.
> Isamu Noguchi is; Louise Nevelson isn't.
> Tony Blum is; Peter Martins isn't.
> Diana Adams is; Margot Fonteyn isn't.
> Shaun O'Brien is; Lucia Chase isn't.
> Allegra (fig. 2.6) is; Suzanne isn't.
> Skin-on-skin is; fully-let-out isn't.
> Iron is; silver isn't.

Lines such as these, suggesting without explaining, have a familiar ring from Ted's writings as well as his sometime stand-alone drawings. By way of insight into Ted's comparison-themed thinking, we have a statement he provided in a preface to a catalogue for *Extraordinary Realities*, a 1973 Whitney Museum of Art exhibition of the same name. It concludes as follows: "the banal is far more mysterious than any of its opposites."[10]

Ted was loath to explain himself or to credit others' interpretations of his often-enigmatic work. Ballet's nonverbal dimensions fit very neatly into the realm of works that entertained and interested him. Similarly, in the instance of ballets that were what Balanchine would call "storyless" — he disliked the word "abstract" — one could, Ted could, take their physical information and read it variously, finding new dimensions with repeated viewings. As Ted wrote to author Peter Neumeyer on October 2, 1968,[11]

Fig. 2.6
Edward Gorey, Invitation
design to celebrate the
publication of *Allegra Kent's
Water Beauty Book* by Allegra
Kent, 1977. Collection of
Robert Greskovic.

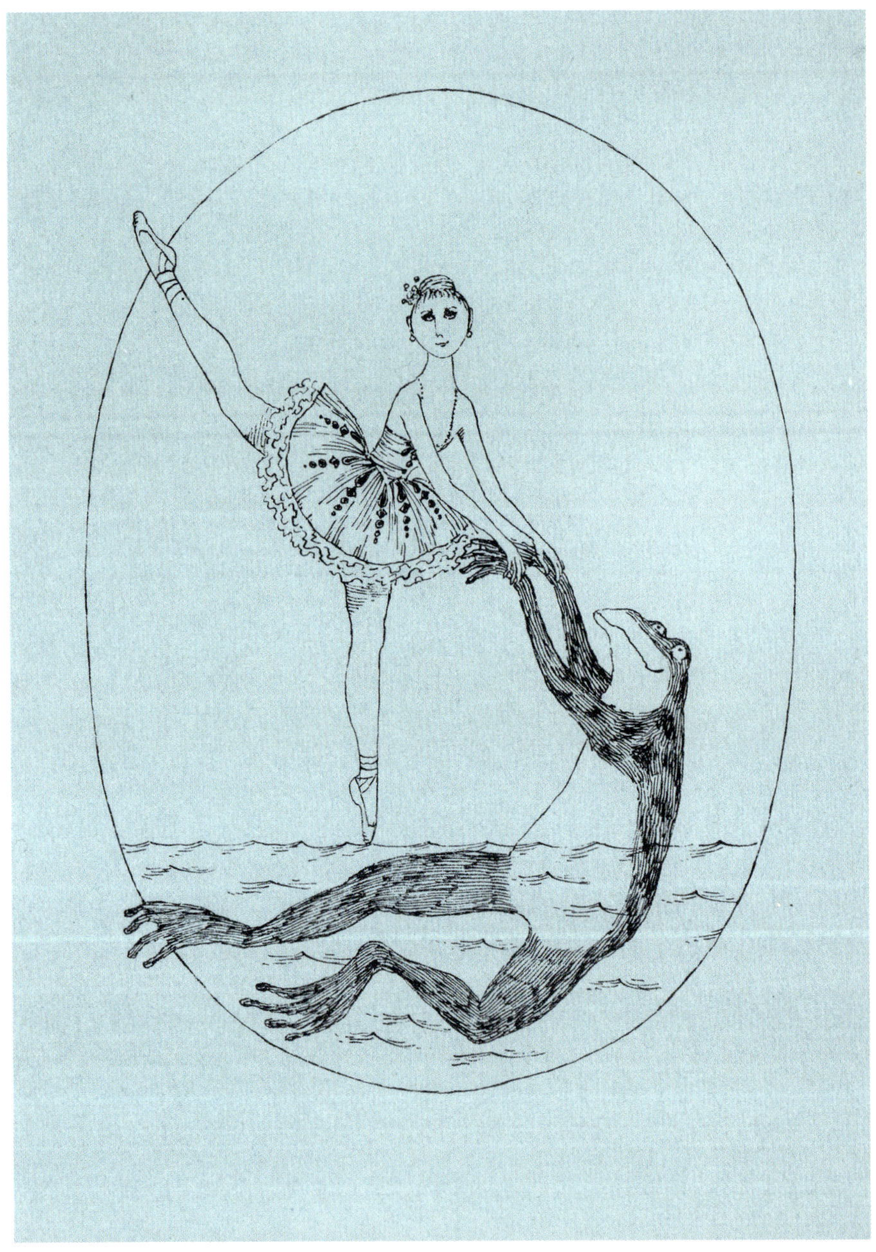

works of art "presumably about some certain thing" are "really always about something else entirely."

On occasion ballet itself became the very subject of Ted's work. As he once related it, this rarefied form of nonverbal theater first came to his attention in 1939, in his hometown of Chicago. He was enticed there as a teen, specifically by a performance of Ballet Russe de Monte Carlo because of the participation of its visual designers. Time was, Ted once reminded me, when you were drawn to the ballet, not by the presence of a particular choreographer, or dancer, which is how his ballet going would eventually be motivated, but by the designer involved. By the time of his NYCB-themed *Lavender Leotard*, in 1973, he'd obviously changed his tune. It was no longer the visual design aspects that piqued his desire to attend a ballet performance; it was the choreographic finesse and inventiveness that enthralled and enticed him. The final plate of his pithy *Leotard* text reads, "Other companies merely put on ballets; we *dance*."

As related in his foreword to *Costumes by Karinska*,[12] Ted recalls that his first look at ballet, as a high school sophomore, was distinguished by the good luck of finding a triple bill with visual designs created by what he calls "the three greatest of all costume designers:"[13] Salvador Dalí, Henri Matisse, and Léon Bakst. It was Dalí who primarily drew Ted to this Ballet Russe program, as this was a time when he enthusiastically admired the work of the flamboyant Spaniard. Later Ted would blush a bit at the thought of such high regard for Dalí.

In the mix of this bill, Dalí's surrealist designs for *Bacchanale*[14] caught Ted's eye, but then so did the more spare ones of Matisse. Matisse's simple but sensual cutout flame shapes on what were then called all-over-tights left lasting impact on his view of stage pictures—especially on the lissome physique of Alicia Markova, the English-born dancer with an adopted Russian name who made a strong impression on Ted in those days with her lightness in lifts and jumps. Likewise the vividness of Bakst's Orientalist decor and costumes for *Schéhérazade*[15] impressed him with their intense color schemes, which Ted liked to dub "ferocious," as dominated by bilious, another favorite word of his, greens and stinging vermilions.

In the case of *Bacchanale*, Dalí's costuming entered the stage pictures by way of Karinska's inimitable art of transferring graphics on paper to wearable dimensions on stage. Ted's foreword specifically recalls the ballet's Lola Montez character "with a whip, twirling about in enormous gold lamé bloomers encircled at their widest part by two rows of white teeth." Yet once Bentley's Karinska book—a pictorial and scholarly study of the costumier's wide-ranging career— was finished, I wonder whether Ted was equally or more struck by the look of an

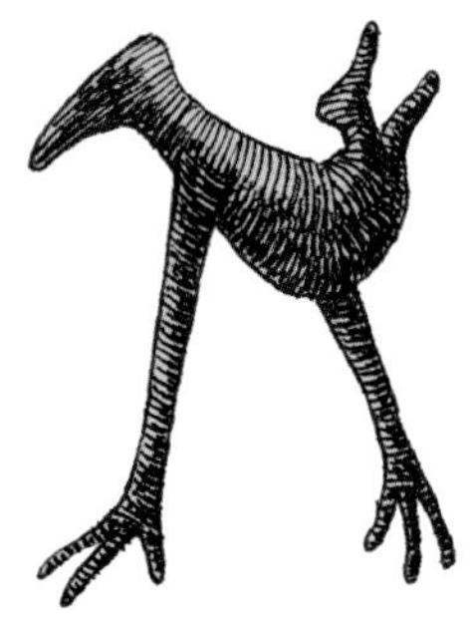

Umbrella figure,[16] which amounts to a closed-up, black, man's umbrella sprouting arms and legs and topped by a skull (fig. 2.7). As Goreyites know, the black umbrella, battered or otherwise, would eventually appear and reappear in Ted's body of work. See, for example, the funereal umbrella held by the death's-head figure over the tots on the cover of *The Gashlycrumb Tinies*, as well as the handleless bumbershoot that makes an appearance in two plates of *The Object-Lesson* (fig. 2.8).[17]

Ted would later learn of an important collection of artworks associated with the ballet as he researched with his usual thoroughness the history of Balanchine's beginnings in the United States. In the very year that Balanchine landed in the States, six years before Ted saw his first ballets in Chicago, with their respective, memorable designs, A. Everett "Chick" Austin Jr., then director of Hartford's Wadsworth Atheneum Museum of Art, had purchased a collection of 188 ballet-related visual works, now known as the Serge Lifar Collection. Among the artworks included in the collection are examples of designs by names that would eventually inhabit Ted's pantheon of artists: Matisse, Bakst, Bérard, Tchelitchew, and Ernst. Arguably, most key for Ted among the pieces in the Wadsworth Atheneum's Lifar Collection, because of their seminal connection to Balanchine's catalogue of works, would be André Bauchant's oil-on-canvas designs, one front cloth and one set design, for *Apollon Musagète* (figs. 2.9a,b).[18] Similarly, there are two companion designs executed in gouache (or tempera) on paper by Georges Rouault for *Le Fils Prodigue* (figs. 2.10a,b). Ted would have known Bauchant's designs only from these pictures or reproductions of them, since by the time he was seeing *Apollo*, as *Apollon* was eventually renamed, Bauchant's faux-naive aesthetic had been replaced by mostly uncredited, simpler, plain, black-and-white or all-white schemes. I never debriefed Ted about Bauchant per se, but knowing his fascination with naifs, among whom Henri Rousseau was a favorite, I suspect he'd have been happy to see these now peculiar-looking design elements in place for a performance of *Apollo*, at least "as a gas," as he might put it. It was no doubt this historic connection to Hartford—where Balanchine was brought by Austin and his chum Lincoln Kirstein with the intent of locating the Russian-born choreographer's ballet career there—that kept the Atheneum on Ted's radar and in his heart, leading him to bequeath to the museum the fine art items of his estate. As witnessed by the history of ballet in America, Balanchine didn't choose to remain in Hartford, but the city remained crucial to launching his US career.[19] As Kirstein's diaries record, it was his opinion that Austin bought the Lifar Collection for the then high-seeming price of ten thousand dollars "because he couldn't have the ballet."[20]

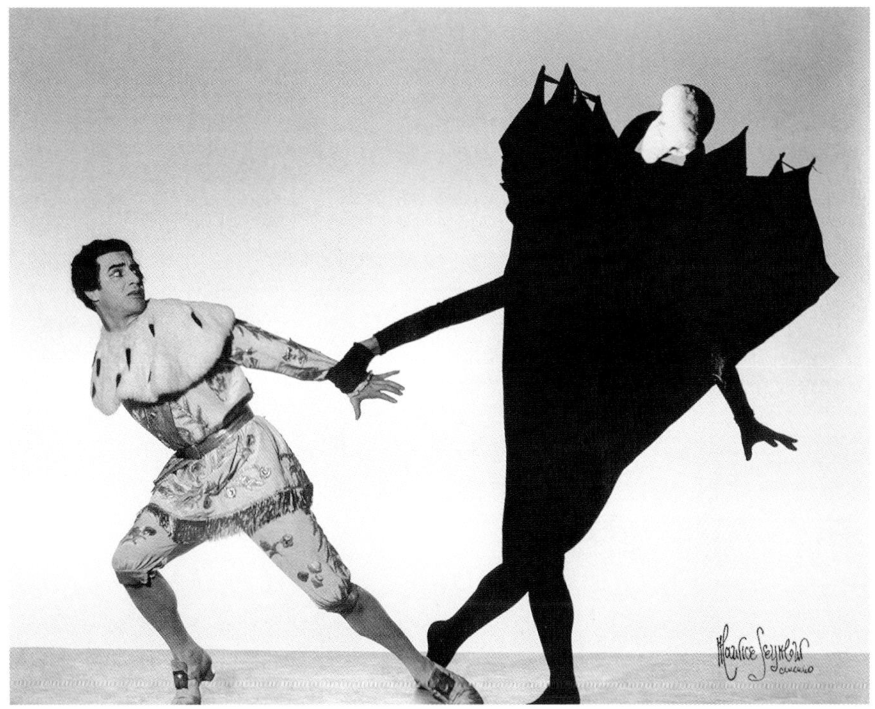

Fig. 2.7

Maurice Seymour (Russian, Maurice Zeldman [1900–1993]) and Seymour Zeldman [1902–1995]), "The Umbrella figure" costume, designed by Salvador Dalí for *Bacchanale* and made by Barbara Karinska, 1939. Photograph. Courtesy of Ronald Seymour.

Fig. 2.8

Edward Gorey, "On the shore a bat, or possibly an umbrella, / disengaged itself from the shrubbery," Illustration in *The Object-Lesson*. Garden City: Doubleday & Company, Inc., 1958.

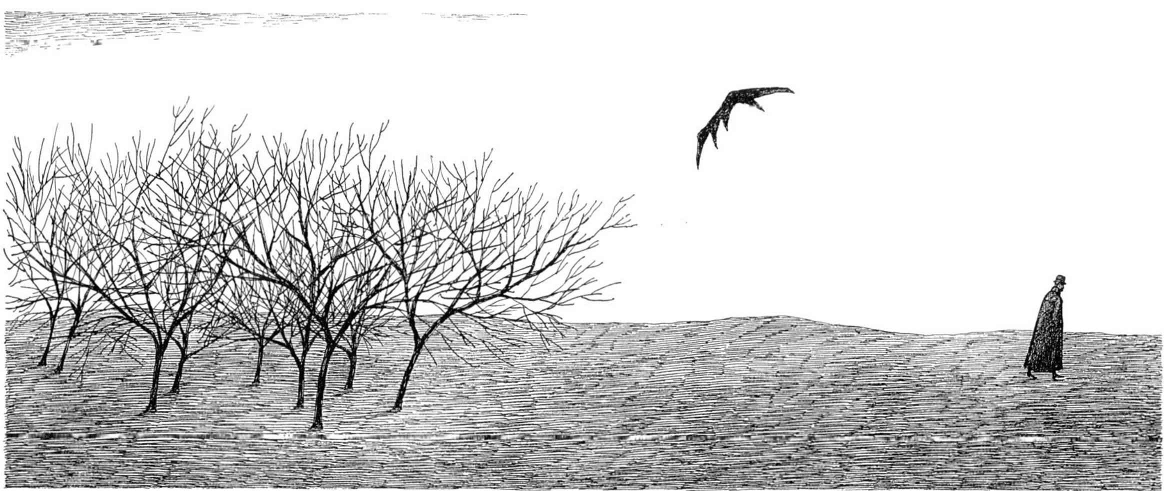

disengaged itself from the shrubbery,

Fig. 2.9a

André Bauchant (French, 1873–1958), *Design for the Front Cloth: Champs-Elysees from "Apollon Musagète,"* 1927. Oil on canvas, 39 ⅛ × 45 ½ in. (99.4 × 115.6 cm). Wadsworth Atheneum Museum of Art, Hartford, Conn. The Ella Gallup Sumner and Mary Catlin Sumner Collection Fund, 1933.395.

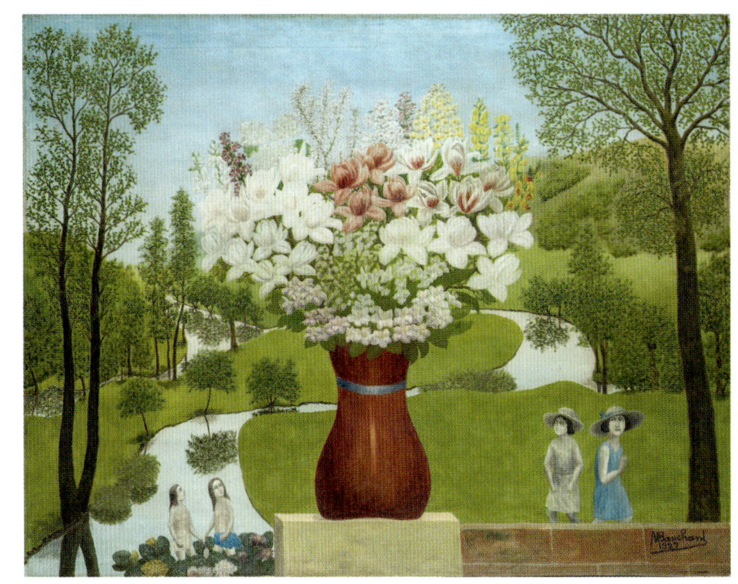

Fig. 2.9b

André Bauchant, *Set Design for "Apollon Musagète,"* 1928. Oil on canvas, 23 ⅝ × 27 ¾ in. (60 × 70.5 cm). Wadsworth Atheneum Museum of Art, Hartford, Conn. The Ella Gallup Sumner and Mary Catlin Sumner Collection Fund, 1933.396.

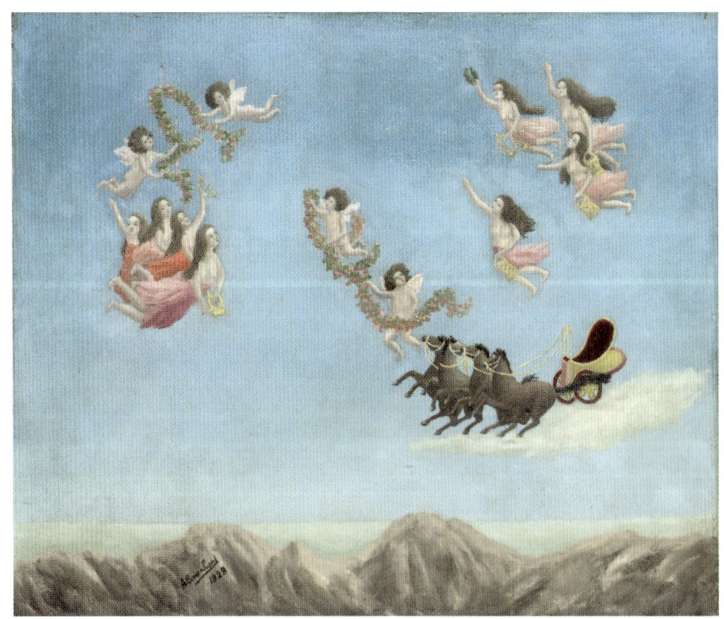

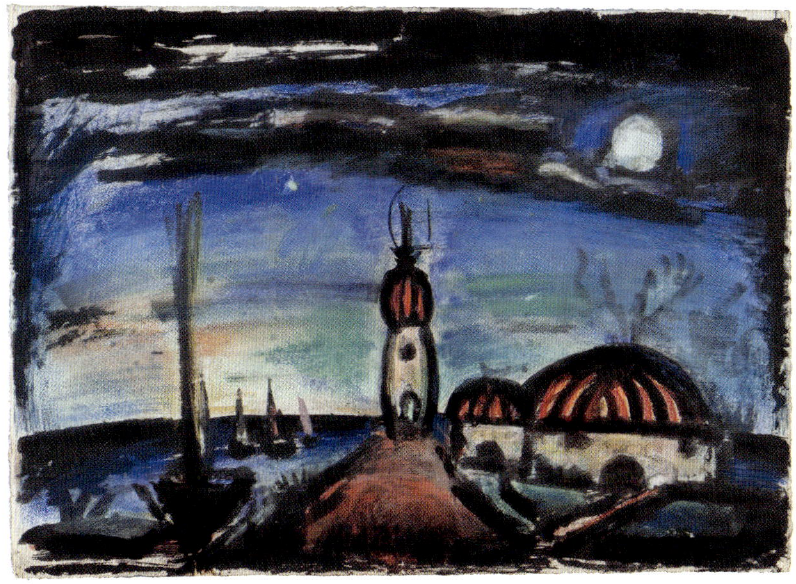

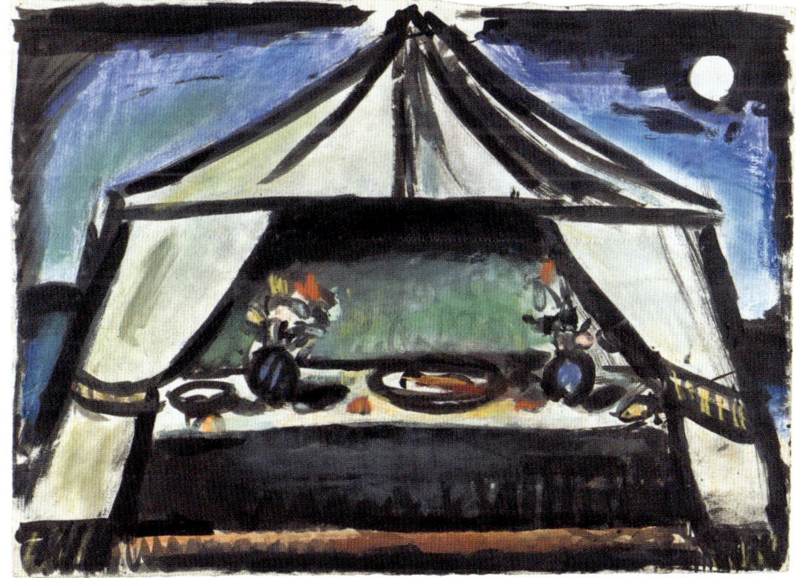

Fig. 2.10a

Georges Rouault (French, 1871–1958), *Design for the Backcloth for Scenes 1 and 3: "Home" from "Le Fils Prodigue,"* 1929. Pastel, ink, tempera, and watercolor, on paper, 20 5/16 × 28 13/16 in. (51.6 × 73.2 cm). Wadsworth Atheneum Museum of Art, Hartford, Conn. The Ella Gallup Sumner and Mary Catlin Sumner Collection Fund, 1933.536.

Fig. 2.10b

Georges Rouault, *Design for the Banqueting Tent for Scene 2: "In a Far Country" from "Le Fils Prodigue,"* 1929. Pastel and gouache on paper, 20 3/4 × 28 7/8 in. (52.7 × 73.3 cm). Wadsworth Atheneum Museum of Art, Hartford, Conn. The Ella Gallup Sumner and Mary Catlin Sumner Collection Fund, 1933.535.

Ted maintained an abiding admiration for Balanchine and his dancers, often in plain stage surroundings and basic costuming that came to be dubbed NYCB's black-and-white look, which was due in good measure to budgetary constraints. But Ted retained a strong interest in more decidedly designed and costumed productions. His all but unqualified admiration for Karinska's costuming at NYCB, however, was not matched by a similarly reliable counterpart in the area of the troupe's scenic efforts. His dislike for some of the "scenic investiture," as he liked to call it, could be stinging. In the case of Peter Harvey's setting for *Jewels*,[21] which framed Karinska's jewel-encrusted, costumed dancers, Ted once suggested that the stage appeared to be set with "cement drapes." He expressed consistent liking, however, for the work of David Hays, who designed lighting as well as visual elements for Balanchine. Overall, Ted admired the spareness, simplicity, and lightness characterizing Hays's scenic efforts. Ted used to say that, in a multiact theatrical work, it was more effective to have fewer visual elements in the end than to have added more and more. Hays's lighting and scenery for *Episodes*,[22] *Liebeslieder Walzer*,[23] and *A Midsummer Night's Dream*[24] all elicited Ted's commendation. In 1985, two years after Balanchine's death, at the behest of Lincoln Kirstein, NYCB presented *Liebeslieder* in a new setting, based on the ornate Amalienburg hunting lodge in Munich, by designer David Mitchell. Ted's assessment of the effort prompted him to say to me, "It looks like a bank." Hays's earlier *Liebeslieder* schemes, with simpler suggestions of a drawing room interior that appeared to breathe the light and air of a mellow evening, struck Ted as more fitting and evocative than the specificity of Mitchell's more architecturally accurate setting. Elsewhere and earlier at NYCB, Ted had utmost praise for the work of Jean Rosenthal, an innovative lighting designer who was also sometimes responsible for striking and yet strikingly simple settings: *La Valse*,[25] with its use of diaphanous, smoky fabrics and sparkler-like chandeliers, is one sterling example of the decor she provided for her lighting, all to Ted's abiding admiration.

Ted's long-standing enthusiasm for the sculpture of Isamu Noguchi easily transferred to the artist's work for NYCB's ballet stage when he designed Balanchine's 1948 *Orpheus*.[26] Already known for the visual elements he provided for the dances of Martha Graham, Noguchi contributed sculptural costuming and props for Balanchine's Stravinsky ballet. He also chose a gossamer, cascading, china silk curtain to isolate the front of the stage for the moment when the characters of Orpheus and Eurydice make their way from the underworld to the world of the living. Ted never found the silk-curtain moment nearly as effective when it was rescaled in 1972 for transference to the larger, higher proscenium

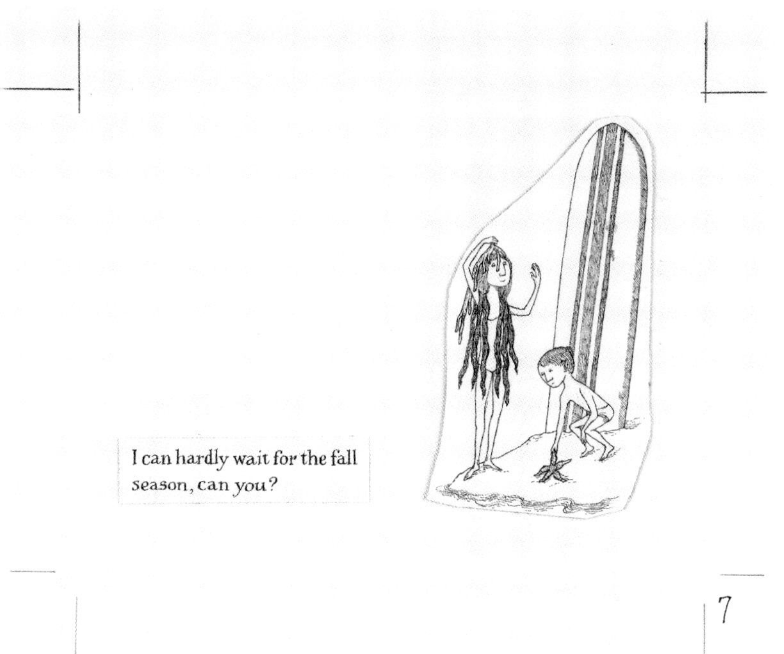

Fig. 2.11
Edward Gorey, "I can hardly wait for the fall season, can you?" Illustration for *The Lavender Leotard: Or, Going a Lot to the New York City Ballet.* New York: Gotham Book Mart, 1973. Pen and ink on paper, 6⅜ × 7¹¹⁄₁₆ in. (16.2 × 19.5 cm). The Edward Gorey Charitable Trust.

stage of the New York State Theater. On the smaller-scaled stage of City Center, where I never saw it and for which it was originally designed, Ted often told of its falling into place in almost gasping tones, specifically describing it as "ravishing" and, in one of his sometime favorite phrases, "to die for."

Another of Noguchi's *Orpheus* effects that Ted found transcendent, as he might say, at least when it was seen at City Center, was the sudden, smooth, and somewhat brief descent of what looked like a sky-blue drip of fresh air, meant, presumably, to indicate the brightness of the upper world awaiting Orpheus and Eurydice when they emerged from the dark of the lower. One plate, the fifth, of his *Lavender Leotard* takes Noguchi's *Orpheus* for its subject (fig. 2.11). Ted felt that some of Noguchi's set elements resembled surfboards, and that the streaming pieces on his costume for Eurydice were seaweed-like; the red sculpture at the mouth of the figure of Pluto was essentially a starfish. The only detail Ted remained less enamored of, and did not depict in this drawing, was the crocheted circle affixed to Eurydice's midsection, which he said "made Maria [Tallchief, the original Eurydice] look like she had a bagel on her stomach."

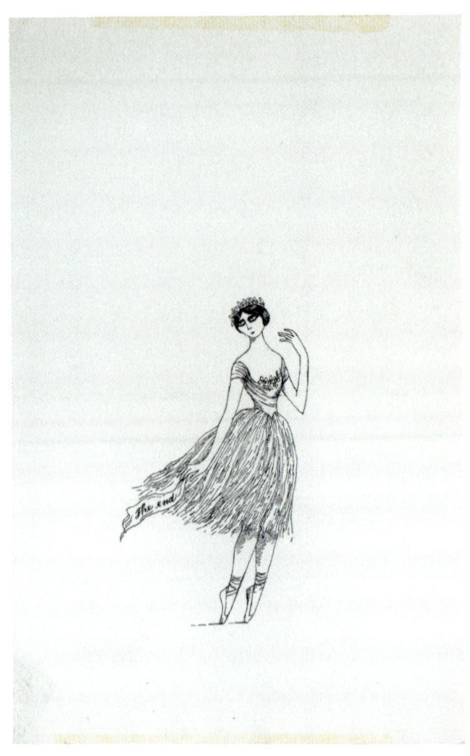

Ted's various ballet world drawings run a gamut, revealing a fascination with the plain and the fancy. Many of these were done gratis for NYCB and for the ballet publications and smaller troupes whose efforts Ted found worthy. For *Ballet Review*, the journal Croce founded in 1965, Ted did any number of drawings; and it was there that he first published his now-classic depiction of the ballet world in all its glamour and drudgery, eventually issued as *The Gilded Bat* (fig. 2.12).[27]

One illustration for a *Ballet Review* benefit captures NYCB's bare-bones visual look, as well as the tone of Balanchine's angular choreography, as seen in works from *Agon* to *Episodes* (fig. 2.13). [28] Another of Ted's designs, for the cover of vol. 4, no. 1, reveals his sense of NYCB's major counterpart in the United States, American Ballet Theatre. There, a single ballerina, dubbed "La Déesse Éclectique," is shown sprouting additional arms and legs, costumed for some nine different kinds of ballets (fig. 2.14). This, again, is not to imply that Ted didn't welcome high-styled costuming. His seventh plate for *The Lavender*

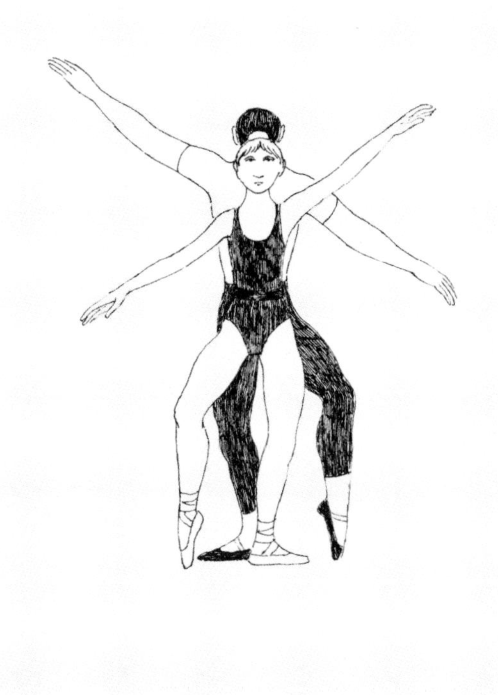

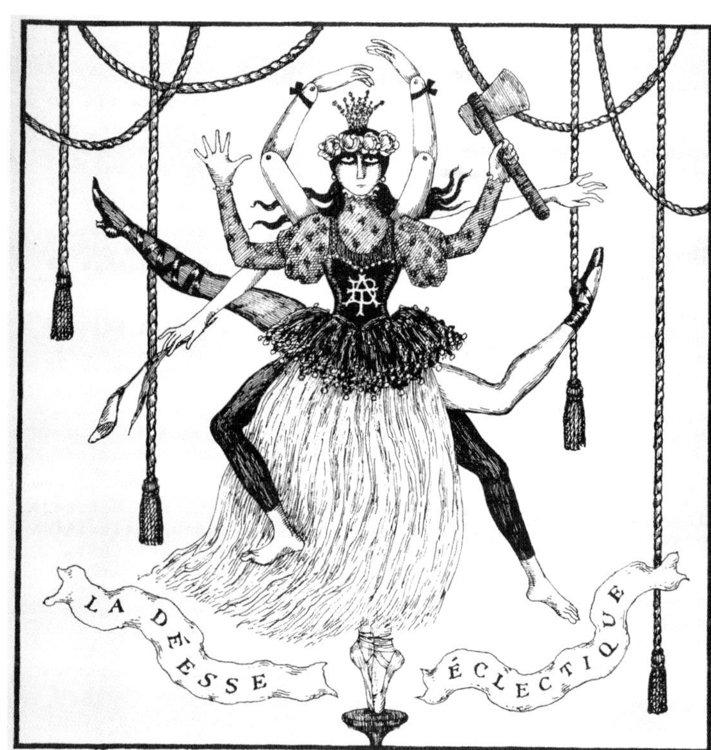
LA DÉESSE   ÉCLECTIQUE

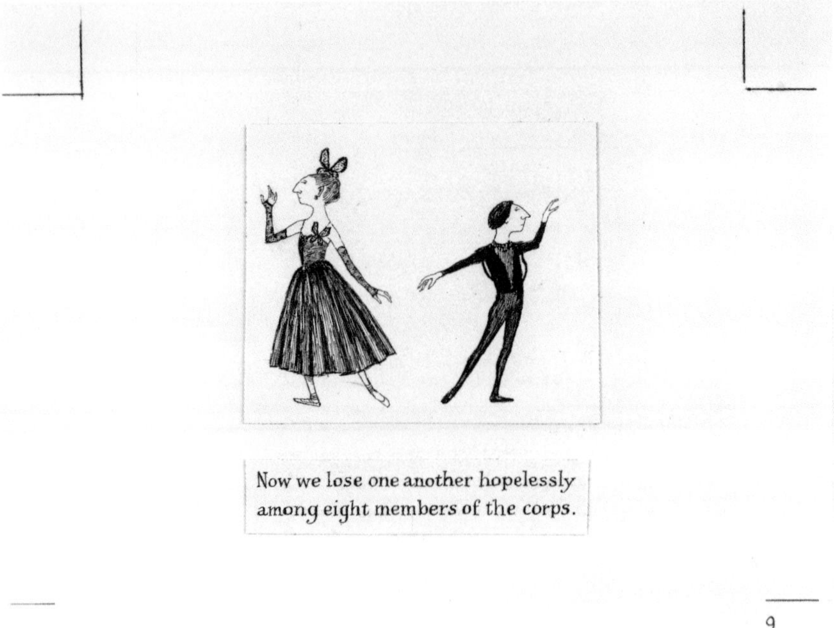

Leotard, the very title of which indicates how weary Ted could become with some of NYCB's more plain costuming,[29] evokes a scene from the second movement of Balanchine's *Bourrée Fantasque*:[30] Ted captures some of the detailing of Karinska's dusky costuming for the woman, with its butterfly hair ornaments and fingerless gloves (fig. 2.15). This ballet to Chabrier's music, which Ted would readily call "zippy," is deftly comedic at the start, lushy romantic at the center, and wildly rollicking at the end. It was a big favorite of his, not least because the ballerina identified in Ted's day with the central role was Diana Adams, the NYCB ballerina he arguably revered above all others. His remembrance[31] of Adams after her death in 1993 is sober and heartfelt. In the essay, Ted sums up his attempts to articulate what he so admired about Adams and her dancing thus: "None of this, however, solves the mystery of her special quality, all the more mysterious for there apparently being no mystery about her at all" (fig. 2.16).

While Ted primarily attended ballet performances in NYC, which he often followed by going to a movie, he also took in other dance events,

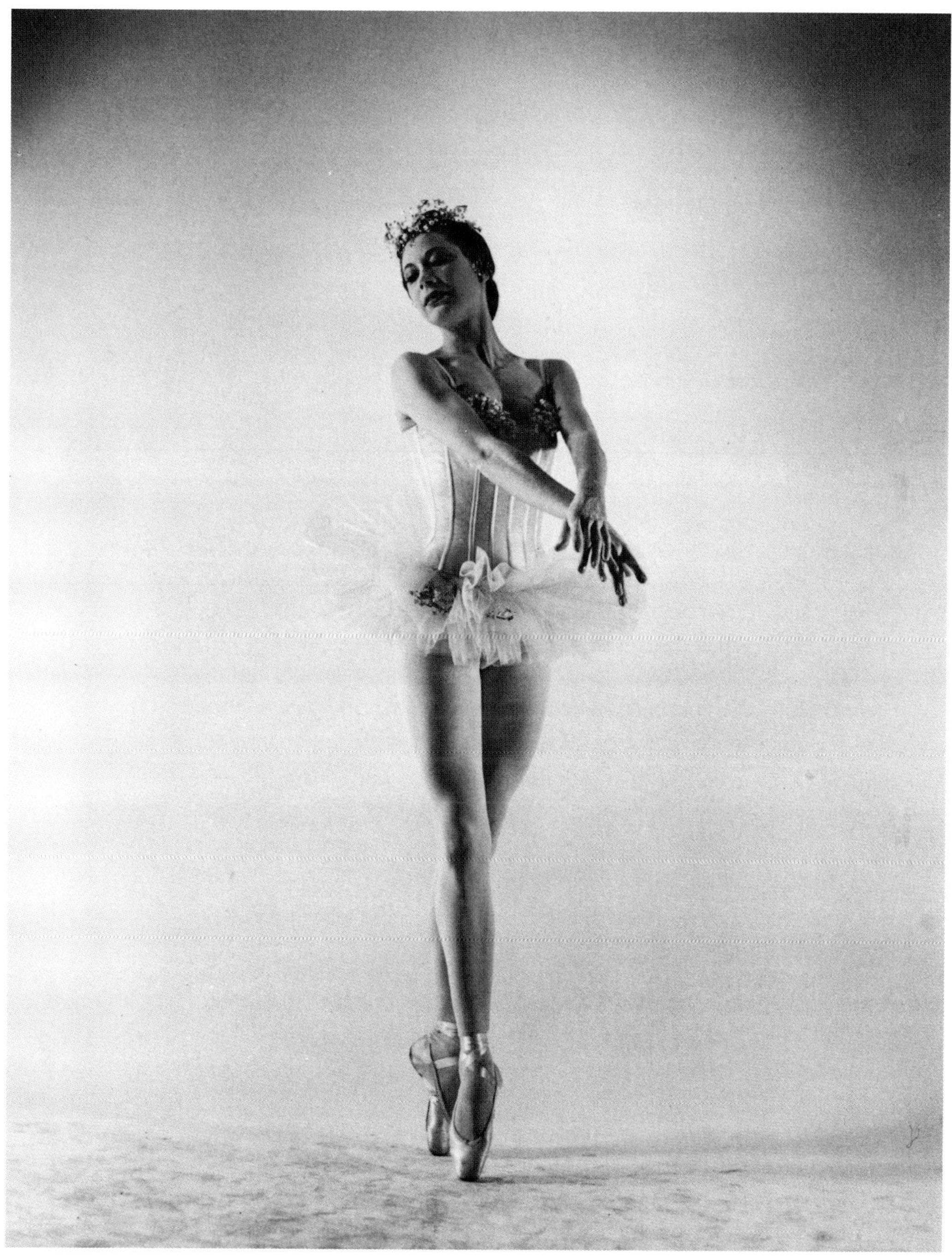

including non-Western dance forms as well as modern and postmodern dance. Of this "other" dance category, as a great admirer of the artistry of Japan he was especially fond of Japan's Bunraku puppet theater and of its Noh drama,[32] as well as of India's often raucous-toned Kathakali theater. After Balanchine died, Ted was most taken with the modern dance works of Paul Taylor. His few jaunts back to town from his home on Cape Cod, once he was settled there year-round, were for seasons of the Paul Taylor Dance Company. He was enthusiastically fond of many of Taylor's dances, in particular those with inspired settings and costume designs by such contemporary artists as Alex Katz and Gene Moore. Katz's *Diggity*,[33] for example, complete with multiple painted, cutout figures of two different dogs was a special favorite of Ted's, as was Moore's work for *Dust*[34] and *Nightshade*.[35] Of this last, I can still hear Ted's appreciative delight in Taylor's dark and, as Ted might have called it, loony sense of theater, as a woman, Victoria Uris, costumed in Moore's long black slip of a dress, rolled around the stage with her head in a woven wicker basket, somewhat as, perhaps, a playful cat might do.[36] *Nightshade* took inspiration from the collage series *Une semaine de bonté* (A Week of Kindness) by the surrealist artist Max Ernst. Ted felt more respect than enthusiasm for Taylor's precursor Martha Graham. With regard to some of the more fraught moments in Graham's often intense dances, Ted could be heard exclaiming, "Oh Martha, come off it!" Of Taylor's contemporary, Merce Cunningham, Ted commented, "I know he's a genius, but he bores the pants off me!"

Of the next, now-called postmodern generation, Ted, as stated above, cared a good deal for Tharp, with whom he was briefly involved as a potential collaborator for what became, without his participation, *When We Were Very Young*.[37] He admired dancer-choreographer David Gordon, for whom he designed the one stage work of his to have been shown at the Metropolitan Opera House. *Murder*[38] was a dance theater work of Gordon's for American Ballet Theatre, and while Ted contributed its look, costumes, press-kit art, and props (figs. 2.17, 2.18), he did so from his place on the Cape, refusing, as he did when his production of *Dracula* opened on Broadway in 1977, to attend the event, let alone take a bow. Later still, Ted eagerly attended performances of Mark Morris's works, sometimes driving in the same night from the Cape to Boston, and back again, to meet me in the city for a performance by the Mark Morris Dance Group.

Approximately three years before Balanchine's death, which more or less gave Ted leave to quit NYC (losing his rent-controlled apartment also played a part), he gave further of his time, artwork, and writing to "A *Ballet*

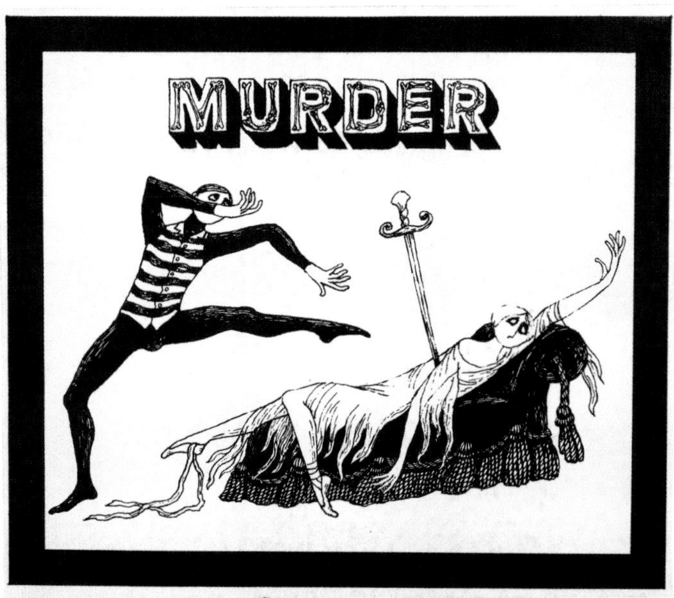

Fig. 2.17

Edward Gorey, Illustrated ephemera in the press kit for *Murder*, a ballet by David Gordon for the American Ballet Theatre. 1986. Collection of Robert Greskovic.

Fig. 2.18

Marty Sohl, *Amy Rose (as an unnamed damsel) and Mikhail Baryshnikov (as a Jekyll/Hyde character) in "Murder,"* 1986. Publicity photo. Collection of Robert Greskovic.

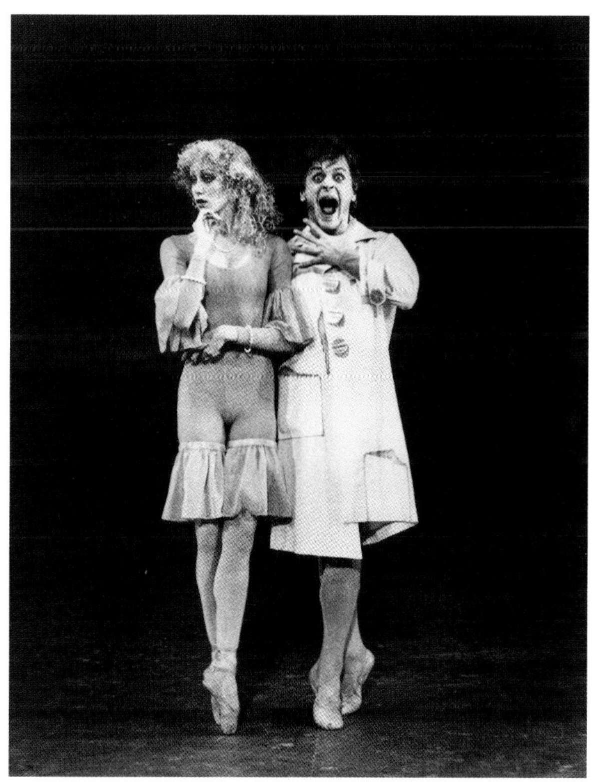

Review Symposium: Directing a Dance Company, and Doing It Properly"
(fig. 2.19).[39] Ted's written contribution[40] takes up twelve pages in the journal.
Among the ballets he proposed for his jeu d'esprit are *L'Avènement des asperges
géantes d'une planète inconnue* ("The advent of giant asparagus from an
unknown planet"), *Patty* (for Patty Hearst), and *One Who Steps Off the Curb*,
a play on a Martha Graham–like statement about stepping into the unknown
of daily life. For each of the twenty-one ballets parceled into nine different
programs, he suggested music, designers, and casting. He also designed
the issue's cover, which shows a garden grown with ballerinas on stems and
tutued in lemon yellow, all suitable for clipping and arranging into bouquets.
The illustration depicts a flower lover, a sun-hat-wearing *jardinier* somewhat
reminiscent of the Gordon Craig character in *The Remembered Visit: A Story
Taken from Life*.[41] The mustachioed man readies his shears for cutting the
flowers he'd like to make into an arrangement; like the man in "Ballet in a
Nutshell," this one might well be Ted himself.

   With Balanchine's death in 1983, Ted would leave his familiar *jardin
de la danse* for the next, and final, phase of his theater-connected life,[42] which
largely took shape on Cape Cod. There, he took in as many movies as he
cared to, among which *Babe*,[43] a talking-animals movie with the tagline "A
little pig goes a long way," won his unbounded enthusiasm. Ted also found
time to work on sundry theatricals or musicales, as he liked to call his musi-
cally underpinned theatricals, as well as on the puppet plays he devised, wrote,
and directed[44] once he was comfortably settled in his house on Strawberry
Lane, in Yarmouth Port.[45] Though quite fond of the Cape home that he would
call "the elephant" because of its weathered, gray exterior, he would blanch
a bit when someone would pigeonhole the address with the words "Oh Ted,
it's so you." To which he'd say something like, "Oh dear, I'm not sure I want it
to be so me."

   To the end, however, I presume Ted did still want to be entertained.

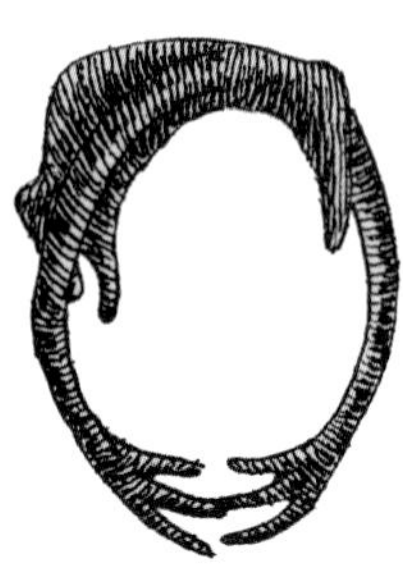

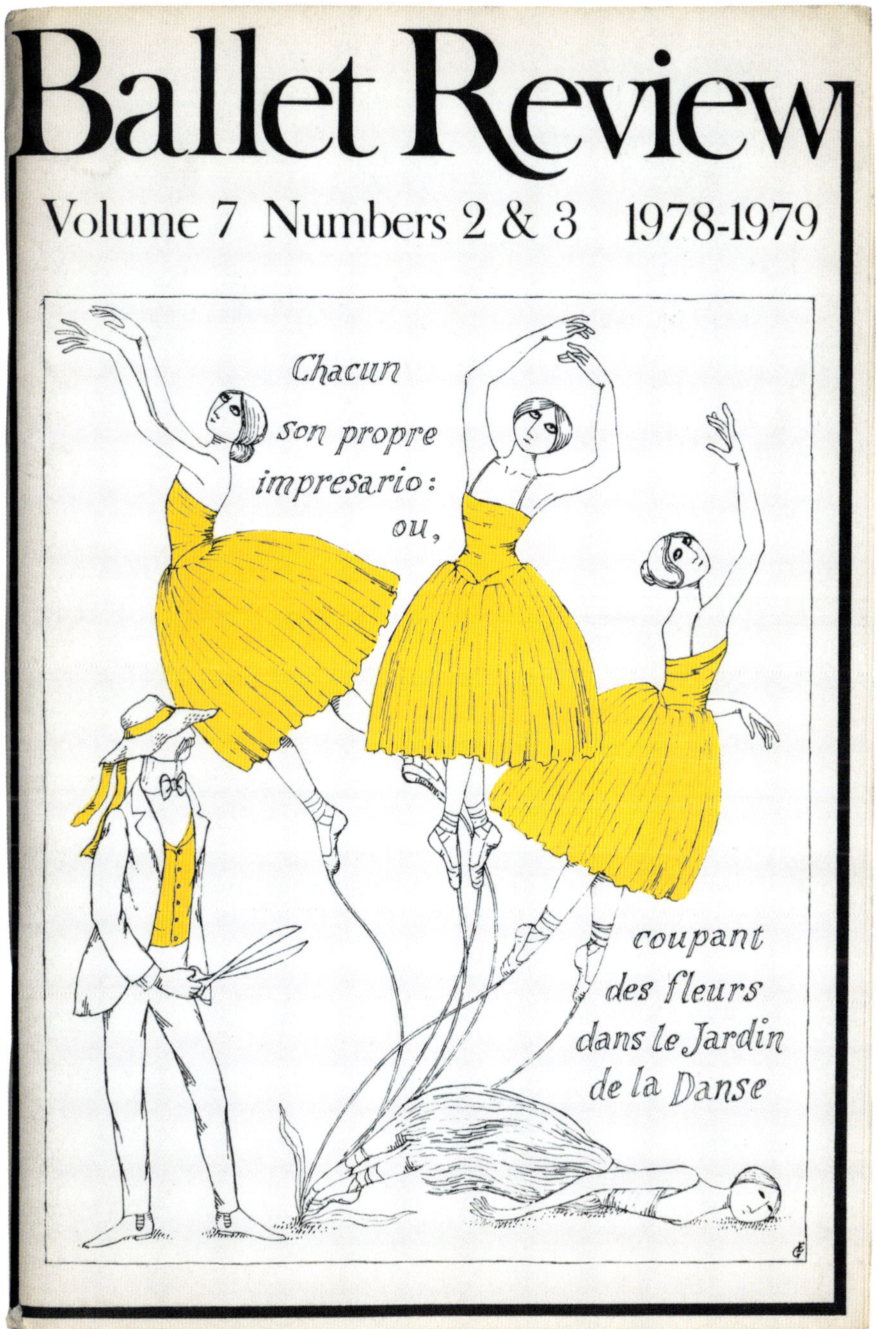

Fig. 2.19
Edward Gorey, Cover illustration for "A *Ballet Review* Symposium: Directing a Dance Company and Doing It Properly," published in *Ballet Review* 7, nos. 2 & 3 (1978–79). Collection of Robert Greskovic.

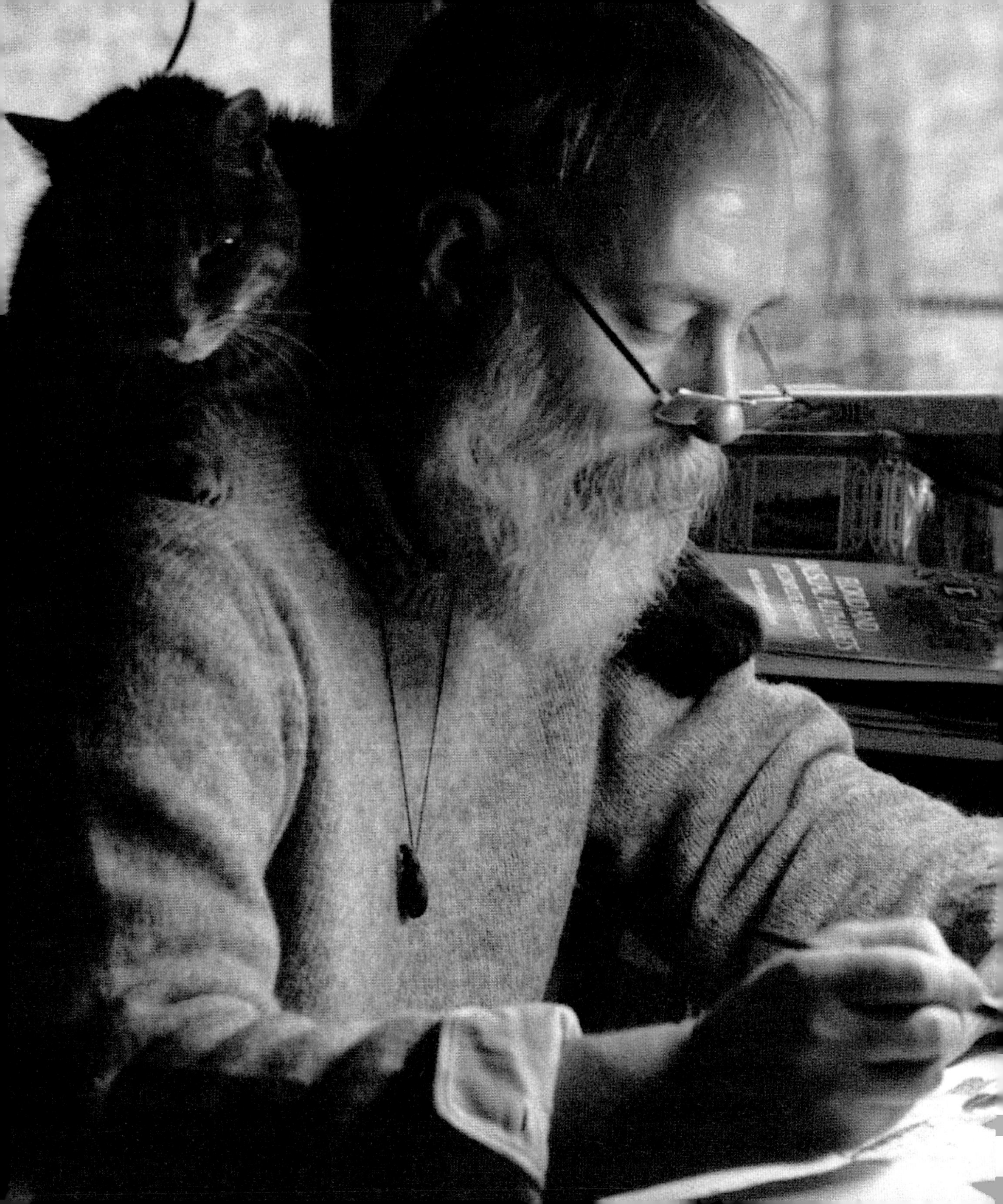

Arnold Arluke

Understanding Gorey's Human-Animal World

A nimals commonly appear in Gorey's own books, in those he illustrated, and in his personal collection of art and objects. Animals appear in Gorey's artwork and collected items because they had incredible significance in his personal life. He spent a great deal of time thinking about and interacting with animals in his house, where he surrounded himself with numerous cats as housemates and friends (fig. 3.1). He also created a charitable trust to support the operation of animal welfare agencies, the protection of a variety of animals, and the work of humane societies. In his artistic work, Gorey's use of animals speaks to a deeper and more complex creative approach to humans' relationship with them than merely fondness of them as pets or concern about their welfare.

TRANSFORMING ANIMALS

Gorey changes the everyday or mundane function, nature, or appearance of his animal creations by transforming them into anthropomorphic creatures, human surrogates, or fantasy animals.

Detail of fig. 3.1

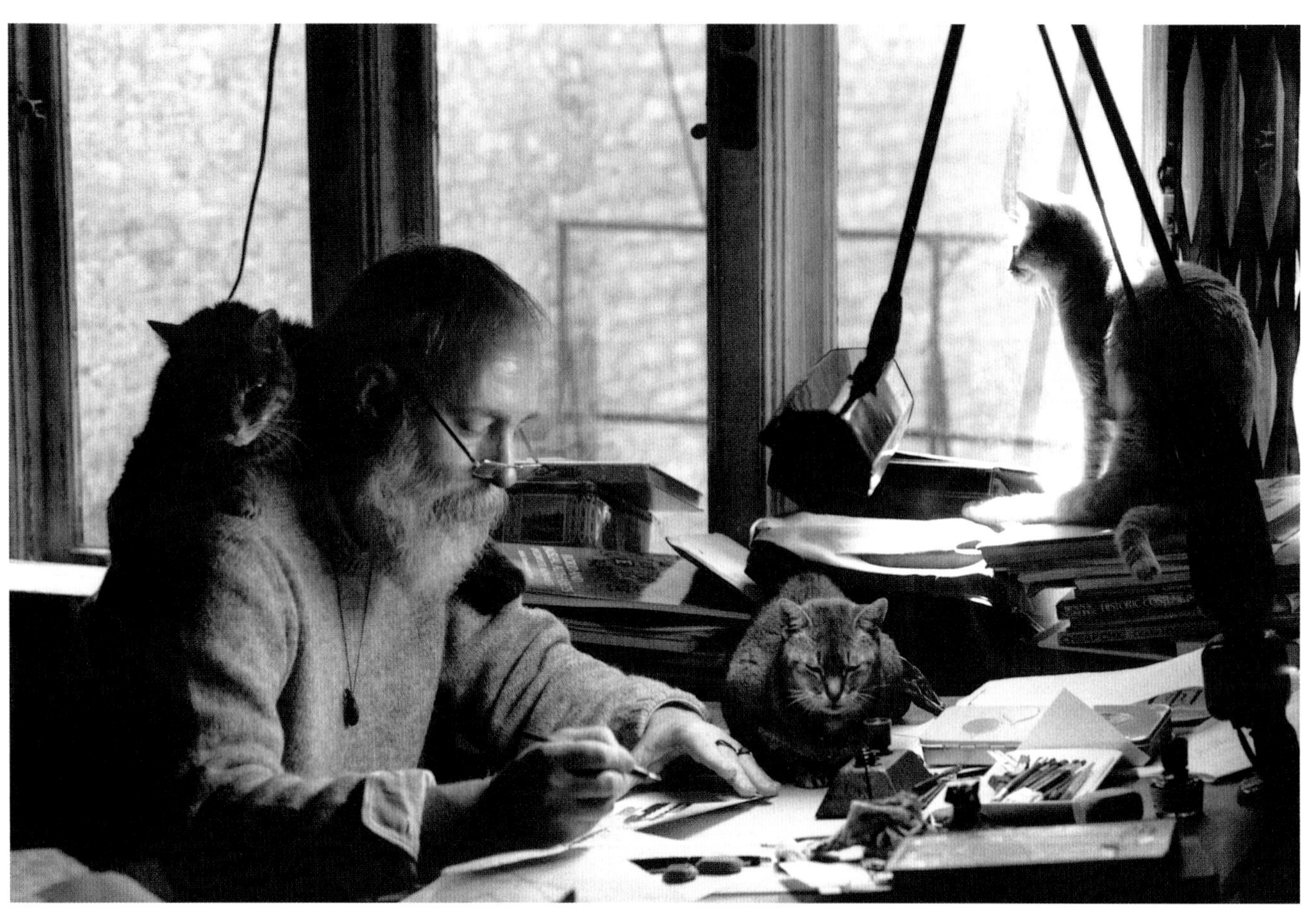

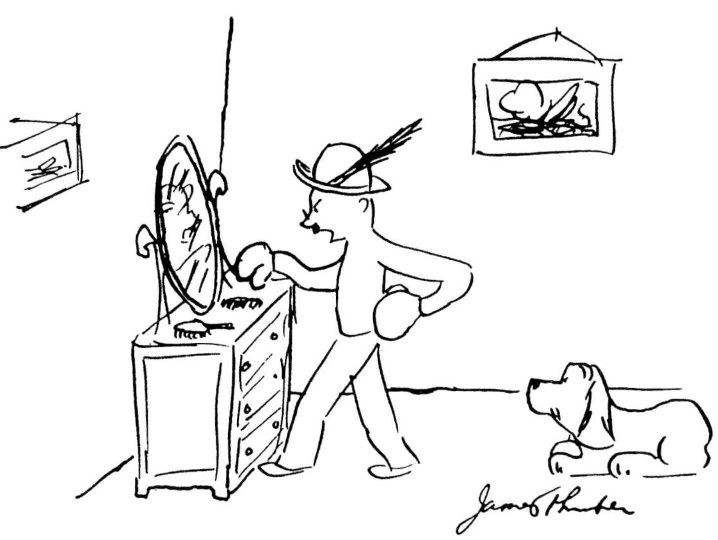

"They're going to put you away if you don't quit acting like this."

Humanoids

To anthropomorphize something is to humanize, to personify; to describe or to explain the nonhuman in human terms; or to attribute human qualities (mental states, physical appearance) to product brands, technical devices and machines, and animals other than *Homo sapiens*. When this is done with animals, boundaries between humans and animals are softened or become completely blurred. Anthropomorphic animals are often used as symbolic protection to distance people from threatening or uncomfortable situations. For example, some people talk through their pets, as though they were human significant others, to express thoughts and feelings they could not otherwise safely articulate. The animal intermediary cushions a communication that would be difficult to undertake more directly. We also find humanizing interesting, even funny, precisely because there exists an underlying culturally supported distinction between humans and other animals that humanizing violates.

Gorey's interest in anthropomorphizing animals is everywhere in his stories and his art, as well as in some of his collected images. One of the latter

Fig. 3.3

Edward Gorey, "Cat with scarf on unicycle, #31." Illustration in *Category: Fifty Drawings.* New York: Gotham Book Mart, 1973.

is James Thurber's "They're going to put you away if you don't quit acting like this," a drawing of a pet dog contemplating his owner's odd behavior while the latter looks into a mirror (fig. 3.2). An equally plausible reading of the drawing suggests that the man and his dog are conversing.

Gorey continues to humanize some of his animals by adorning them with human clothing: they wear sneakers, scarves, top hats, derbies, and they hold umbrellas and read books. They participate in human activities: they play musical instruments, dance, and ride unicycles (fig. 3.3). Even dangerous animals are often depicted whimsically, as in a series of etchings Gorey made featuring elephants. Elephants cavort, carry figures on their backs, shower, and hold dapper canes. His ballet cats dance as gracefully as their human counterparts. His animals even have human mental and emotional states. One of his creatures demonstrates curiosity as it peeks around the letter *I* in "Indecency" (fig. 3.4). And his cats wear bewitching smiles, whether they are standing atop a unicycle or leaning against a gravestone; they seem carefree and sprightly, in happy contrast to Gorey's more gothic creations.

Surrogates

While anthropomorphized animals are given attributes that make them human-like, some animals can serve as stand-ins for humans, substituting for a range of human ties[1]—from friends and authority figures to imagined or lost dependents. Animals have served as sex objects, transitional phenomena, symbols of enemies, and significant others for individuals, families, and groups, such as sailors at sea[2] or adult couples without children.[3] Animals, especially those treated as companions, can easily become "virtual persons"[4] because they are perceived as empathic but do not question or judge.[5] By substituting for human bonds, these real or imaginary ties with animals can provide children and adults with unique experiences not readily available from fellow humans.[6] Indeed, the ability of animals to substitute for human companions may account for many of the positive effects that pets allegedly have on humans.[7]

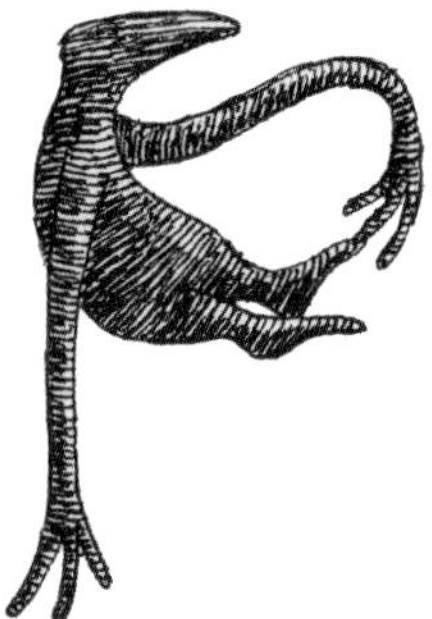

Many of Gorey's animal characters appear to substitute for missing humans in the images' stories—whether the absent person is supposed to be someone's playmate, best friend, or parent. For example, in *The Osbick Bird*,[8] a man and his feathered friend appear to enjoy their companionship and share cups of tea "frequently," as might two people who have a warm and close relationship (fig. 3.5).

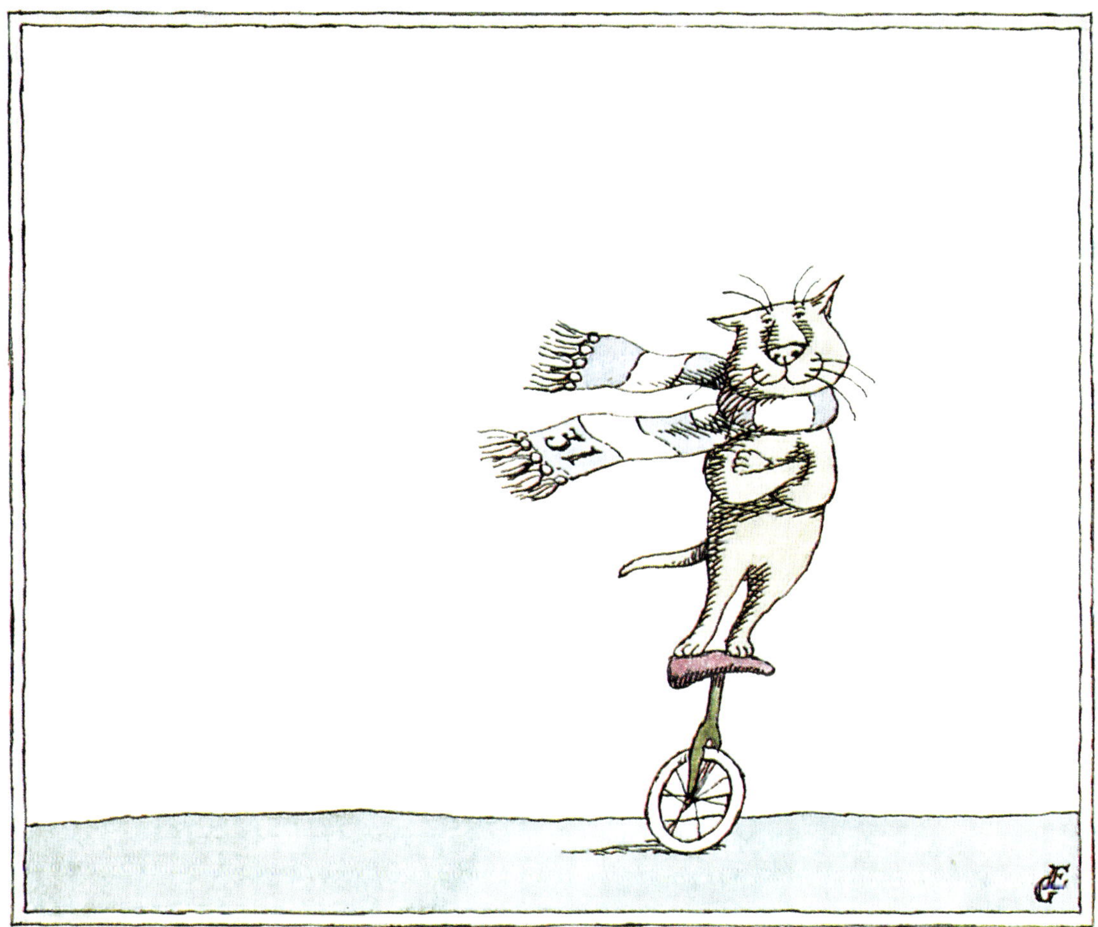

Fig. 3.4

Edward Gorey, "Indecency."
1980. One of thirteen cards
from *Dogear Wryde Postcards:
Interpretive Series*.

Fig. 3.5

Edward Gorey, "The top of the
zagava tree / Was frequently
where they had tea."
Illustration in *The Osbick Bird*.
New York: Fantod Press, 1970.

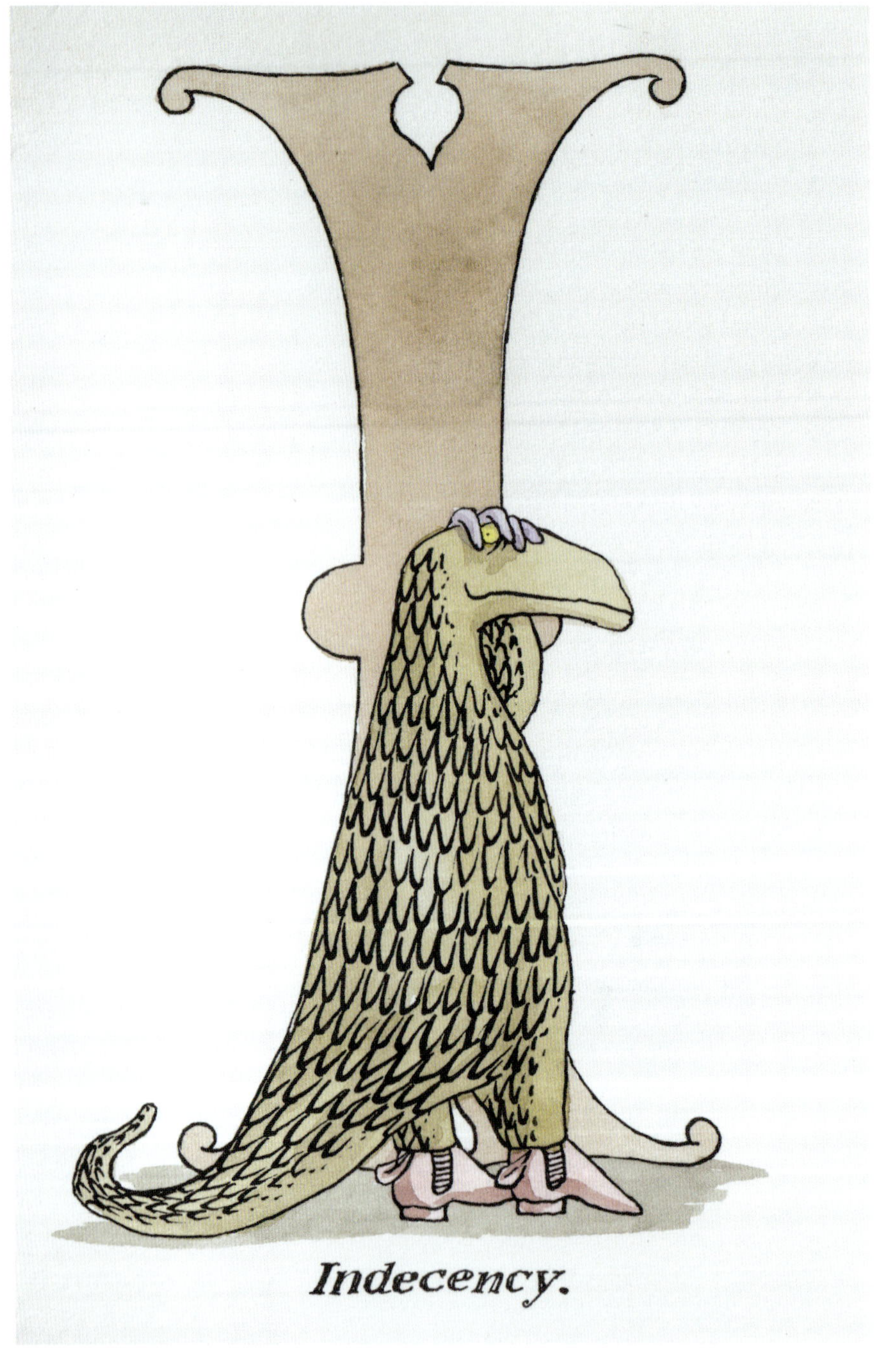

Indecency.

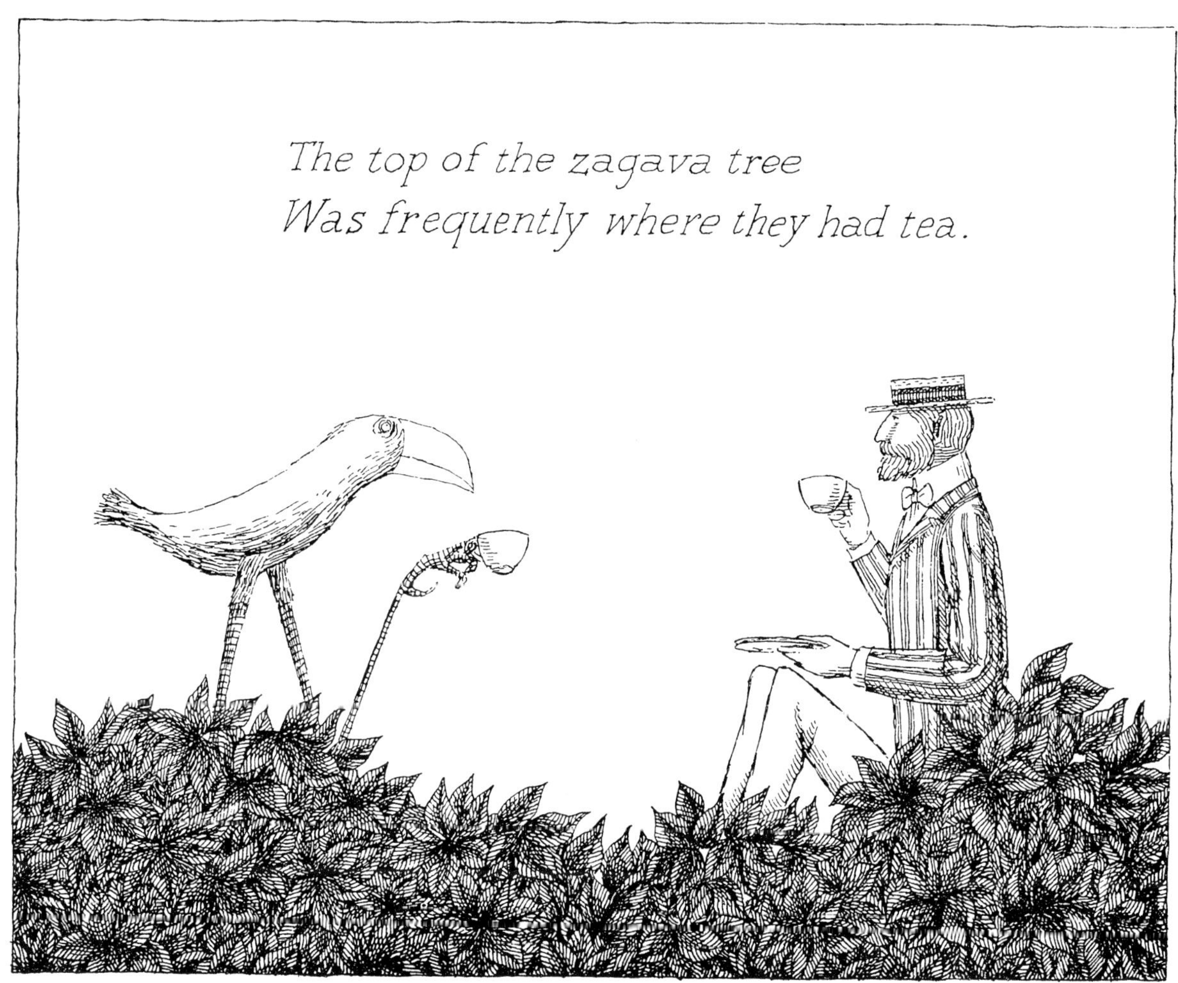
The top of the zagava tree
Was frequently where they had tea.

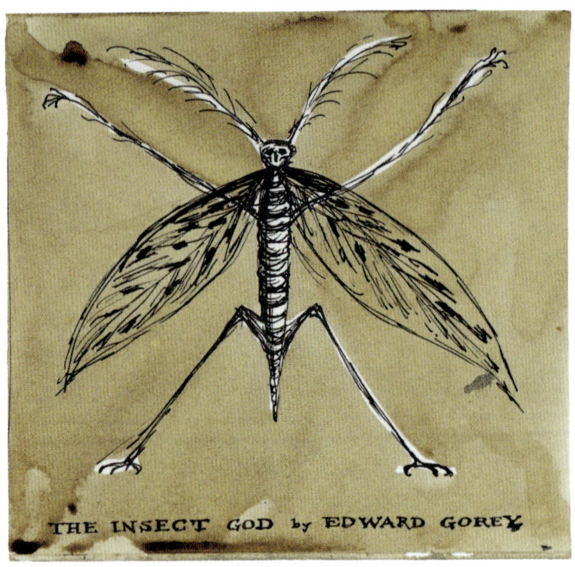

Inventions

Hybrid animals are common in literature and visual arts, but less so are truly
fantastic creations that are original and bizarre.[9] Whether hybrid or fantasy, these
artistic inventions breathe new life into borrowed bits and pieces of animals in
order to create something altogether challenging and new.

Some of Gorey's animal creations are hybrids that combine aspects of
actual animals—heads, tails, legs, claws—with those from other animals, while
others are surreal inventions that have no real-world counterparts. Some of
these fantastic creatures can vaguely resemble actual animals, or at least parts
of them, while others are unlike any real animal. One of Gorey's hybrid animals,
the "insect god," has an insect's body, a skull for a face, and butterfly wings
(fig. 3.6). Some of these invented creatures can be oddly endearing. His moody
and stubborn creature known as the Doubtful Guest resembles a furry penguin
wearing high-top sneakers and a striped scarf. Gorey refers to this character as
"it," suggesting it is unique and without gender (fig. 3.7).

Other Gorey animal creations are more fantastic than hybrid because they
have no counterpart in reality in terms of their body parts, expressions, proportions, gaits, or skin coverings. He invented an alphabet of twenty-six strange
and unique creatures in *The Utter Zoo.*[10] One example from this book is Gorey's
Twibbit, a most unusual, one-of-a-kind being (fig. 3.8). While not as inventive or

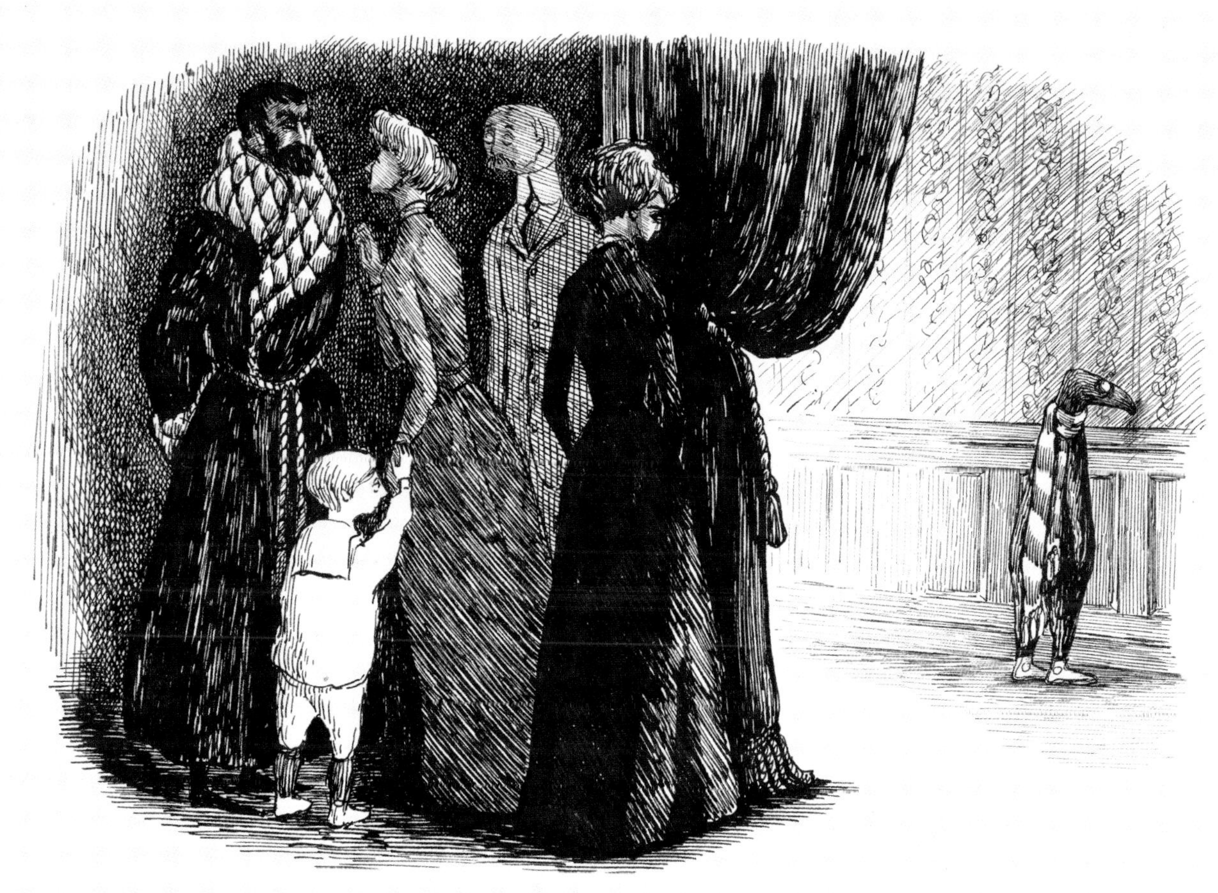

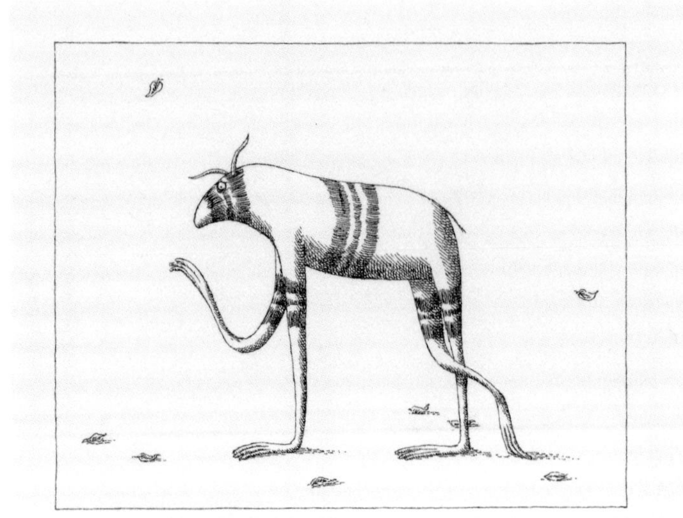

unique as Gorey's hybrid and fantastic animals, a similar playfulness toward the
shape and form of animals appears in a drawing of a horse by Bill Traylor, part
of Gorey's own art collection (fig. 3.9). The horse's strange proportions may have
influenced the animals in Gorey's invented zoo and animal characters.

Counterpoints

Most of Gorey's animals are transformed in some manner, whether into humanoids,
stand-ins, or surreal creatures, but he depicts some in their everyday form. Unlike
his transformed animals, these animals have more realistic appearances, and their
interaction with humans is closer to what we would expect from them in everyday
life. Michael Lynch[11] calls this the "naturalistic animal," or the animal found in
ordinary perception and interaction, as opposed to animals that have been rendered
or transformed.

Although conventional human-animal relationships are a minority of Gorey's
animal depictions, they do occur in his work. In these counterpoints to his typical
animal depictions, the animals are often rendered somewhat realistically and
threaten people, who in turn then victimize or harm the animals. In one example,
an alligator surprises a brother and sister on their bicycle; Embley kicks it and
causes its death (figs. 3.10a,b).

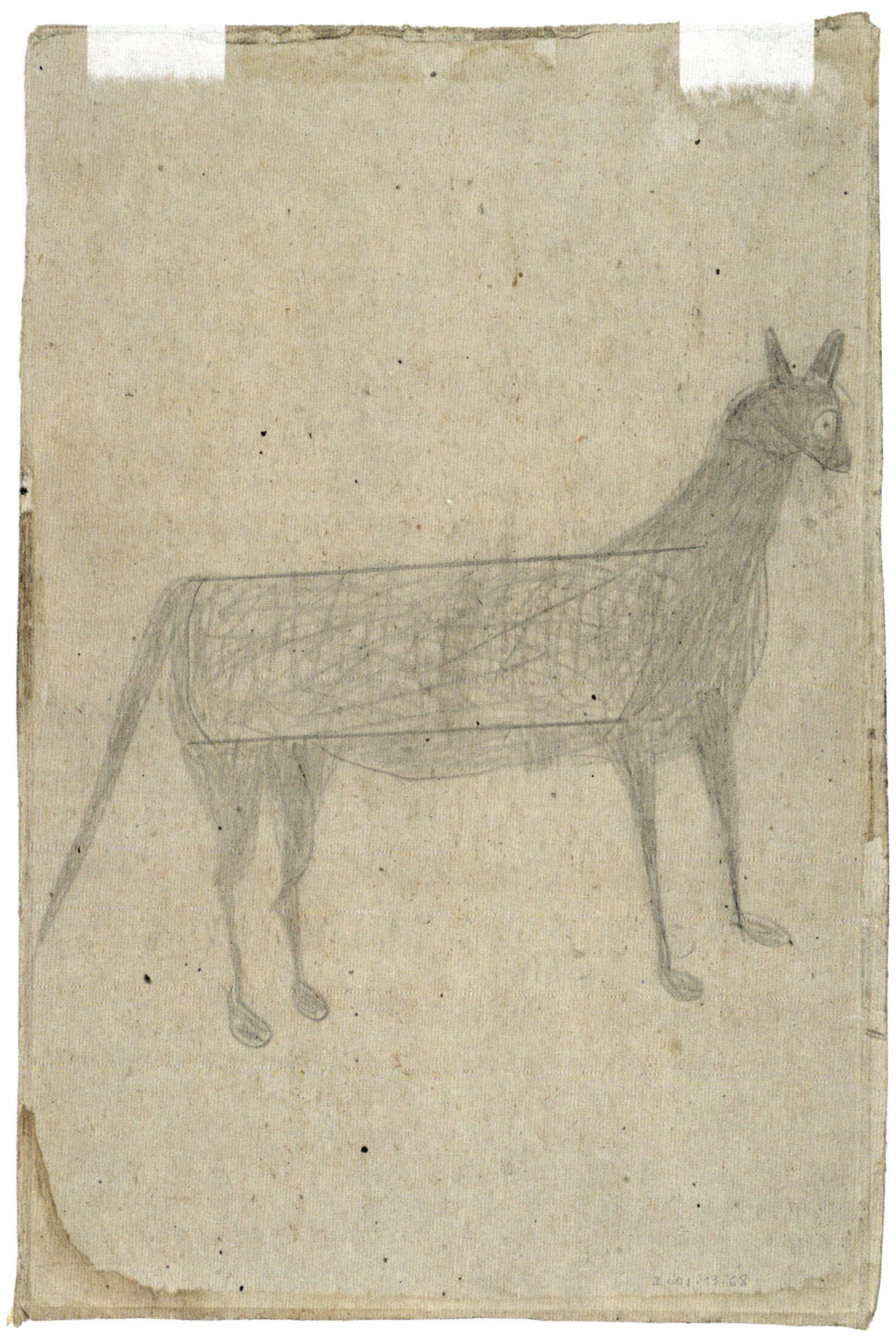

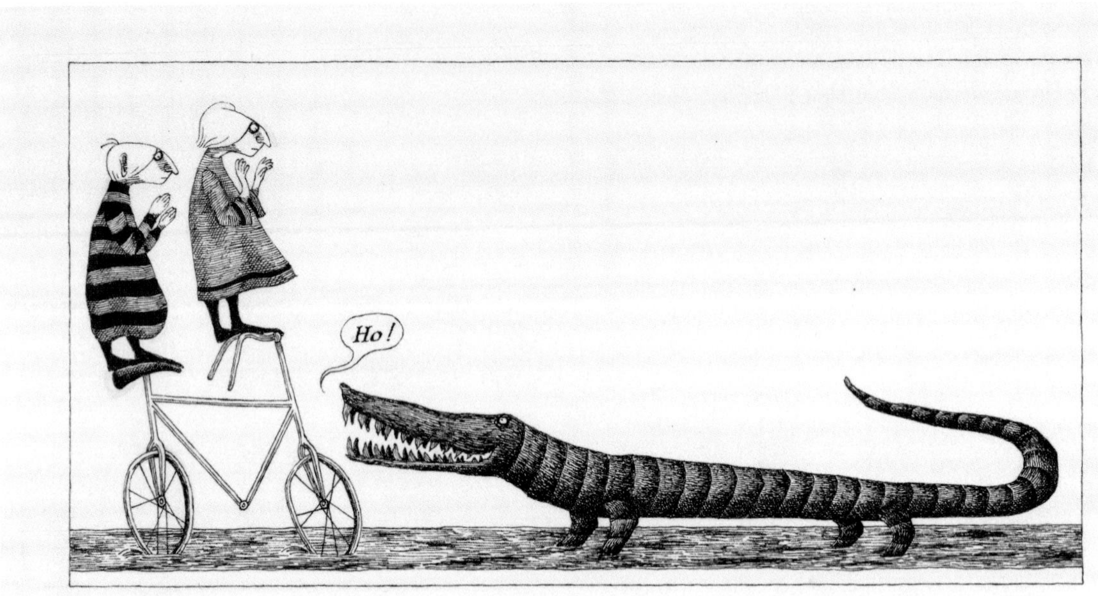

an alligator rose up in front of them;

Fig. 3.10a

Edward Gorey, "An alligator rose up in front of them." Illustration for *The Epiplectic Bicycle*. New York: Dodd, Mead & Company, 1969. Pen and ink on paper, 6 × 9 in. (15.2 × 22.9 cm). The Edward Gorey Charitable Trust.

Fig. 3.10b

Edward Gorey, "Embley kicked it on the end of its nose, and it expired." Illustration in *The Epiplectic Bicycle*. New York: Dodd, Mead & Company, 1969.

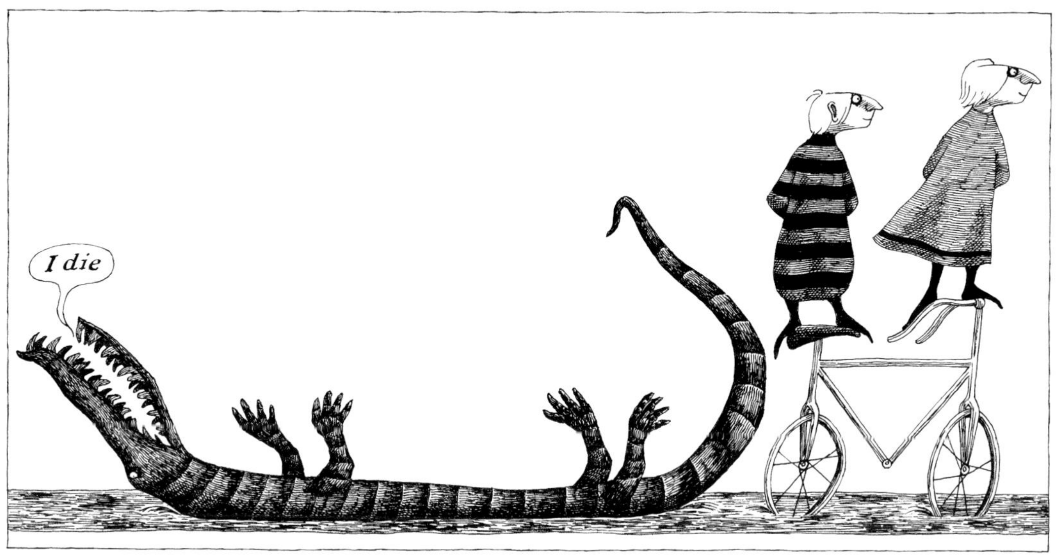

Embley kicked it on the end of its nose, and it expired.

CASTING ANIMALS

Fig. 3.11

Edward Hicks (1780–1849). *The Peaceable Kingdom*, c. 1833. Oil on canvas, 17 ½ × 23 ¹¹⁄₁₆ in. (44.5 × 60.2 cm). Worcester Art Museum. Museum purchase, 1934.65.

Gorey's transformations of the appearance and behavior of animals gave him enormous flexibility to cast these creations in various roles. Rather than being static depictions of animals in different forms, these transformations allowed his animals to behave in unconventional if not unnatural ways, whether as friends, tricksters, or monsters.

Friends

Edward Hicks, an early nineteenth-century folk artist, created a series of paintings called *The Peaceable Kingdom* in which the animals he depicts do not threaten people or other animals in the scenes, even though he included animals regarded as potentially dangerous in everyday life (fig. 3.11). Tigers, lions, and various livestock are positioned comfortably near people as friends. Like Hicks, Gorey's human-animal world can also resemble a peaceable kingdom. Humans are not always threatened when depicted with dangerous animals. For example, one of Gorey's dragon creations has people around the dragon in leisurely poses—one lies on the dragon's back, another over its large claws, and yet another along its meandering tail; one child even balances upside down on the animal's beak: none seem to be the slightest bit concerned or alarmed by their proximity. And in another example, Gorey draws a man sitting with two lions as though they were pets.

To emphasize friendly human-animal relationships, Gorey sometimes pairs exaggeratedly huge animals with small children, but again no threat is implied. In one such composition, he depicts an enormous bear feeding a cookie to a small boy (fig. 3.12).

Some of his work even pairs humans and wild animals living peacefully as family members or close friends. Again, in *The Osbick Bird*, a bird arrives one day to live with a man. The two become best friends, playing music and cards together, drinking tea and going on excursions, occasionally getting into fights. As the story unfolds, eventually the man dies and the bird perches on his gravestone.

Even when the text indicates danger or violence to children or adults, Gorey's work is open to interpretation because his images often suggest a more peaceful or benign story than does the text. For example, in Gorey's *The Gashlycrumb Tinies*, the image in "B is for Basil assaulted by bears" merely depicts a child standing between two enormous bears (fig. 3.13).[12] Rather than showing an impending assault on the boy, the scene might be interpreted as representing all three communicating or making a peaceful journey together.

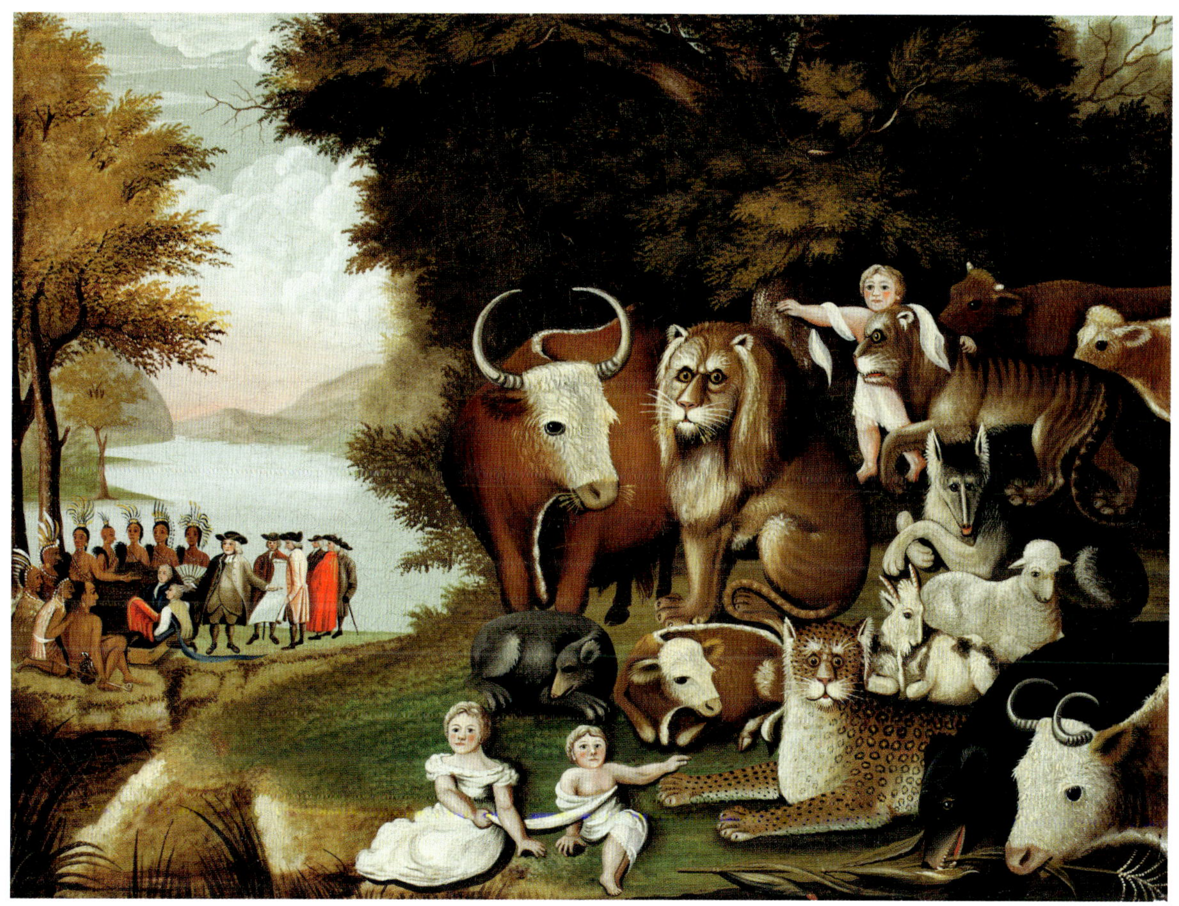

Fig. 3.12

Edward Gorey, "A Future Unremembered Poet of the Seventeenth Century accepts a Christmas Cookie from the Great Veiled Bear." Limited Christmas cards, 1977.

Fig. 3.13

Edward Gorey, "B is for Basil assaulted by bears." Illustration in *The Gashlycrumb Tinies: Or, After the Outing*. New York: Simon and Schuster, 1963.

Fig. 3.14

Eugène Delacroix (French, 1798–1863), *Tigre Couché Dans le Désert (Tiger Sleeping in the Desert)*, 1846. Etching on wove paper, 3 ¼ × 4 ¹⁵⁄₁₆ in. (8.3 × 12.6 cm). Wadsworth Atheneum Museum of Art, Hartford, Conn. Bequest of Edward Gorey, 2001.13.39.

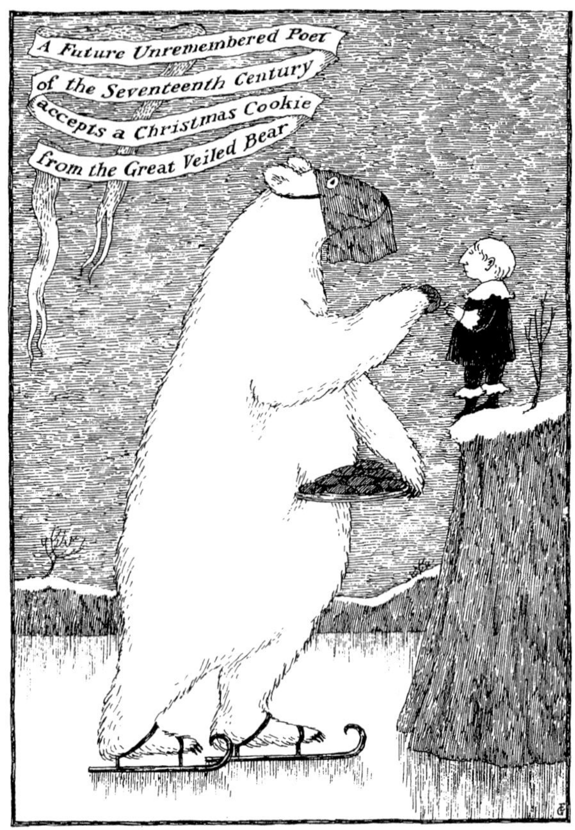

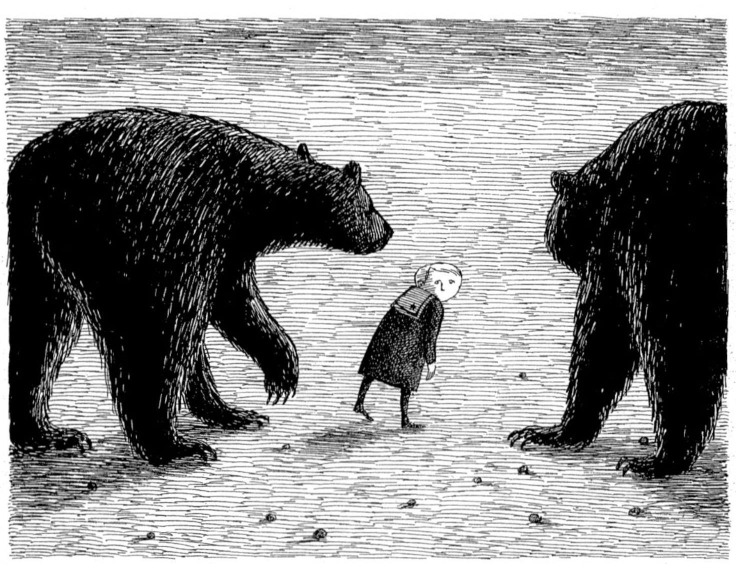

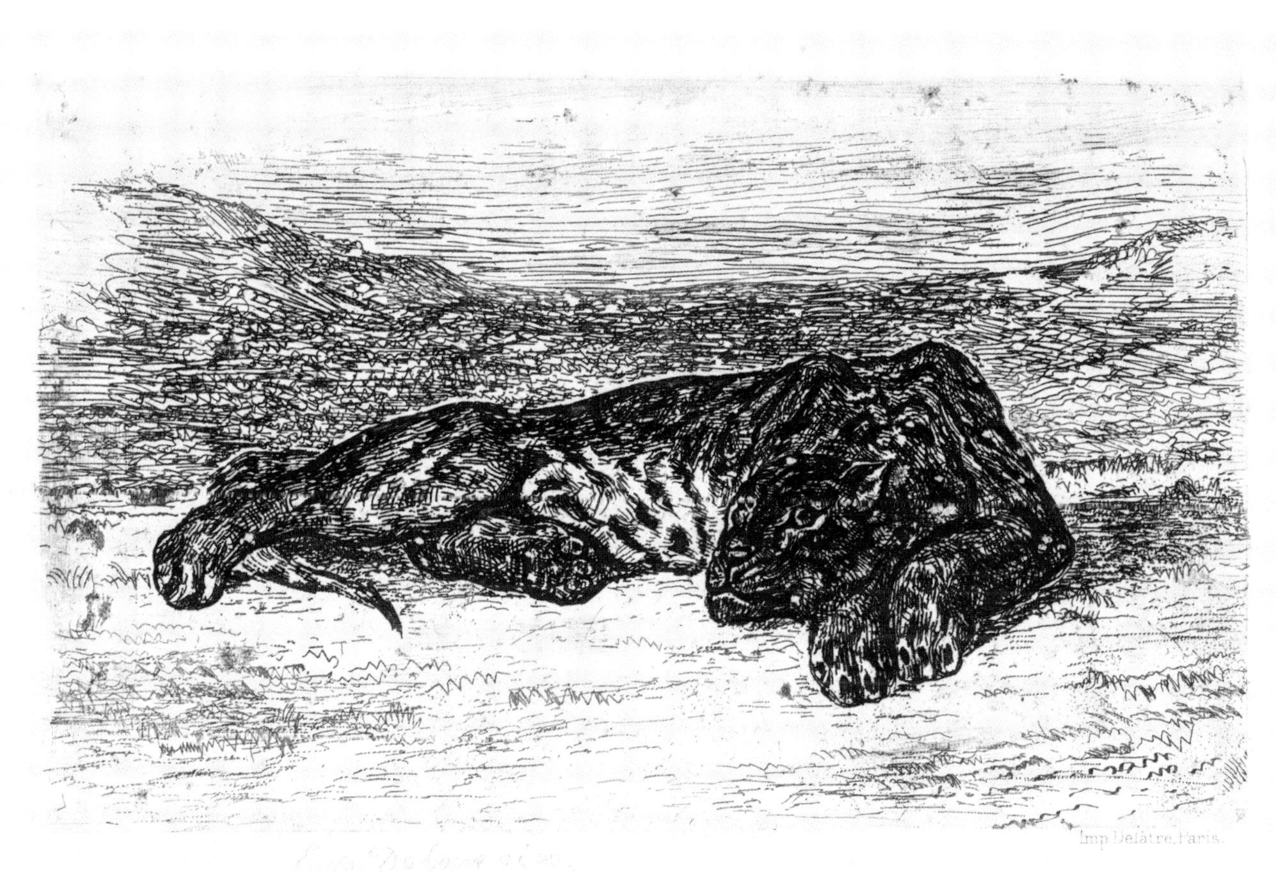

Friendly depictions of harmful animals also appear among the works Gorey collected. For example, in his print by Eugène Delacroix, *Tiger Sleeping in the Desert*, the tiger appears not ferocious or dangerous, but gentle and approachable (fig. 3.14).

Tricksters and Monsters

However, not all of Gorey's images suggest friendly, cooperative, orderly, and compatible interactions between the species. In some depictions his animals behave unpredictably and disturb everyday tranquility, suggesting that all is not so peaceful in Gorey's human-animal world. These animals are Gorey's tricksters—animals that assume human qualities and, like bratty children, create mischief and become nuisances.[13]

In *The Doubtful Guest* a scarf-wearing penguin-like creature suddenly appears in the home of a Victorian family.[14] The creature consistently behaves strangely, performing unsettling and destructive acts, such as carrying off books and dropping them in the pond or breaking a gramophone. As Gorey's text explains, "It wrenched off the horn from the new gramophone, / And could not be persuaded to leave it alone," and "It would carry off objects of which it grew fond, / And protect them by dropping them in the pond" (fig. 3.15). The Doubtful Guest, we are told, arrived seventeen years ago and has shown no intention of leaving; its longevity in residence only adds to its disturbing effect.

There is also a darker side to Gorey's human-animal world. Some of his creatures are ghastly, violent, or spooky, although even his depictions of vampires seem more delicate and pretty than threatening or scary. Indeed, when Gorey depicts monsters interacting with humans, the visuals and captions are sometimes only ambiguously threatening, with harm or violence suggested but not displayed. For example, in *The Tuning Fork*, a girl encounters "a monster of alarming size," but in the subsequent illustrations, Gorey backs off from depicting any harm, asserting that it was the monster that was "surprised" (figs. 3.16a,b). It is also unclear whether the monster is about to victimize the girl or move away from the scene.

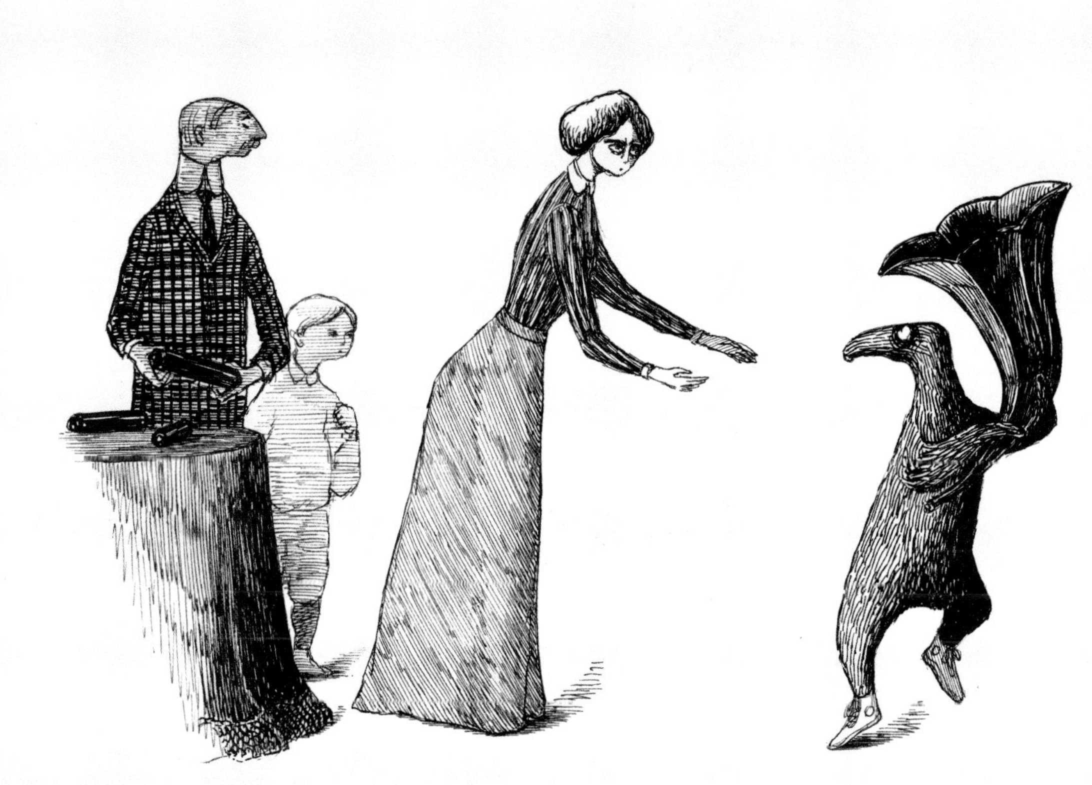

Fig. 3.16a

Edward Gorey, "Despite this sudden change of fate, / She soon began to perorate." Illustration for *The Tuning Fork*, drawn in 1966, first separate edition published by New York: Fantod Press, 1990. Pen and ink on paper, 7 ¼ × 7 ¾ in. (18.4 × 19.7 cm). The Edward Gorey Charitable Trust.

Fig. 3.16b

Edward Gorey, "The simple creature was aghast / At hearing of her cruel past." Illustration for *The Tuning Fork*, drawn in 1966, first separate edition published by New York: Fantod Press, 1990. Pen and ink on paper, 7 ¼ × 7 ¾ in. (18.4 × 19.7 cm). The Edward Gorey Charitable Trust.

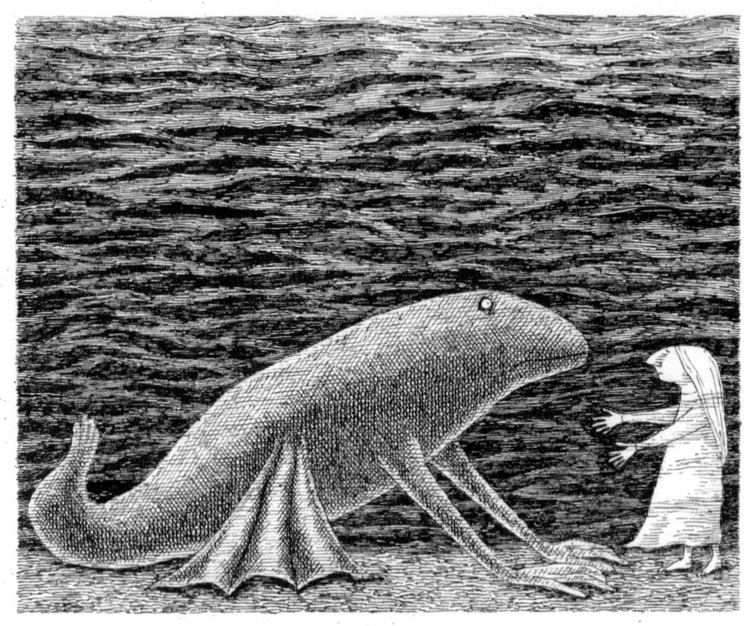

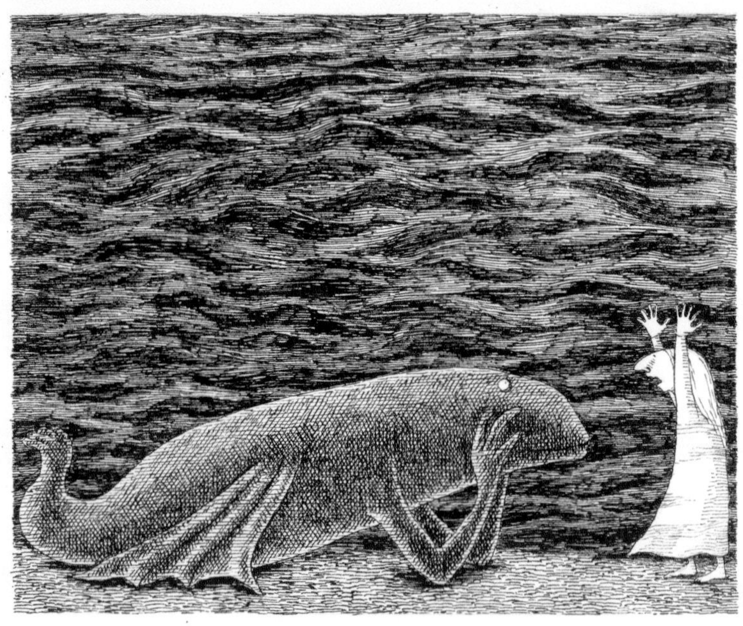

UNDERSTANDING GOREY'S ANIMALS

We should be hesitant to interpret Gorey's animal depictions too narrowly or literally. Gorey himself offered no explanations. Moreover, whatever meaning they have may simply be part of his goal to create literary nonsense for children and adults.[15] His use of animal images may have been a tool, along with his verse, to create that nonsense. But nonsense literature has a complex nature,[16] suggesting that it is not meaningless.

In part, nonsense literature acquires meaning because readers will interpret and have an emotional reaction to it from their own perspectives, whether or not the author deliberately sought to communicate such meaning or feeling. Animal images, in particular, can elicit these reactions because they are very flexible and potent devices that can serve many ends, both for those who create the images and for those who see them. They can symbolically function as complex and ambiguous others[17] to tell stories in media, literature, and the arts.[18] Commonly in children's stories, talking animals instead of human adults are used to teach moral lessons to young readers. They can be allegories communicating real social and political agendas using fictional characters—for example, George Orwell's *Animal Farm* (1945) and Art Spiegelman's *Maus* (1980–91). And they can also reflect or mirror a group's perspective or its anxieties and concerns.

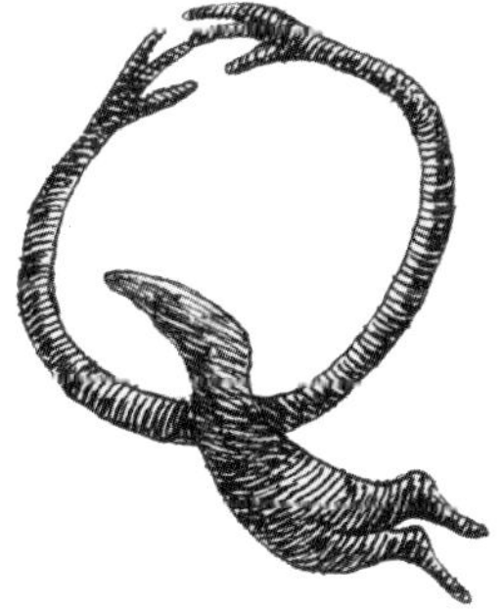

Indeed, animals represent one of the richest windows for understanding ourselves, and it is at this level that scholars may find great opportunities when exploring Gorey's human-animal world. In an oft-quoted passage, the anthropologist Claude Lévi-Strauss[19] observed, "Animals are good to think." By this Lévi-Strauss meant that animals act as metaphors, as powerful cultural labels that well-socialized members of a society use to understand, and share an understanding of, culturally significant ideas and experiences. How we think and act toward animals may reveal our most essential conceptions of the social order, unmask our most authentic attitudes toward people, and expose our conceptions of the experience of being human.

For example, Gorey's depictions of animals express a childlike wonder. They often appear and behave as children might imagine them or as children might think and act themselves. That Gorey provides a child's take on animals that is often innocent and make-believe must be understood in the context of his work in general. While Gorey intensifies the pathos of his child protagonists by having them victimized in a cruel world, he does the reverse with his animal protagonists, saddling them with sweet, curious, playful, and silly

Fig. 3.17

Edvard Munch (Norwegian, 1863–1944), *The Woman and the Bear*, 1908–9. Lithograph on wove paper mounted on wove paper, approximately 9¼ × 8¾ in. (25.6 × 22.7 cm). Wadsworth Atheneum Museum of Art, Hartford, Conn. Bequest of Edward Gorey, 2001.13.61.

childlike qualities, or at least features that estrange them from their expected animal behavior. Many of Gorey's animals are like a child's imaginary friend who shares the child's curiosity and joys. They appear to be happy, or at least they are usually not portrayed as victims. They are carefree, whimsical, impulsive, sprightly, mischief-creating playmates.

Gorey may also have intended to make his readers uneasy. In this respect, much of his work is like the strange creature in *The Doubtful Guest*— it is something you invite in; you are put at ease by its charming appearance, only to end up somewhere unexpected or troubling. In particular, his use of anthropomorphism may be unsettling for some readers. Although people have always anthropomorphized animals, and the tendency occurs everywhere— media, literature, commercials, propaganda, everyday language—there is something culturally taboo about violating human-animal boundaries. In the ancient world, animals and people were considered to be closely related, with borders between the two frequently crossed with ease,[20] but in the modern world, distinctions became more rigid between species, and border crossings more restricted. Anthropomorphism makes us uneasy because at a moral or aesthetic level it feels wrong to mix species. Humanized animals are strange; they are alienated from both human and animal worlds, between the two and not purely one or the other. Gorey's humanoid animals subvert taboos about traditionally rigid distinctions between humans and animals, perhaps leaving viewers somewhat confused or even disturbed, while simultaneously amused by their strangeness, as in some of the works of art in his personal collection. For example, Gorey owned one of Edvard Munch's prints from the pictorial fable *Alpha and Omega* (fig. 3.17). The imagery in *The Woman and the Bear* clearly violates human-animal taboos because Omega has sex with various animals and gives birth to animal hybrids.

Finally, animals in Gorey's work may also function as a cautionary tale for his adult readers. There is arguably a message for adults in Gorey's use of animal characters—namely, do not forget how you used to feel as a child. It is mainstream society, with its sterile lack of imagination and insistence on conformity, that is the true monster, demanding in exchange for adulthood the sacrifice of childish wonder, sympathy, and creativity.[21]

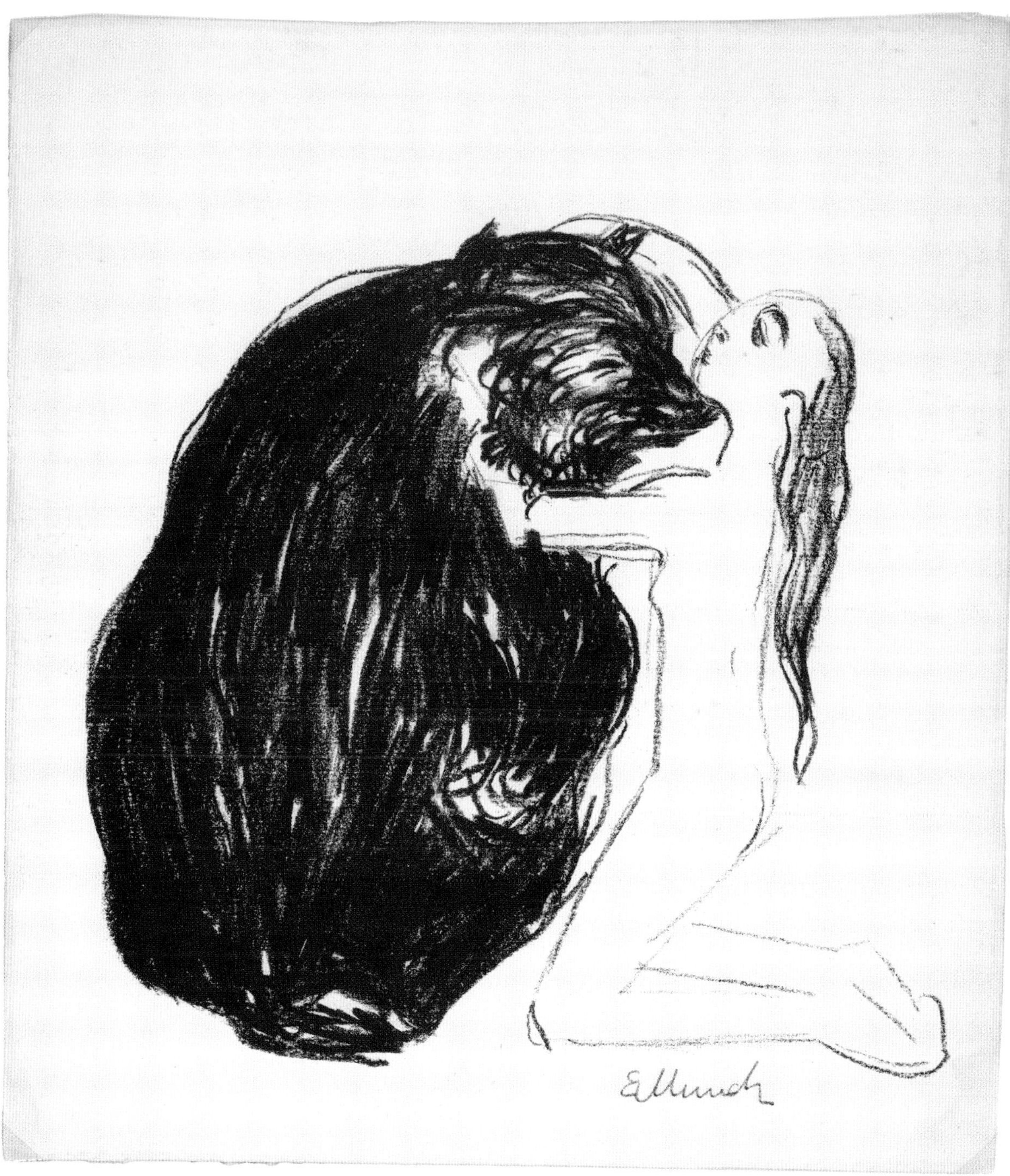

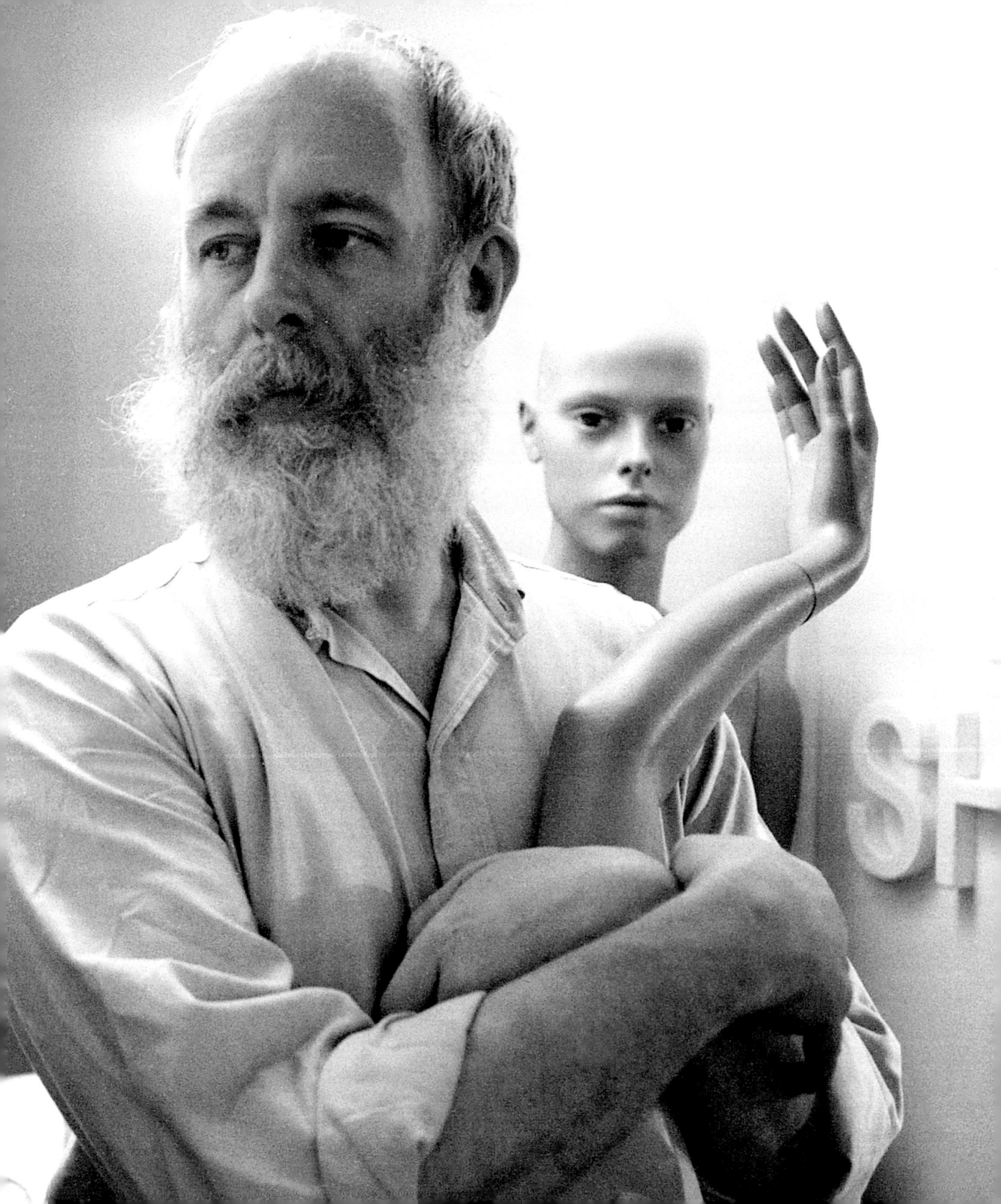

Kevin Shortsleeve

Edward Gorey: Nonsense, Surrealism, and Silent Matter

E dward Gorey's texts and illustrations were influenced by many forms of artistic expression: surreal, modern, minimalist, and postmodern art and literature, Japanese art and literature, nineteenth-century illustrations, Victorian novels, children's cautionary tales, the New York City Ballet, and silent films, to name a few. Yet while each of these movements, genres, and institutions influenced his work, no single genre was as foundational to him as literary nonsense. Gorey often felt misunderstood, his work routinely mislabeled "macabre" or "horror." But as *New Yorker* columnist Stephen Schiff reported, Gorey "insisted that his books were not in the Gothic tradition . . . What he's up to has more to do with nonsense, Lewis Carroll and Edward Lear."[1] As Gorey said, "Carroll and Lear are two of my favorite people . . . I'm an extravagant admirer of both of them."[2] So, if one is to understand Gorey and his artistic passions, it makes sense to trace his interests through the lens of literary nonsense, a genre that, like Gorey himself, is little understood. This essay, then, explores the unbound surreal aesthetics of literary nonsense, and shows how the genre is akin, in important ways, to Gorey's writing and illustration, as well as to the art Gorey collected or admired.

To begin, one must understand that what Gorey appreciated most in any piece of art or literature is what we might term "silent matter." In his letters to Peter Neumeyer, Gorey discusses what he calls his "Great Simple

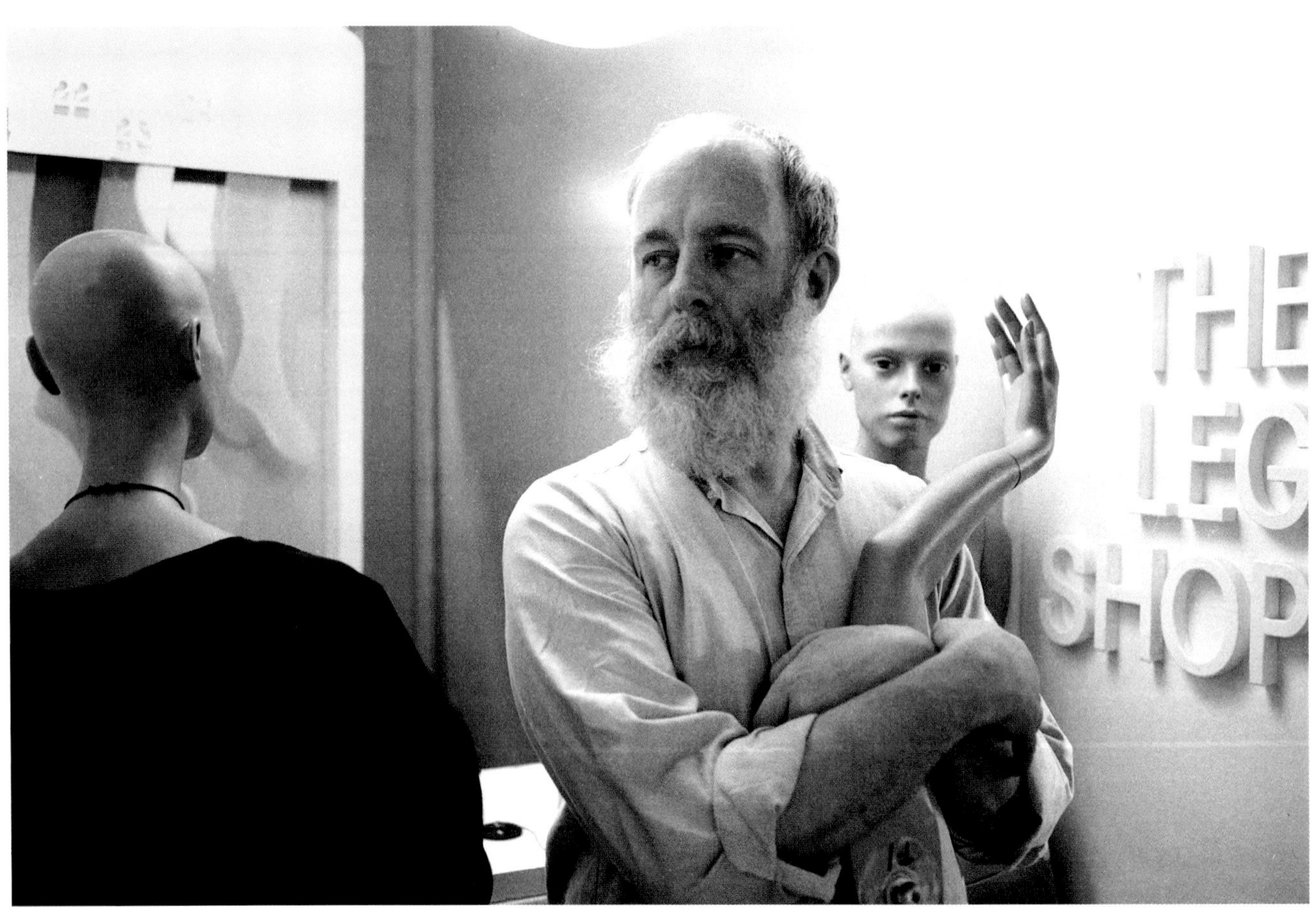
22
23
THE
LEG
SHOP

Theory About Art." Gorey posits that beyond the surface meaning found in any great work of art (or literature), there is the sense that the work is "really about something else entirely."[3] He describes it as "the extra something in a good work that you find you cannot pin down."[4] Gorey explains his own work in similar terms to Schiff: "The way I write, since I do leave out most of the connections, and very little is pinned down, I feel that I'm doing a minimum of damage to other possibilities that might arise in the reader's mind."[5] Nonsense poems are especially good at leaving out "the connections." Consider the "possibilities that might arise in the reader's mind" when faced with the most famous stanza of nonsense ever written, the opening to Lewis Carroll's poem "Jabberwocky":

> Twas brillig, and the slithy toves
> Did gyre and gimble in the wabe;
> All mimsy were the borogoves,
> And the mome raths outgrabe. [6]

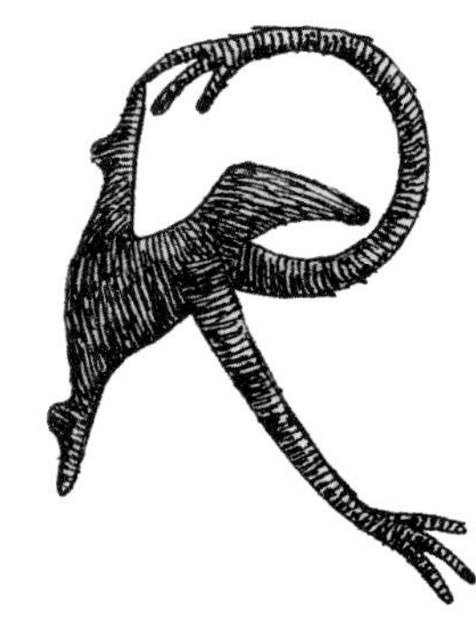

Fig. 4.1
Harry Benson, *Edward Gorey at Henri Bendel's The Leg Shop, New York City,* 1978. Gelatin silver print, 30 × 24 in. (76.2 × 61 cm). Collection of the artist. © Harry Benson

It is not the bewildering vocabulary that matters most here; the bewildering vocabulary is a means to an end—and that end is a provoked reader, one who must consider the silent matter and is left with the suspicion that this text is "really about something else entirely."

One of the hallmarks of literary nonsense is its excessive randomness, the seemingly disparate, chimerical constructions of a piece of nonsense suggesting a disregard for narrative convention. Samuel Foote's text "The Grand Panjandrum," first published in 1755, is an oft-quoted (and early) example of literary nonsense:

> So she went into the garden to cut a cabbage-leaf, to make an apple-pie; and at the same time a great she-bear, coming up the street, pops its head into the shop. "What! no soap?" So he died, and she very imprudently married the barber.[7]

In discussing his own stories, Gorey commented, "I do tend to sort of write things that would make as little sense as possible." When asked which of his own works are his favorites, Gorey answers, "*The Object-Lesson* [1958] because that doesn't make any sense," and notes that his text "grew out of [Samuel] Foote's poem, "The Grand Panjandrum."[8] And indeed, comparing the text above to *The Object-Lesson* reveals their kinship:

He descended, destroying the letter unread,
and stepped backwards into the water for a better view.
Heavens, how dashing! Cried the people in the dinghy,
and Echo answered: Count the spoons![9]

Add to this comparison the fact that Gorey chose as the title for his anthologies *Amphigorey*, a play on the word "amphigory," which means a nonsense
verse, and his commitment to the genre is rendered all the more certain.

Another way to spot nonsense from a distance is by its tendency to posit
temporal confusion. The nonsensical children's street rhyme, "One Dark Day in
the Middle of the Night"[10] suggests a bewildering temporality, and sounds very
like the impossible time implied in the opening line to Gorey's *The Epilectic
Bicycle* (1969): "It was the day after Tuesday and the day before Wednesday."[11]

Nonsense is also typified by wordplay and linguistic invention. Gorey's
strangely named creatures, like the Wuggly Ump and Throbblefoot Spectre,
are comparable to Lewis Carroll's Jabberwock and Edward Lear's Yongy-
Bongy-Bò. Lear's playful linguistic inventions, such as "Twikky mikky bikky,"
"Quangle Wangle," or "Ploffskin Pluffskin Pelican Jee," are also readily compared
to Gorey. A book Gorey considered one of his best, *The Untitled Book* (1971),
is an assemblage of Learesque nonsense words: "Flappity flippity . . .
Thumbleby stumbleby . . . Rambleby rumbleby"[12] (fig. 4.2).

As I've suggested elsewhere, Lear was perhaps Gorey's single greatest
influence.[13] Gorey had a lifelong interest in Lear's work and identified with
him in many ways. A verse from Lear's *The Dong with a Luminous Nose* (1877)
features the brooding melancholy that so inspired Gorey.

Till morning came of that hateful day
When the Jumblies sailed their sieve away
And the Dong was left on the cruel shore
Gazing — gazing — for evermore.[14]

A similar mood is achieved in Gorey's *The Iron Tonic* (1969):

The Light is fading from the day. The rest is darkness and dismay.
They've gone and left it all alone: An absolutely useless stone.[15]

Gorey's intimate connection to Lear is further established by the fact that
Gorey chose to illustrate Lear's poems, and those illustrations were considered

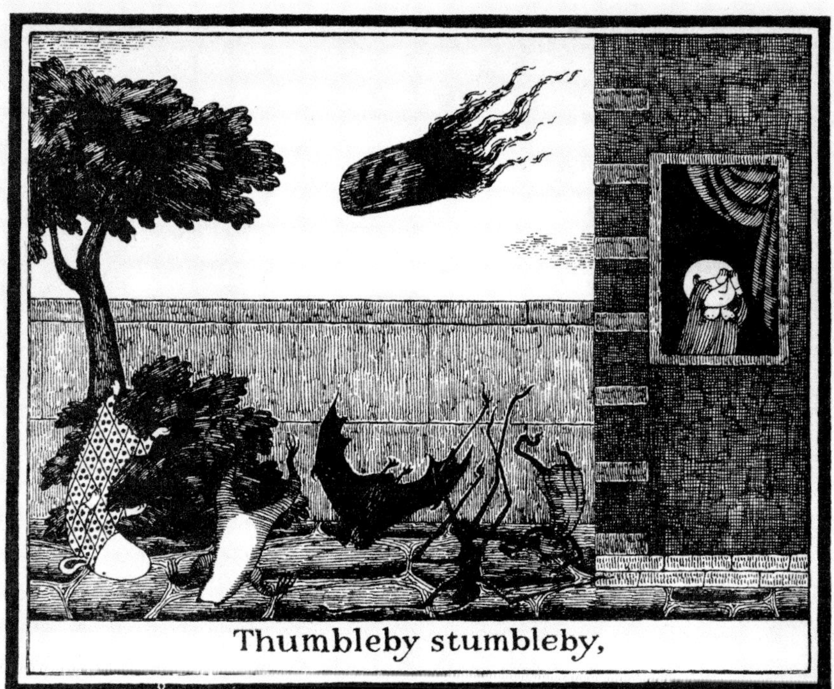

Fig. 4.2

Edward Gorey, "Thumbleby stumbleby," Illustration in *The Untitled Book*. New York: Fantod Press, 1971.

by many to be a defining moment, described as "the most inventive and tonally complex of his drawings."[16] The *London Times* reported that "Gorey's greatest achievement was to provide Lear's *The Jumblies* and *The Dong with a Luminous Nose* with drawings that match the atmosphere of poems so resistant to illustration."[17] Alison Lurie saw a deep connection between the two authors and noted that the "overall effect" of an Edward Gorey book "is not tragic, but comic, just as it is in the work of Edward Lear, whom Gorey greatly admired."[18] And, while noting their differences, Hendrik van Leeuwen points out that "the two certainly [also] exhibit similarities, such as the sing-songy musicality of the verse, the use of playful rhymes and the (nonsensical) limerick form, and in a fascination with dance."[19] A close associate of Gorey's, owner of the Gotham Book Mart, and co-executor of Gorey's estate, Andreas Brown, has even suggested that Gorey's beard was worn, in part, in emulation of Lear, the father of Victorian nonsense.[20]

Sometime between 1954 and 1971 Brown gave Gorey a drawing by Lear of an Egyptian landscape, *Hagar and Silsilis* (1856) (fig. 4.3). The watercolor

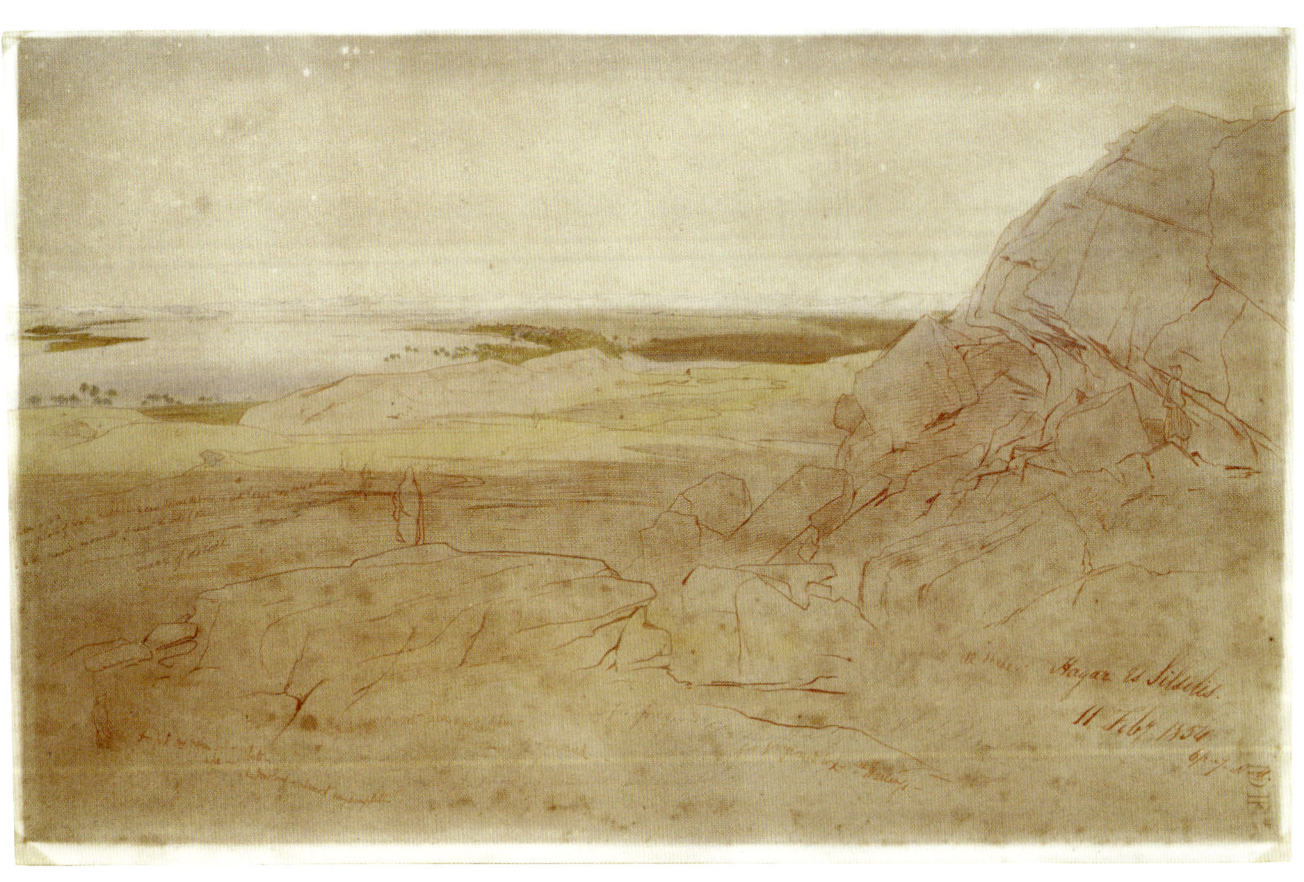

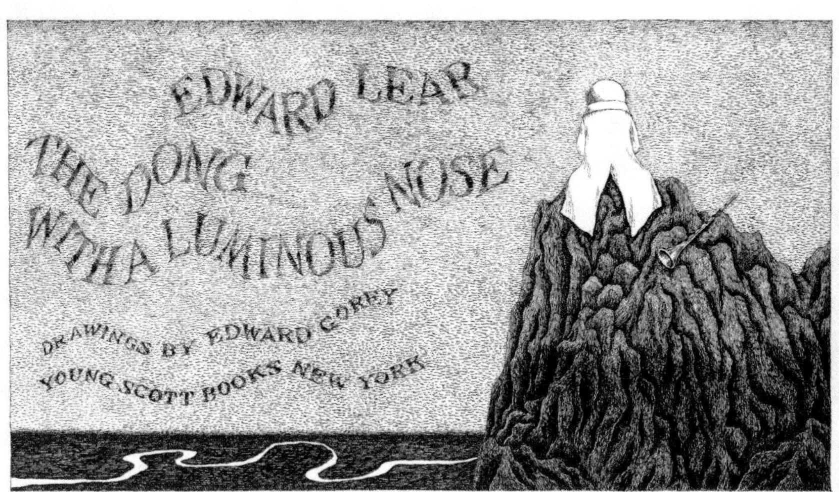

Fig. 4.3

Edward Lear (English, 1812–1888), *Hagar and Silsilis, Egypt*, 1856. Watercolor and pencil on paper, 11 1/16 × 17 15/16 in. (28.1 × 45.6 cm). Wadsworth Atheneum Museum of Art, Hartford, Conn. Bequest of Edward Gorey, 2001.13.51.

Fig. 4.4

Edward Gorey, Title page for *The Dong with a Luminous Nose*, story by Edward Lear, illustrated by Edward Gorey. New York: Young Scott Books, 1969. Pen and ink on paper, 7 1/4 × 9 3/4 in. (18.4 × 24.8 cm). The Edward Gorey Charitable Trust.

might have influenced the work Gorey was doing on his Lear projects in the late 1960s. Lear's composition, with its lifeless heap of stones, spare flat landscape, and water in the distance, resembles the title page of Gorey's illustrated version of *The Dong with a Luminous Nose* (fig. 4.4).

Lear was also fond of drawing cats—well, one cat: Foss. Lear's beloved pet of seventeen years was the object of the author's devotion and the subject of hundreds of playful ink sketches, the famous feline often posing in the margins of personal correspondence (fig. 4.5). In *The Jumblies* (1968), Gorey reproduces Lear's cat on the dedication page and notes, "The drawings are for Foss" (fig. 4.6a).[21] Gorey, who had numerous cats, also delighted in picturing them in myriad poses. He adorned the front and back covers of his first two anthologies, *Amphigorey* and *Amphigorey Too*, with playfully posing cats reminiscent of Foss. Gorey's cat (as with Lear, it is always the same cat), with his slightly rotund physique and striped shirt, recalls Foss's fat body and stripes. The poses offered in Gorey's counting book *Category: Fifty Drawings* (1973) recall a number of memorable Foss stances (fig. 4.6b).[22]

Another illustrator who regularly portrayed animals in his work is *New Yorker* cartoonist George Booth, whose drawings Gorey collected. Two of his drawings of dogs are reminiscent of Lear. His *Study of Six Dogs* has a narrative sequence that features a humor and honesty reminiscent of Lear's treatment of Foss (fig. 4.7). Like Lear, Booth sketches the terrier in a range of positions and emotions, and the ultimate effect of the sequence is a tender portrait of a silly pet.

Fig. 4.5

Edward Lear, *Illustration of his cat Foss*, n.d. Published in *Edward Lear: A Biography* by Peter Levi. New York: Scribner, 1995.

Fig. 4.6a

Edward Gorey, Dedication page to Foss in Edward Lear's *The Jumblies*, illustrated by Edward Gorey. New York: Young Scott Books, 1968. Pen and ink on paper, 6 ¾ × 9 ¼ in. (17.1 × 23.5 cm). The Edward Gorey Charitable Trust.

Fig. 4.6b

Edward Gorey, "Cat in striped sweater on ladder, #39." Illustration in *Category: Fifty Drawings*. New York: Gotham Book Mart, 1973.

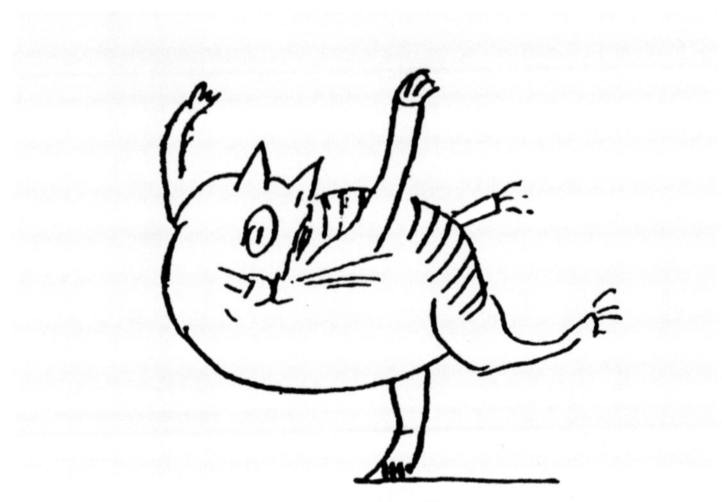

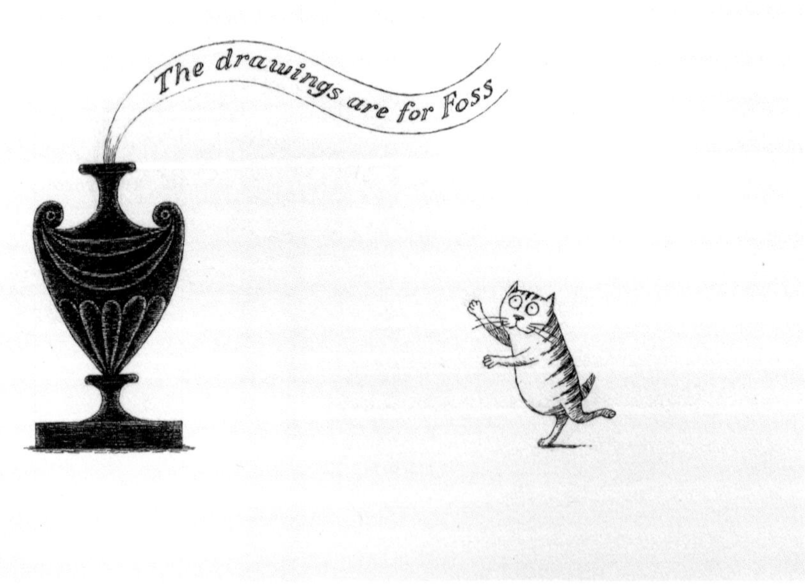
The drawings are for Foss

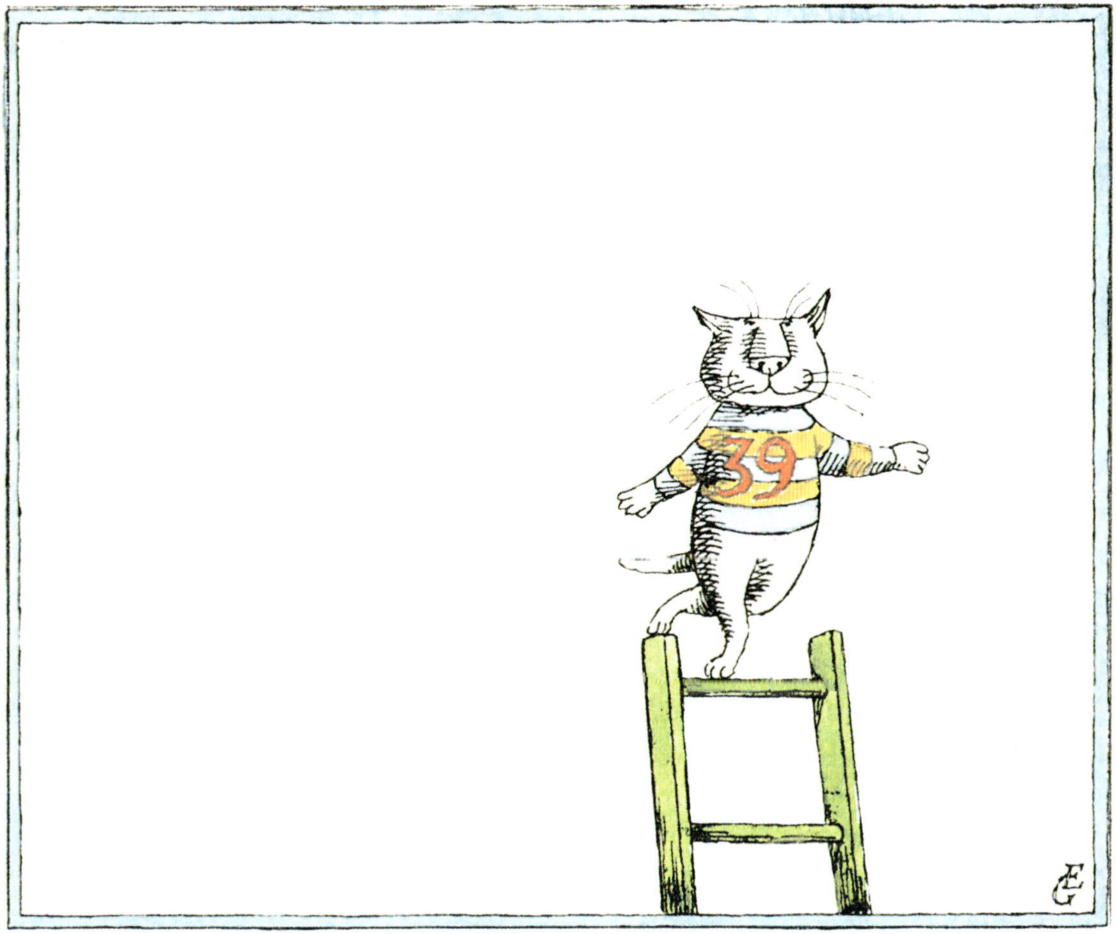

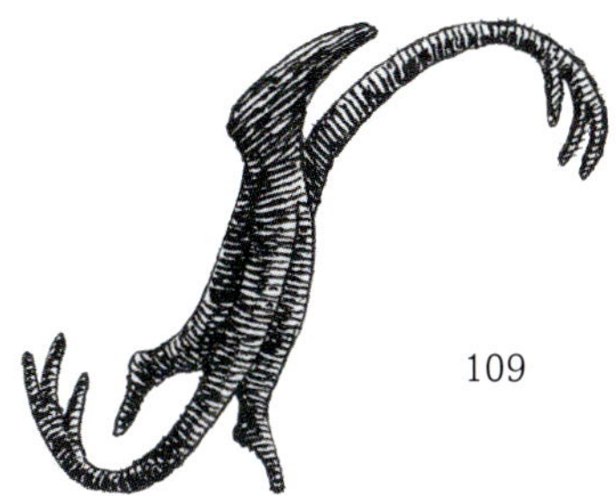

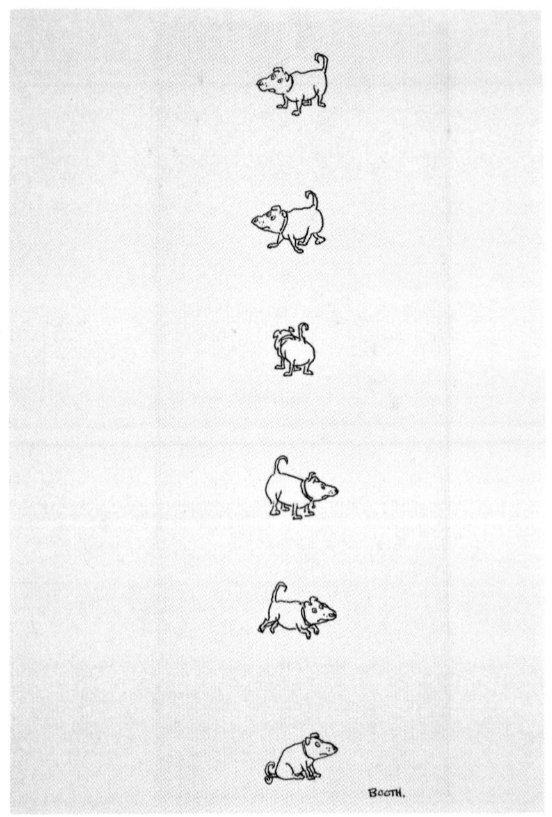

Fig. 4.7

George Booth (American, b. 1926), *Study of Six Dogs*, c. 1980. Ink on paper, 12 × 8 ¼ in. (30.5 × 21 cm). Wadsworth Atheneum Museum of Art, Hartford, Conn. Bequest of Edward Gorey, 2001.13.30.

Gorey also had a lifelong devotion to another father of Victorian nonsense, Lewis Carroll. As Gorey commented, "*Alice in Wonderland* is one of the earliest books I read and one of the books I know best."[23] Recalling the *Alice* books perhaps, one of Gorey's books, *The Eleventh Episode* (1971), features a heroine who falls down a hole (in this case a well). Like Alice, this anonymous heroine lands unscathed and finds that the hole leads to a tunnel. Her disorienting adventure, again like Alice's, includes travel by train and boat. And while Alice undergoes a series of existential dilemmas, even temporarily forgetting her own name in *Through the Looking-Glass and What Alice Found There*, we learn that in the course of her adventures Gorey's anonymous heroine decides to change her name, leaving her past behind.

Another connection between Gorey and Carroll is evidenced by an engraving of a dragon that Gorey owned, which resembles the Jabberwock illustrated by John Tenniel for *Through the Looking-Glass* (fig. 4.8). Gorey claimed it was one of his favorite engravings and hung it on the wall of his studio (fig. 4.9).[24] Gorey knew Tenniel's work intimately, as well as that of other nineteenth-century engravers such as the French artist Gustave Doré and the English brothers George and Edward Dalziel.[25] Perhaps Gorey would have recognized the Jabberwock as a descendent of Tenniel's earlier dragons published in the humor magazine *Punch*. Tenniel's *St. George and the Dragon* (1852), which predates the Jabberwock by many years, is of particular interest, as it has been guessed that his Jabberwock might have been inspired by the Renaissance artist Paolo Uccello's *Saint George and the Dragon* (c. 1470, National Gallery, London).[26] Interestingly, Gorey counted Uccello as a "strong direct influence" on his work. Along with artists like Vermeer, Balthus, and Francis Bacon, Uccello drew Gorey's admiration because of his ability to capture what the latter called the "frozen moment."[27] Both Uccello's *Saint George* and Tenniel's Jabberwock depict such a moment, staged dramatically and suspended in time a second before resolution.

Tenniel could have seen Uccello's dragon—or dragons like it— somewhere else, as the creature portrayed in both Tenniel's Jabberwock illustration and the engraving Gorey collected resembles the wingless, bipedal Lindworm of Norwegian, Swedish, Danish, and German tradition.[28] Gorey would have enjoyed owning a nineteenth-century engraving of a dragon whose pedigree may have been in conversation with the world of Tenniel. Gorey was fond of drawing dragons, and the creatures he placed on the back cover of *The Hapless Child* (1961) or the Quingawaga in *The Utter Zoo* (1967) may owe a debt to one of his favorite images (fig. 4.10).

Another strong link between Carroll and Gorey is through the twentieth-century artist Balthus. In an interview Gorey was asked, "Which living person do you most admire?" His answer is unequivocal: "Balthus."[29] Gorey owned three drawings by Balthus; in his correspondence with Neumeyer, Gorey describes Balthus as "one of his three favorite painters," along with René Magritte and Francis Bacon. He explains to Neumeyer that he is attracted to the "beauty" and "strangeness" of Balthus's work.[30]

A number of critics observe that, like Gorey, Balthus had an abiding interest in Lewis Carroll and the illustrations of John Tenniel.[31] Beyond the direct influence of images from the *Alice* books, Sabine Rewald observes that Balthus had a muse in the model Thérèse, while Carroll had a real-life muse, in the person of Alice Liddell. She suggests that Balthus's controversial paintings of Thérèse and Carroll's provocative photographs of Alice reveal a shared

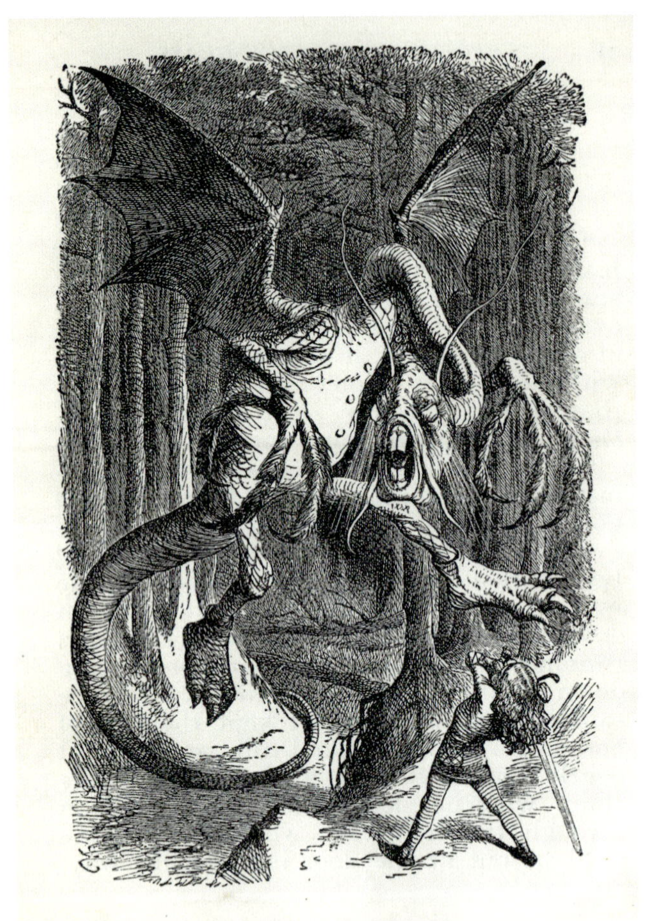

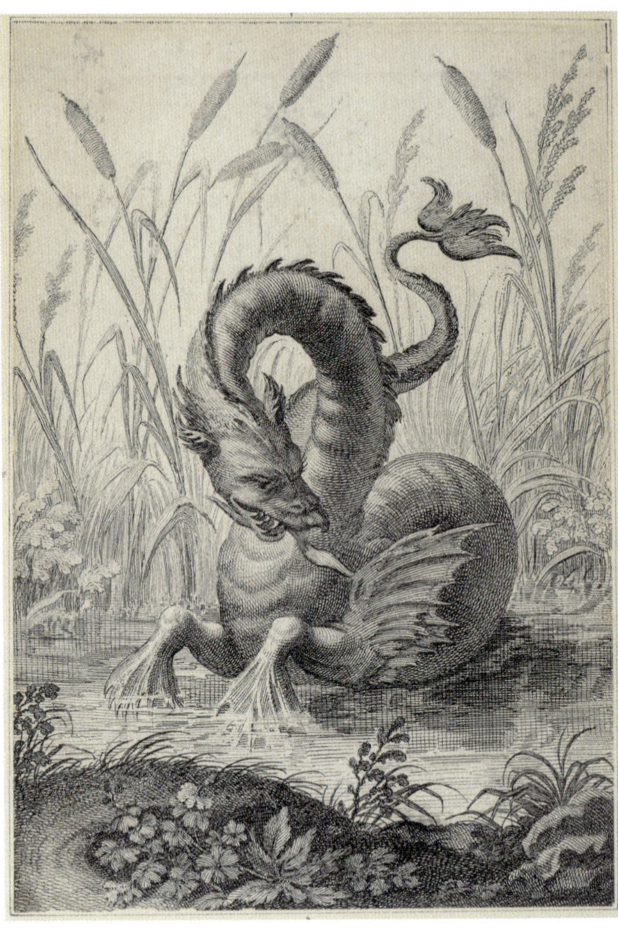

Fig. 4.8

John Tenniel (British, 1820–1914), "The Jabberwock" from Lewis Carroll's *Through the Looking-Glass, and What Alice Found There*, 1871.

Fig. 4.9

Unidentified Artist, *Dragon*, n.d. Engraving on paper, 10 1/16 × 8 in. (25.8 × 20.3 cm). Wadsworth Atheneum Museum of Art, Hartford, Conn. Bequest of Edward Gorey, 2001.13.69.

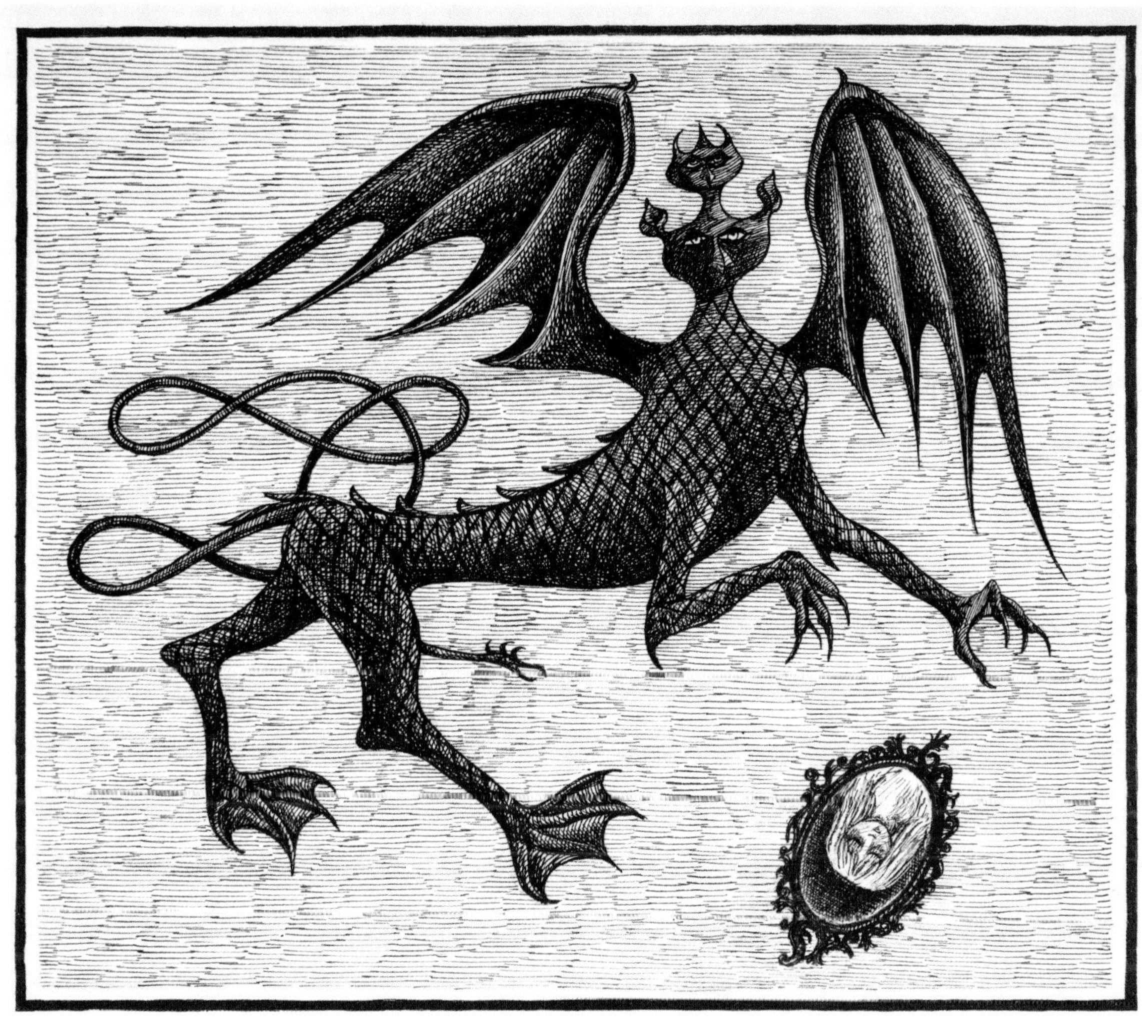

Fig. 4.10

Edward Gorey, Illustration for
the back cover of *The Hapless
Child*. New York: Ivan
Obolensky, Inc., 1961. Pen and
ink on paper, 8 ¹⁵/₁₆ × 9 ⅜ in.
(22.7 × 23.8 cm). The Edward
Gorey Charitable Trust.

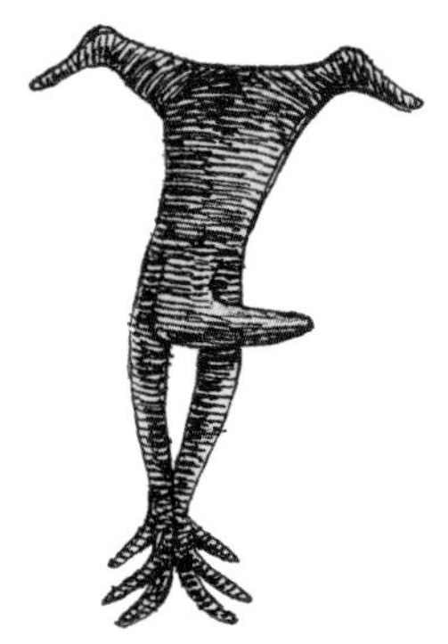

"kinship or intuitive insight into [their] young sitters,"[32] if not also a latent eroticism regarding "dreamy children."[33] While Gorey's innocent young ladies are not eroticized like Balthus's or Carroll's photographic subjects, his young heroines are nevertheless romanticized. Rewald draws comparisons between Balthus's girls and literary counterparts in the works of Rainer Maria Rilke, Jean Cocteau, and Vladimir Nabokov, whose female subjects also possess "remoteness," "lassitude," and "loneliness." Like many of Gorey's young women, these girls are depicted in a "semi-conscious" state in which they "float immersed" with a "fey grace."[34] Karen Wilkin sees the connection and writes that Balthus's "oddly stiff, but vulnerable adolescents, who seem violated by the artist's gaze, permeate many of Gorey's works."[35] Gorey's subjects who pose with their cats, like Drusilla in *The Remembered Visit* (1965) or Sara in Gorey's illustrations for Alphonse Allais's *Story for Sara* (1971), are similar to the moody or brooding young innocents featured in Balthus's paintings (fig. 4.11).

Interestingly, parallels between Balthus and Gorey intensify when one moves from the subject to the setting. Choosing terms that evoke direct comparison to Gorey, Rewald discusses Balthus's Biedermeier interiors as "uncluttered," "severe," "empty rooms."[36]

I suspect that Gorey also liked the cats. Like Gorey, Balthus had a house full of cats and featured cats prominently in his art. Rewald notes, "[Balthus's] cats added a wonderful sense of childish playfulness and that was a large piece of the artist's personality."[37] Balthus's *The Mediterranean Cat* (1949), with his odd behavior and striped sweater, has a surreal whimsicality that reminds one of so many of Gorey's playful felines (fig. 4.12). Balthus, in fact, launched his career with a critically acclaimed wordless picture book about a cat, *Mitsou* (1921). In discussing *Mitsou*, Rewald observes the meticulous attention Balthus gave to detailed wallpapers and floorboards and notes also the use of provocative window views,[38] features that remind one of Gorey. *Mitsou*'s hero, a young boy, is the picture of Goreyesque innocence in his Little Lord Fauntleroy suit and kneesocks. Again, evoking comparisons to Gorey's picture books, one contemporary critic called *Mitsou* "imponderable and strangely moving."[39]

Returning to the subject of nonsense, we may explore Gorey's interest in "silent matter" via his preference for illustrations that diverge in meaning from their accompanying text. In a letter to Neumeyer, Gorey describes himself searching around children's bookshops for interesting illustrators and reveals a frustration with illustrations that do not go beyond the text: "Oh dear. Competence everywhere, and no . . . sense of illustration except literal

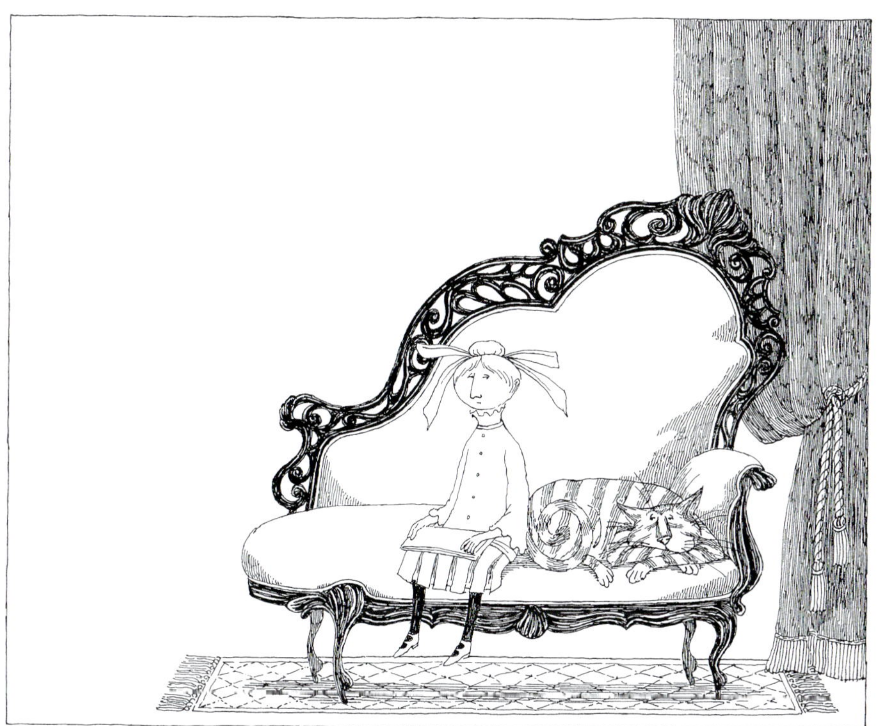

Fig. 4.11

Edward Gorey, Illustration for the back cover of *Story for Sara: What Happened to a Little Girl*, story by Alphonse Allais, translated and illustrated by Edward Gorey. New York: Albondocani Press, 1971.

Fig. 4.12

Balthus (Balthasar Klossowski de Rola), *Le chat de la Meditérrranée (The Mediterranean Cat)*, 1949. Oil on board, 18 × 24 in. (46 × 61 cm). Private Collection.

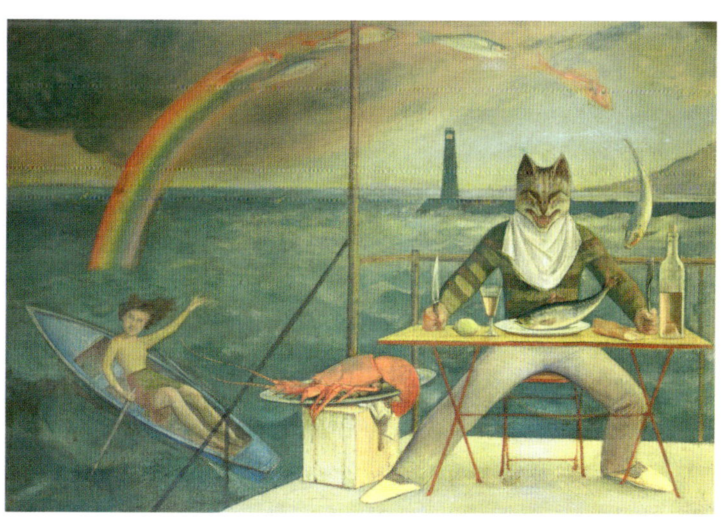

renditions of the text."[40] Gorey, in fact, often actively avoided making clear connections between text and image. Wilkin notes, for example, that the close-ups featured in Gorey's *The Iron Tonic* "are dislocated, divorced from their apparent context," and therefore the surreal narrative is rendered that much more "unintelligible" (fig. 4.13).[41] Meanwhile Jane Doonan and Lisa Ede argue separately that the illustrations for the works of Carroll and Lear are especially effective when there is a divergence or extension of meaning between the texts and illustrations that serves to produce a heightened level of reader participation.[42] In "The Liaison of Visual and Written Nonsense" van Leeuwen concurs, and posits the work of American artist Saul Steinberg as an example of this idealized tension. As Steinberg himself comments, "The purpose of the drawings is to make people feel that there is something else beyond the perception."[43] In chapter 2 of *Alice's Adventures in Wonderland*, Tenniel's interpretation of the heroine floundering in the stream is (like much of Gorey's work) a densely crosshatched black-and-white drawing. While Tenniel is more known for literal interpretations of a text, this particular illustration can take on an eerie quality. Is Alice staring at something out of frame? What she *might* be seeing is never explained in the text.

Gorey was enamored with this sort of disconnect, and he collected and admired works of art and literature where text and image diverge or work to create an enigma. He owned, for example, a drawing by humorist James Thurber (see fig. 3.2). A middle-aged man wearing a plumed hat and boxing gloves looks at himself in the mirror. His dog looks on placidly. In its published form, the caption runs, "They're going to put you away if you don't quit acting like this." It's what's left out of this illustration (and caption) that gives the reader pause. Who is saying this? The man or his dog? What is going on here and what led to this moment? Many Thurber drawings are enigmatic and remind one more directly of Gorey. In *A New Natural History*, two fictional creatures stare at each other. Their expressions are hard to read—either concerned or bored. Thurber's caption reads: "A Trochee (left) encountering a Spondee" (fig. 4.14).[44] Nothing more is offered by way of explanation. A similar disconnect between text and image is evidenced in several drawings Gorey owned by the British artist Glen Baxter, including *The Desecration of the Tennis Courts Has Produced a Very Difficult Situation* and *Today Was No Exception* (figs. 4.15a,b). In these examples, the artist has purposefully avoided providing a clear narrative connection between text and image.

Gorey also very much admired the work of the surrealist artist Max Ernst. He often cited Ernst's *Two Children Are Threatened by a Nightingale*

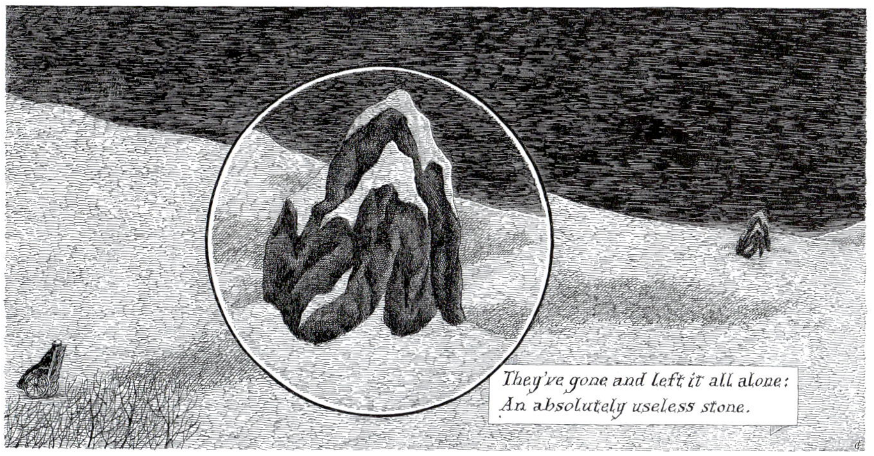
They've gone and left it all alone:
An absolutely useless stone.

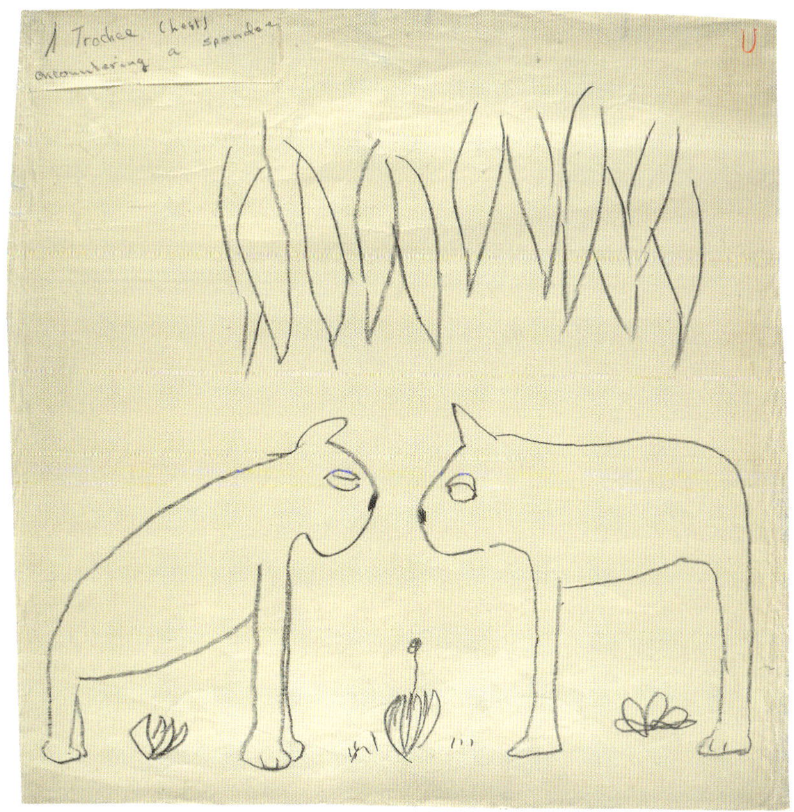
A Trochee (chest)
encountering a spondee

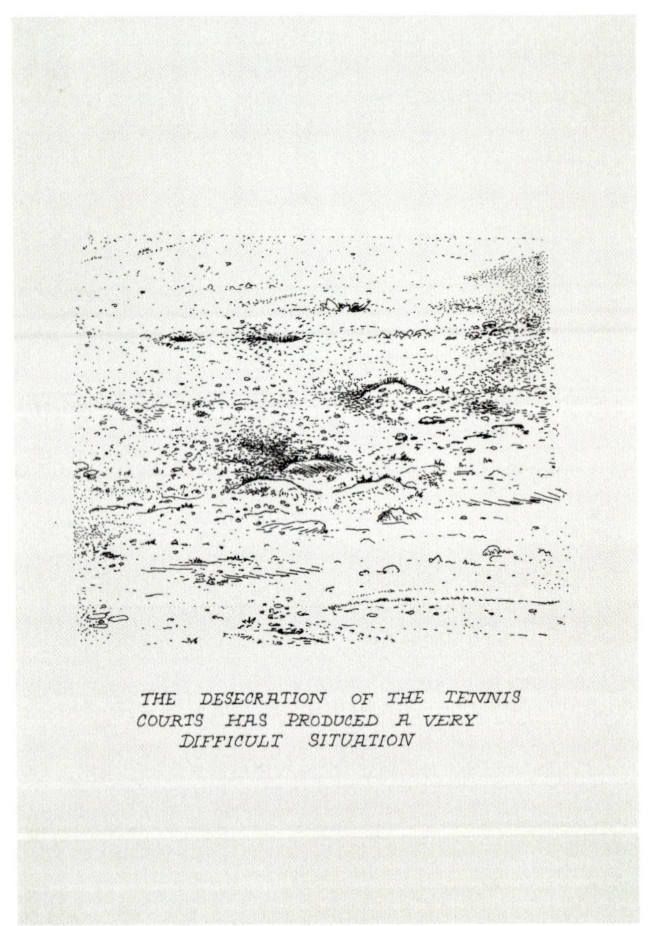

THE DESECRATION OF THE TENNIS
COURTS HAS PRODUCED A VERY
DIFFICULT SITUATION

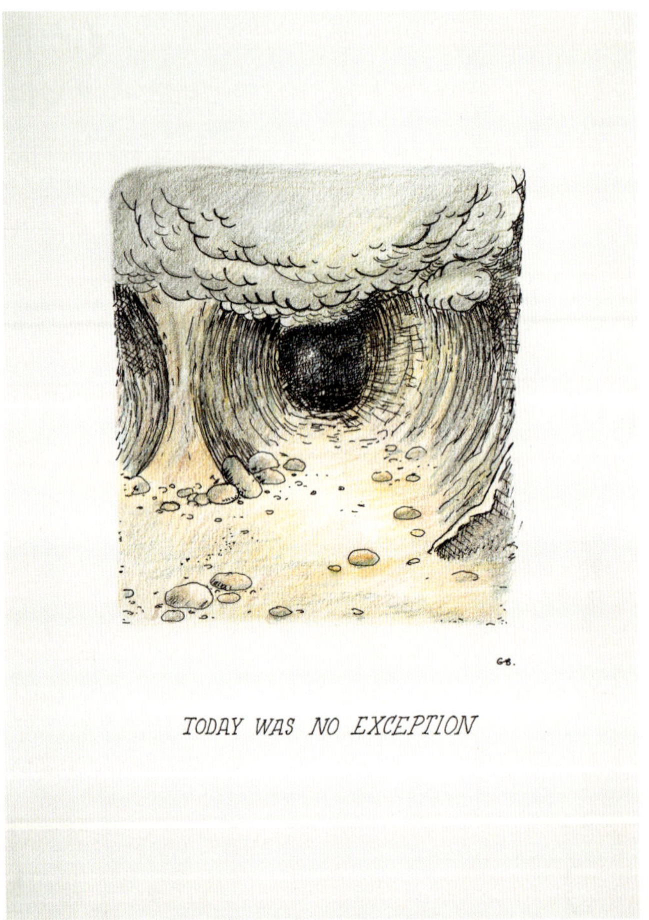

TODAY WAS *NO EXCEPTION*

(1924) (Museum of Modern Art, New York), a collage painting with the title, in French, written across the bottom of the frame (fig. 4.16).[45] Amid a number of inexplicable objects placed in proximity to each other with no obvious connection, including a melting urn, Ernst has placed the two children, one fleeing and the other being rescued from a cute little bird. The bird is tiny in scale, despite having a central role in the title. While this feathery fright might be a touch territorial, it is an exaggeration to call it "threatening." As the "rules" of nonsense illustration would dictate, a tension between text and image is achieved. Like Ernst and Baxter, Gorey created numerous works where similar tensions are exploited, among them *The Glorious Nosebleed* (1975), which is an alphabet book featuring single-panel drawings, one of which shows an inexplicable spiny sea beast flopped on the end of a dock. Three children stand at a safe distance, staring at it. The text reads, "The creature regarded them Balefully" (fig. 4.17).

Another link between Gorey and Ernst is Gorey's recurring character/ motif, Figbash. This furry, stretchy creature never speaks but dances through surreal texts such as *The Raging Tide: Or The Black Doll's Imbroglio* (1987), where, within desolate or surreal landscapes, it performs various acts of wanton silliness amid a coterie of nonsense creatures; *Figbash Acrobate* (1994), where it silently contorts itself into each letter in the alphabet (as reproduced in the margins of this book); and *Ten Impossible Objects* (2006), Gorey's ode to M. C. Escher, where Figbash explores impossible spaces the way a child explores trees. Figbash spilled over into so many other Gorey productions, such as plays, posters, and beanbags, that, as Alexander Theroux recalled, it became "Gorey's icon."[46]

According to Gorey, his Figbash was inspired by Ernst's birdlike alter ego Loplop[47] (fig. 4.18a). The Loplop was featured in Ernst's collages and in his comic *Une semaine de bonté* (1934), an extended surreal five-volume work that features illustrations from Victorian novels and encyclopedias that had been cut up and reorganized for surreal effect. In volumes 4 and 5 (*Mercredi* and *Jeudi*) this peculiar avian changeling pops into juxtaposition with the weird backgrounds and surreal images. Similarly, Gorey's Figbash, less sinister than Loplop, dances and contorts himself in and out of Gorey's imagined worlds. A visual cousin to Figbash is Gorey's earlier creation, and his most famous character, another furry penguin-like creature, the Doubtful Guest (fig. 4.18b).

But the Loplop/Figbash connection is perhaps made more intriguing in a somewhat mysterious, untitled, unpublished (until now) Gorey collage

Fig. 4.15a

Glen Baxter (English, b. 1944), *The Desecration of the Tennis Courts Has Produced a Very Difficult Situation*, 1976. Pen and ink and colored pencil on paper, 16½ × 11¾ in. (41.9 × 29.8 cm). Wadsworth Atheneum Museum of Art, Hartford, Conn. Bequest of Edward Gorey, 2001.13.22.

Fig. 4.15b

Glen Baxter, *Today Was No Exception*, 1976. Pen and ink and colored pencil on paper, 16⅝ × 11¾ in. (42.2 × 29.8 cm). Wadsworth Atheneum Museum of Art, Hartford, Conn. Bequest of Edward Gorey, 2001.13.23.

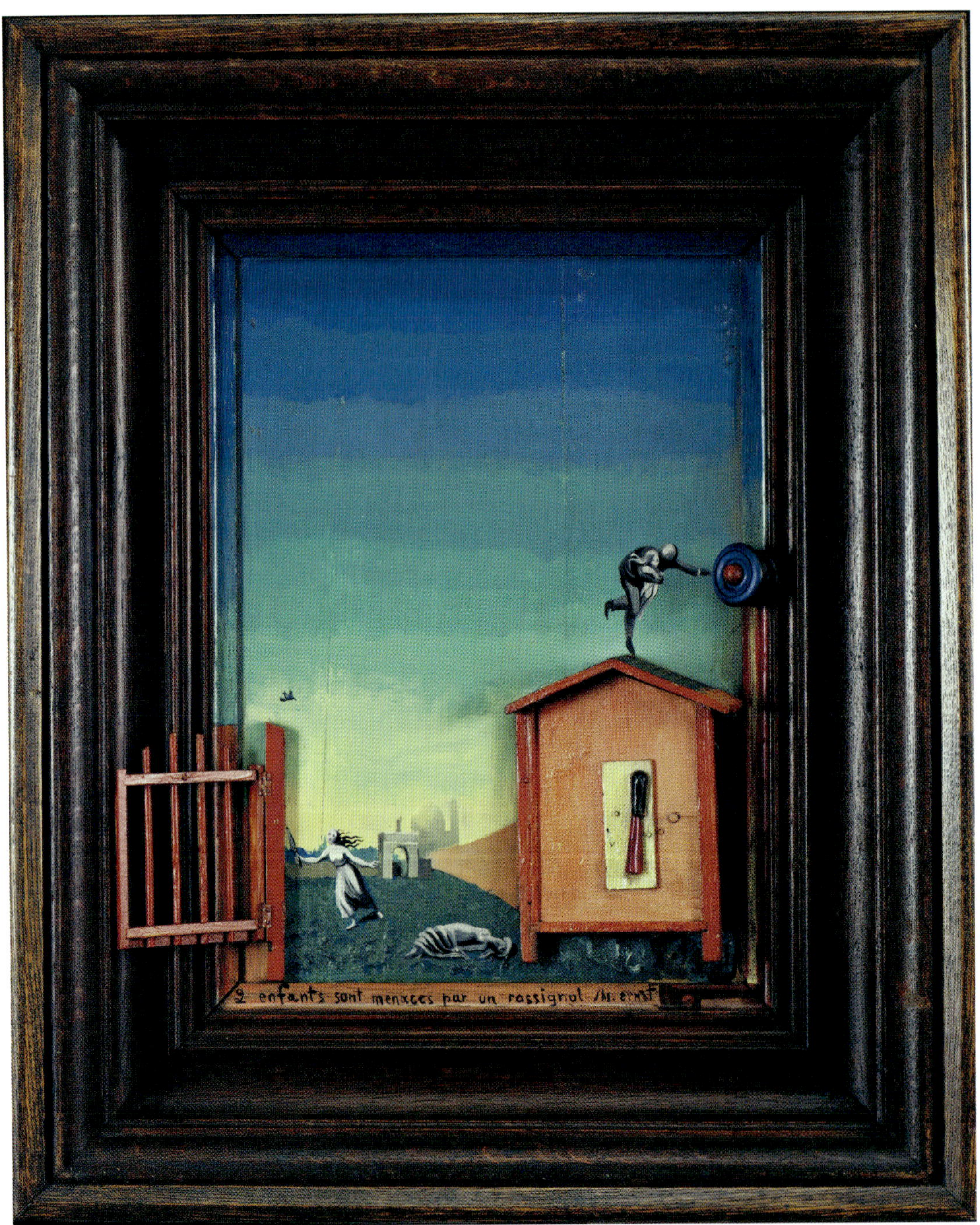

2 enfants sont menaces par un rossignol /M. ernst

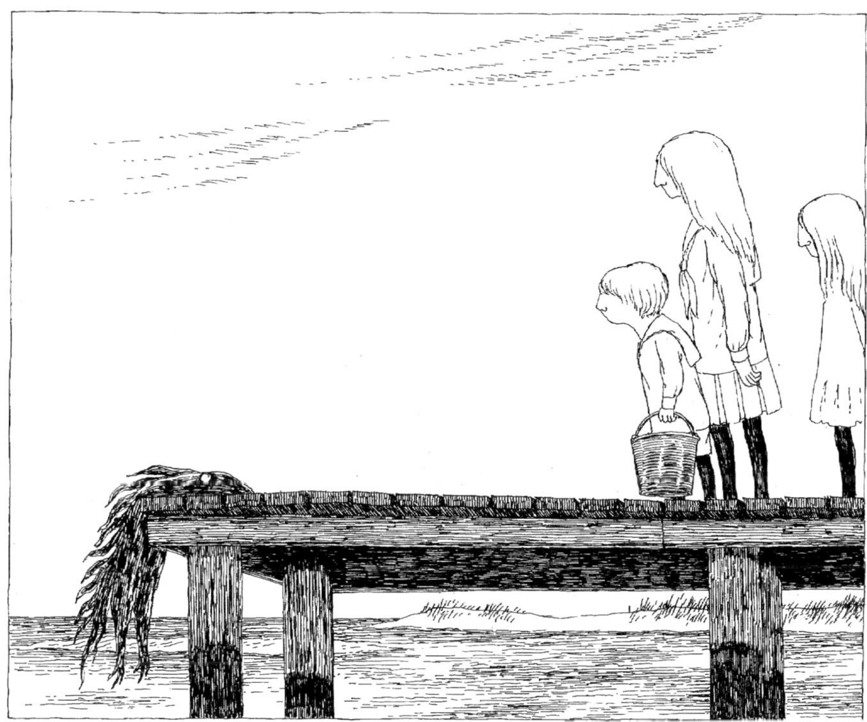

The creature regarded them Balefully.

Max Ernst, Illustration in *Une Semaine de Bonté ou les Sept Éléments Capitaux Roman: Quatrième Cahier Mercredi.* Original collages published in five volumes by J. Bucher, Paris, 1934.

Edward Gorey, Mockup of the cover for *The Doubtful Guest*, c. 1957. Offset lithograph on board, 5 × 7 ½ in. (12.7 × 19.1 cm). The Edward Gorey Charitable Trust.

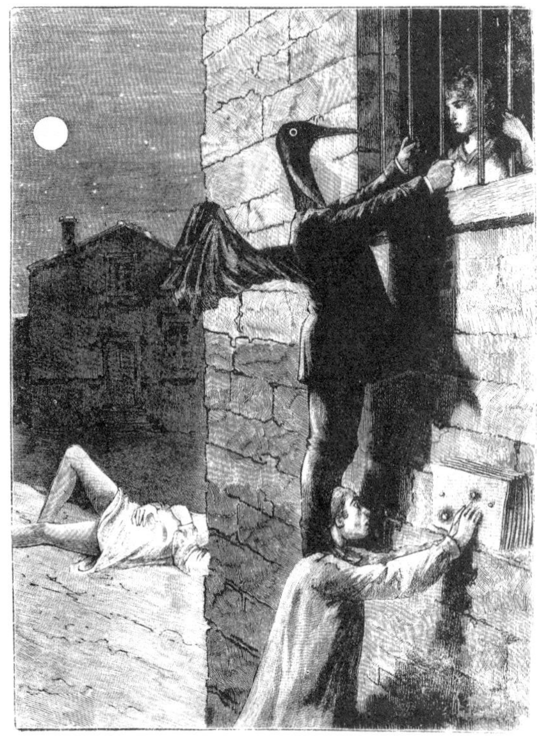

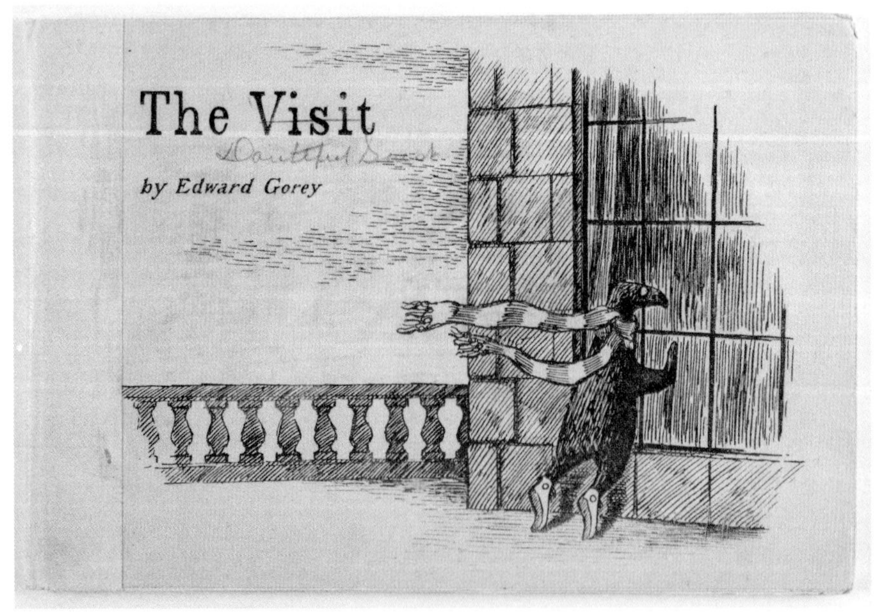

(fig. 4.19). The work was donated to the Art Institute of Chicago by the daughter of one of Gorey's childhood neighbors, along with several letters Gorey wrote in the late 1940s, suggesting that it might date to that period. Gorey collaged phrases in English and French that have apparently been cut out of magazines or catalogues, such as "slightly damaged goods" and "subject to this sort of madness." He then drew an odd shrew-like character in two different positions, one looking up philosophically, and the other sitting dejectedly in a chair. Other than a sort of wanton madness, peppered with claustrophobia and mixed with malaise, it's not possible to draw any certain conclusions about the meaning of this collage. The character could simply be a randomly invented nonsense creature, or, with its pointed nose and placement in a surreal setting, it may represent one of Gorey's earliest reinterpretations of Loplop. The creature can also be understood as an ancestor to Gorey's Doubtful Guest, and other Figbash-like creatures to follow.

The image is also interesting for its use of cut-up bits of language. Confronted with Gorey's seemingly random texts, as in *The Object-Lesson*, Schiff compared Gorey to William Burroughs, known for cutting out lines from newspapers and reassembling them at random. But this wanton treatment of written language was recommended much earlier by Lewis Carroll in his poem "Poeta Fit, Non Nascitur" (1869):

> First you write a sentence,
> And then you chop it small;
> Then mix the bits, and sort them out
> Just as they chance to fall:
> The order of the phrases makes
> No difference at all.[48]

Another of the Baxter images that Gorey owned, *The Fourteen*, features an enigmatic landscape (and no text) (fig. 4.20). A colorless villa sits in the distance amid a "forest" of gently tinted, oddly hulking trees and trimmed bushes. In the foreground a figure stares at something white on the ground. She is touching it, as if perhaps she is examining a tear in the painting itself. When asked to explain the meaning of the painting, Baxter replied, "It doesn't have to MEAN anything, nor does the figure in the picture—I want the viewer to make up their own mind about this."[49] With Baxter, then, we move from artfully rendered tensions between text and image to a general idealization of ambiguity that Gorey also embraced.

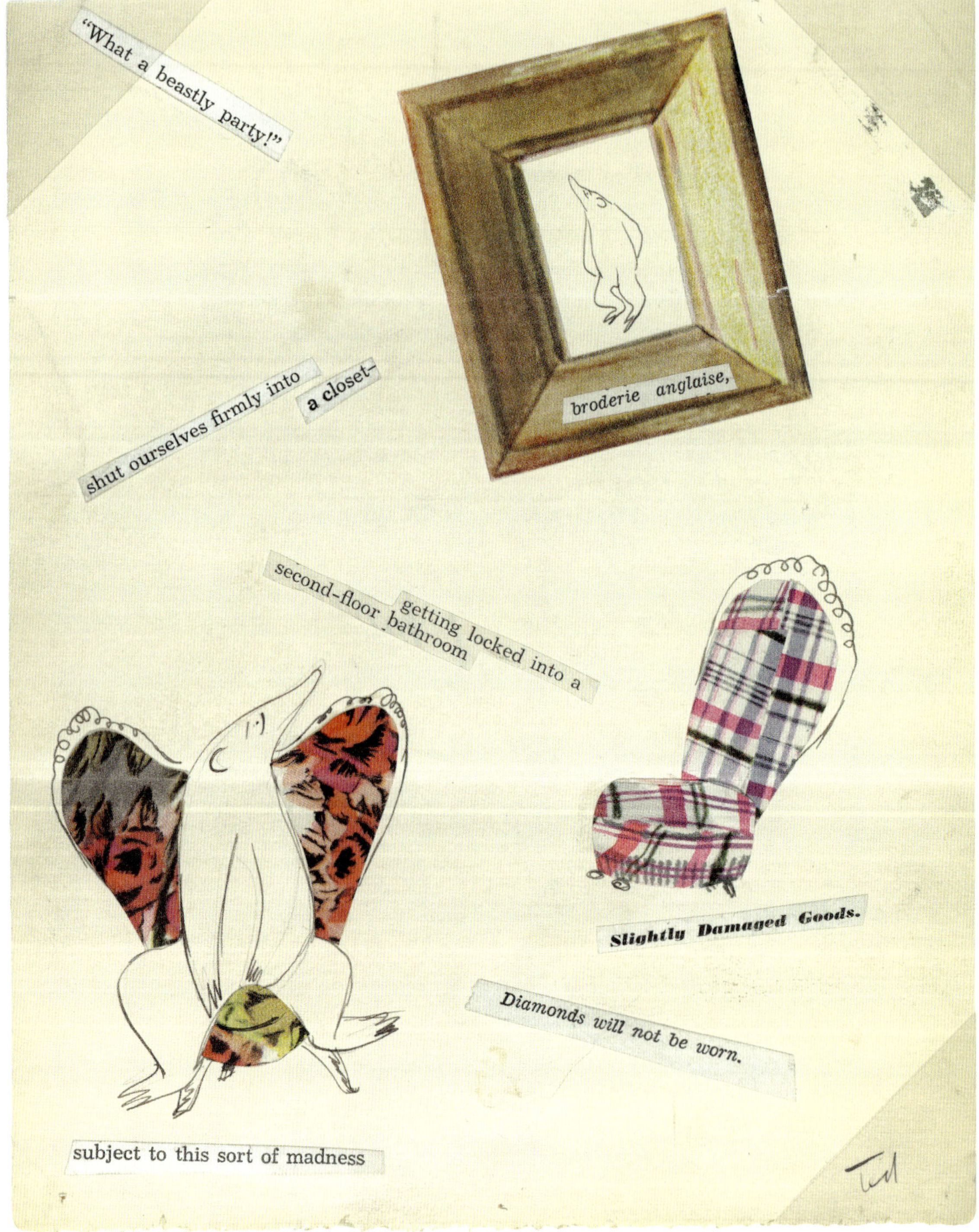

"What a beastly party!"
shut ourselves firmly into a closet–
broderie anglaise,
second–floor bathroom getting locked into a
Slightly Damaged Goods.
Diamonds will not be worn.
subject to this sort of madness

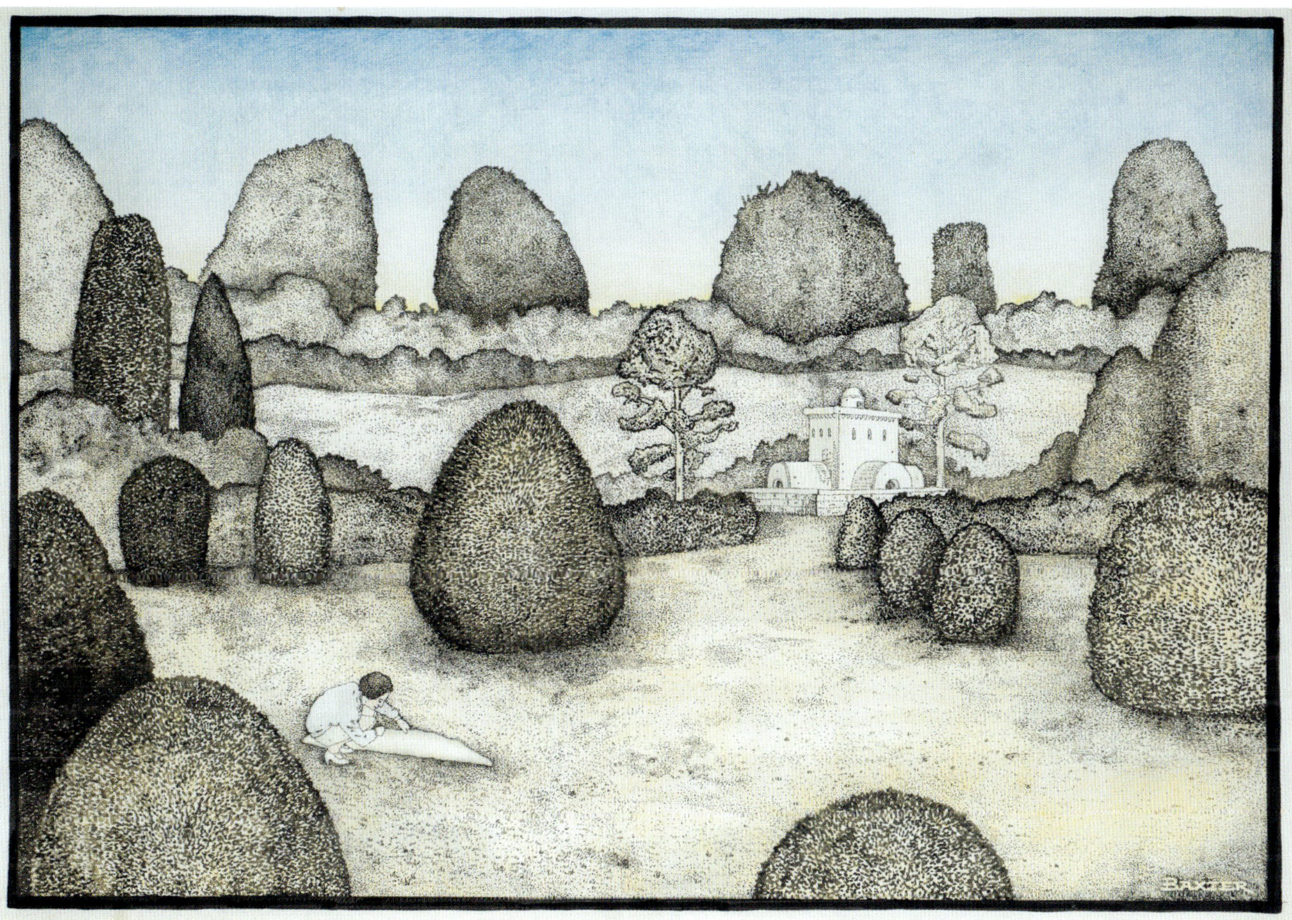

Fig. 4.19

Edward Gorey, *What a Beastly Party!*, n.d. Pen and black ink, with cut and pasted paper elements, on cream wove paper, 7½ × 6 in. (19.3 × 15.5 cm). The Art Institute of Chicago. Bequest of Sylvia Sights, 2009.993.

Fig. 4.20

Glen Baxter, *The Fourteen*, 1977. Pen and ink and colored pencil on paper, 21⅞ × 32³⁄₁₆ in. (55.6 × 81.8 cm). Wadsworth Atheneum Museum of Art, Hartford, Conn. Bequest of Edward Gorey, 2001.13.25.

While the focus of this essay is to interpret Gorey's interest in art through the lens of nineteenth-century literary nonsense, it should be acknowledged that the ambiguity nonsense embraces was also embraced in later movements, such as twentieth-century modernism and surrealism, which clearly influenced Gorey. The pedigree, however, is important to trace. Writing in 1901, critic and nonsense poet G. K. Chesterton asserted that nonsense literature was "a new type of literature" that may represent a "literature of the future."[50] Many would concur. Michael Holquist, for example, in "What Is a Boojum? Nonsense and Modernism,"[51] links writers like James Joyce, Franz Kafka, Samuel Beckett, Vladimir Nabokov, Jorge Luis Borges, Jean Genet, and Alain Robbe-Grillet in terms of the tropes and conventions they inherited from Victorian nonsense. And in her study *Alice to the Lighthouse: Children's Books and Radical Experiments in Art*, Juliet Dusinberre traces the influence of Lewis Carroll on modernist writers and their experiments with story structure and meaning.[52] Gorey's oeuvre can be understood similarly, comfortably situated in both worlds, nonsense and modernism.

Gorey may have tied his work to the modernist movement via his settings. In an attempt to demarcate the literary boundaries of modernist writers such as Joyce and T. S. Eliot, Virginia Woolf claimed that "on or about December 1910, human character changed."[53] After this moment in history, Woolf contended, humans, and their stories, were transformed. Characters began to speak to one another in "disconnected lines,"[54] and a story might end "without any point to it."[55] Certainly well aware of Woolf's oft-quoted essay, Gorey frequently mentioned or conceded in interviews that his books were situated on or about 1910. His introduction to *The Black Doll* situates the action "In the year 1910, more or less."[56] Nearly every "prop" in Gorey's settings, from clothing to automobiles, confirms this date, locating Gorey's worlds at the mythological birth of modernism.

Gorey also aligned himself with surrealism. He commented, "[Surrealism] is my philosophy, if I have one, certainly in a literary way."[57] Among the surrealists Gorey mentioned were Charles Cros, Alphonse Allais, and André Breton — all authors. And while he disliked Salvador Dalí, he admired Ernst and Magritte. Wilkin notes that in Gorey's art "Magritte's paintings are often invoked . . . particularly those without accompanying words. The ambiguous interiors of *The West Wing* [1963] with their ominous, over-scaled cracks . . . and their ordinary objects wrenched out of context, altered in scale, and released from normal physical laws, read like tributes to the Belgian artist."[58] Indeed, Magritte's *The Invisible World* (1954) (fig. 4.21)

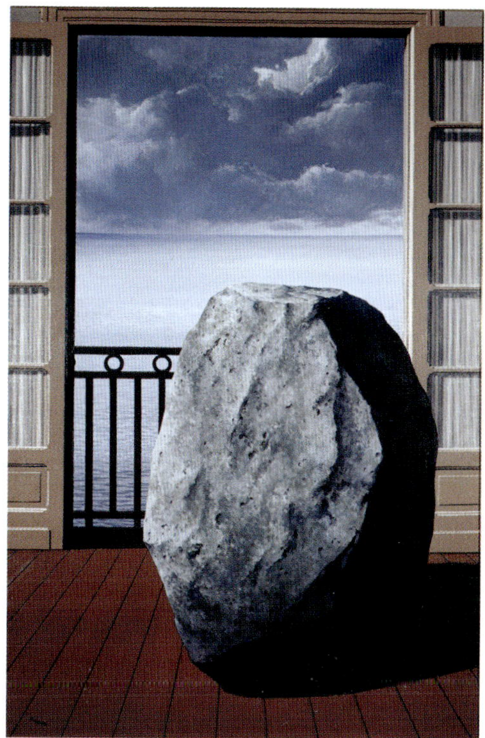

Fig. 4.21

René Magritte (French, 1898–1967), *Le Monde Invisible (The Invisible World)*, 1954. Oil on canvas, 76¾ × 51 3⁄16 in. (195 × 130 cm). Private Collection.

compares easily to the image of a boulder mysteriously resting on a table in a vacant room in Gorey's *West Wing*.

It should be noted here that surrealism—initially a literary movement—embraced Lewis Carroll from the beginning. Breton, author of *The Surrealist Manifesto*, later explained the origins of the movement in "On Surrealism in Its Living Works" (1953), commenting that "Surrealism, as an organized movement, was born of a far-reaching operation having to do with language." He points to several nineteenth-century authors who struggled to liberate language and words "from their . . . narrow utilitarian usage . . . [T]his need to counteract . . . the depreciation of language was felt . . . in England by Lewis Carroll."[59] Breton is probably referring to Carroll's fascination with puns, neologisms, and portmanteau words, and his surreal poetry, which resists logical interpretation. The dreamlike quality of Carroll's writings also comports well with surrealism's fascination with Freud and the understanding of the subconscious, where the deepest meaning lies concealed yet still resonates with

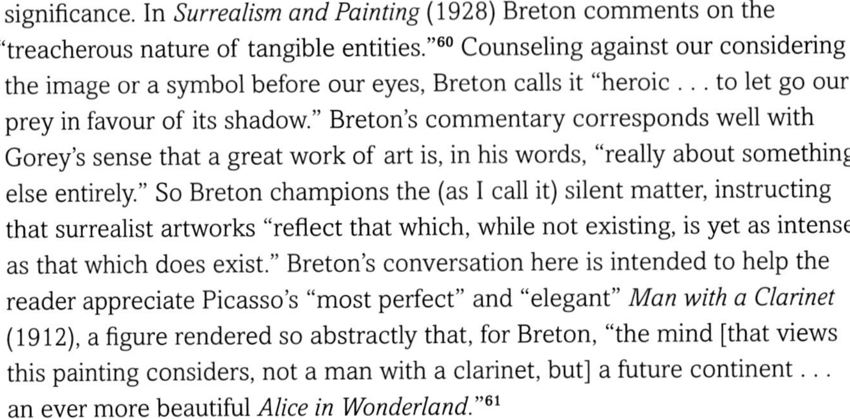

significance. In *Surrealism and Painting* (1928) Breton comments on the "treacherous nature of tangible entities."[60] Counseling against our considering the image or a symbol before our eyes, Breton calls it "heroic . . . to let go our prey in favour of its shadow." Breton's commentary corresponds well with Gorey's sense that a great work of art is, in his words, "really about something else entirely." So Breton champions the (as I call it) silent matter, instructing that surrealist artworks "reflect that which, while not existing, is yet as intense as that which does exist." Breton's conversation here is intended to help the reader appreciate Picasso's "most perfect" and "elegant" *Man with a Clarinet* (1912), a figure rendered so abstractly that, for Breton, "the mind [that views this painting considers, not a man with a clarinet, but] a future continent . . . an ever more beautiful *Alice in Wonderland*."[61]

Like Gorey, Alfred Jarry is another writer-artist who can be interpreted across several genres. While he is known formally as symbolist, his writings—such as the poem "Le Homard et la boîte de corned-beef . . . ," in which a can of corned beef falls in love with a lobster—are sometimes collected in anthologies of nonsense literature.[62] Jarry is also widely regarded as a precursor to modernism, Dada, surrealism, futurism, and theater of the absurd. Like later surrealist artists, the symbolists suggested that art should evoke rather than describe. Stéphane Mallarmé, one of the movement's chief proponents, instructed that the symbolist should depict not the thing, but the effect the thing produces.

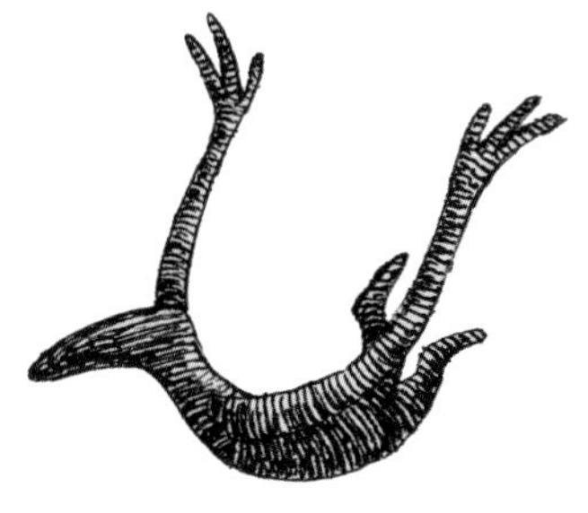

Jarry went out of his way not to depict things, and the effect his art created could be quite disorienting. For example, toward the end of his short but storied career, he founded an absurdist pseudoscience he called pataphysics. Jarry offered no single definition of pataphysics, preferring to present numerous contradictory definitions. A central tenet was that pataphysics concerned itself with imaginary solutions to imaginary problems. In Jarry's novel *The Exploits and Opinions of Dr. Faustroll* (1911), this new "science" is discovered by the title character, a man who was born at the age of sixty-three.

For Gorey, then, there was a lot to love about Alfred Jarry. He owned three prints related to the 1898 staging of Jarry's absurd carnivalesque play *Ubu Roi*, featuring illustrations for, among other things, "La Chanson du Décervelage" or "The Disembraining Song," which celebrates the weekly public lobotomies held in a Paris marketplace (fig. 4.22). *Ubu Roi* is notorious for its wildness, blasphemy, crude humor, and generally chaotic nature. In scene 2, for example, the boorish main character, Père Ubu, and his wife set

Fig. 4.22

Alfred Jarry (French, 1873–1907), *La Chanson du Décervelage (The Disembraining Song) from "Ubu Roi"* from the *Répértoire des Pantins (Puppet Theater)*, 1898. Lithograph on paper, 13 9/16 × 10 5/8 in. (34.5 × 27 cm). Wadsworth Atheneum Museum of Art, Hartford, Conn. Bequest of Edward Gorey, 2001.13.59.

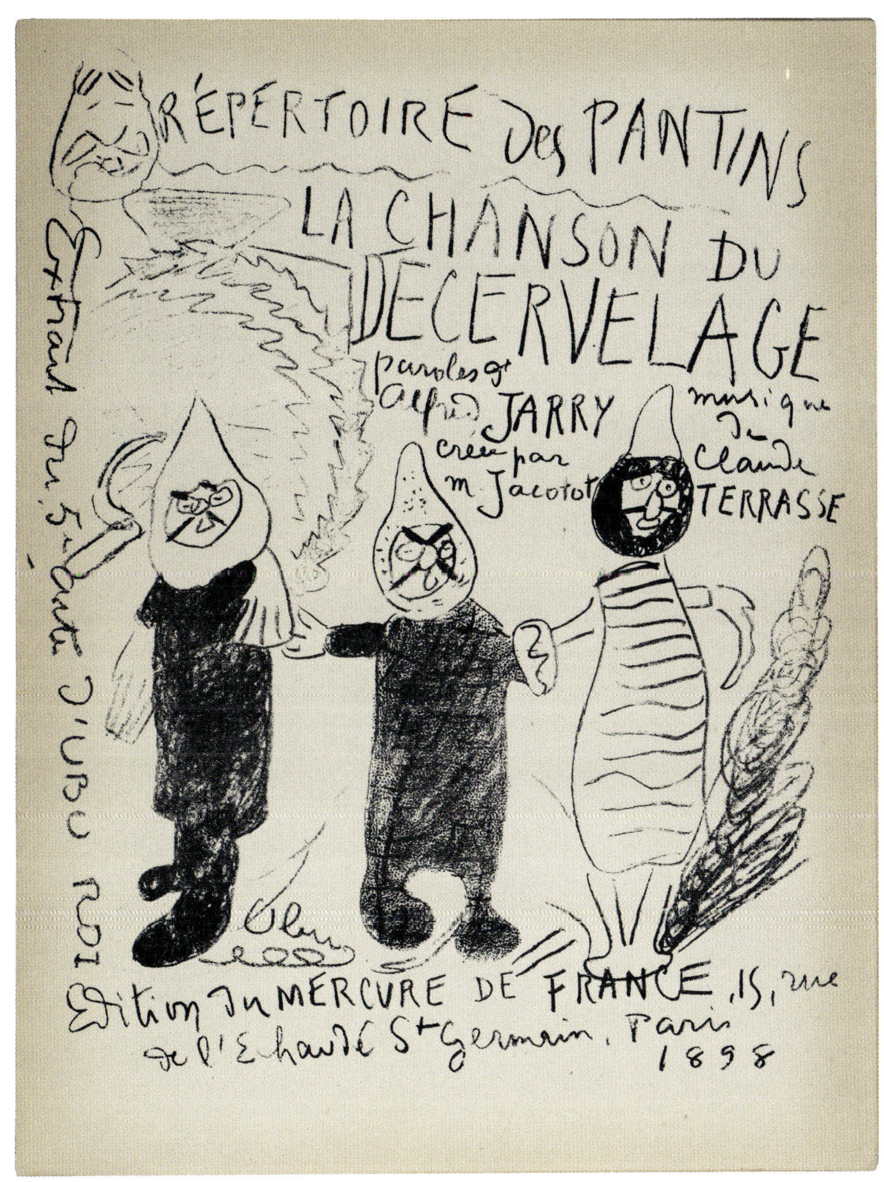

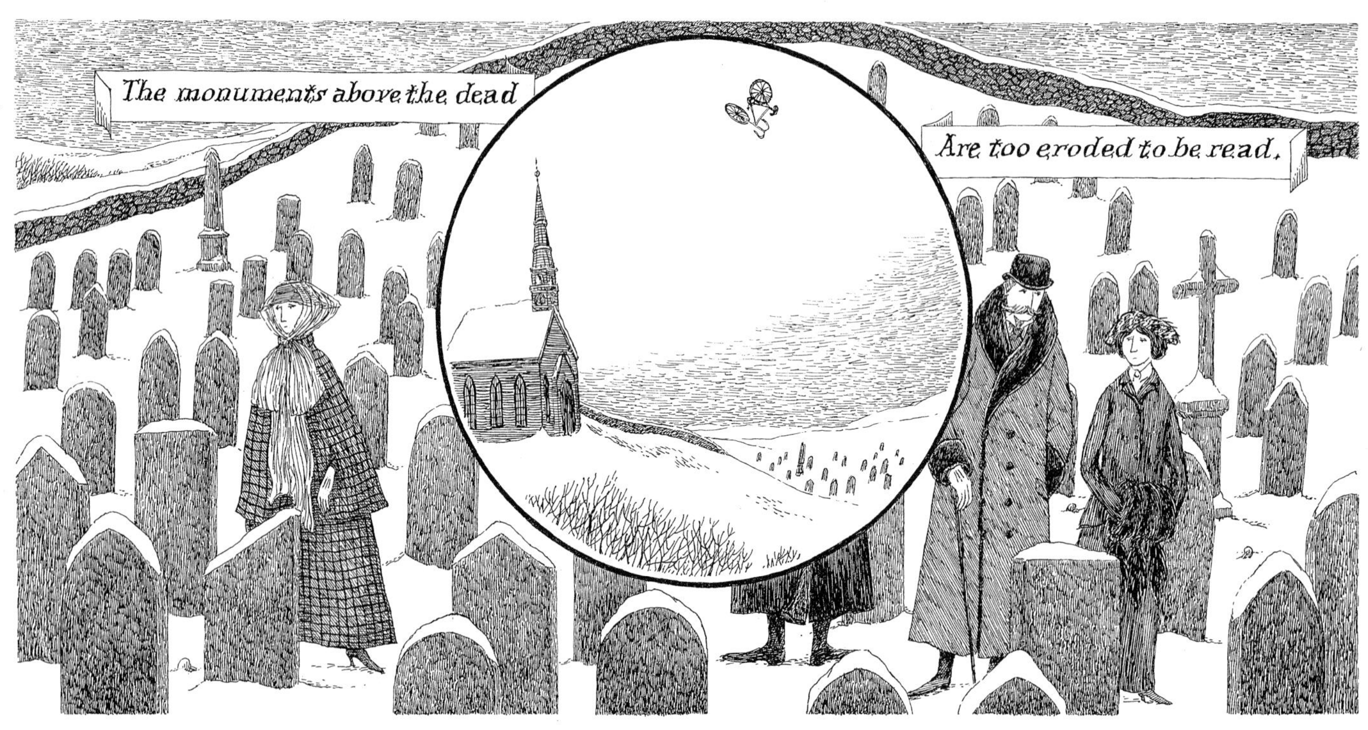

The monuments above the dead

Are too eroded to be read.

out a table prepared for guests with "wombat cutlets," "pâté of dog," and "pope's noses." While the 1896 stage premiere resulted in a riot, the 1898 advertisements that Gorey owned refer to an ostensibly "safer" presentation, performed this time with marionettes. Gorey, himself a creator of absurd puppet shows, would have admired *Ubu Roi* for its nonsense and its irreverent, darkly humorous tone.

Gorey also owned a number of pieces by Charles Meryon, another artist whose works are sometimes regarded as precursors of surrealism. In *Le Ministère de la Marine* (1865/66), the Ministry of the Navy, in Paris, is being attacked by a fantastic hoard of Maori canoes, flying horseman, mystical sea creatures, and airborne whales (see fig. 1.12). Meryon reveled in communicating cabalistic secret meaning through obscure symbolism,[63] and his works were often greeted with confusion and sometimes understood as evidence of a mania that grew as the artist aged. In Meryon's mind, however, it is possible that this particular image functioned more like a political cartoon; according to one interpretation Meryon is venting his anger about the French navy's failure to aid New Zealand in its colonial struggles.[64] Regardless of Meryon's intentions, what is left is an enigmatic scene that one may only puzzle over. It is likely that *Le Ministère de la Marine* intrigued Gorey for its surreal quality. It reminds one of several images in such books of Gorey's as *L'heure Bleue* (1975), which features oars floating in the air over a pond, or especially several images from *The Iron Tonic*, in which objects such as clocks and bicycles float in, or fall from, the sky (fig. 4.23). Of note is that a copy of *Le Ministère de la Marine* is featured in the collection of the Art Institute of Chicago, thus making it possible that Gorey first encountered the image during his studies there at age eighteen in 1943.

In a 1978 interview Gorey comments, "If a book is only what it seems to be about, then somehow the author has failed."[65] And while Wilkin is correct that Gorey was "at home with a wide range of traditions,"[66] it is within a particular spectrum of the arts, from literary nonsense to surrealism, that Gorey explored and exploited that silent matter—the same provoking ambiguity that so fueled his keenest appreciations of art and literature, and that marks as distinct and idiosyncratic the art he chose to surround himself with at home and in his studio.

Notes

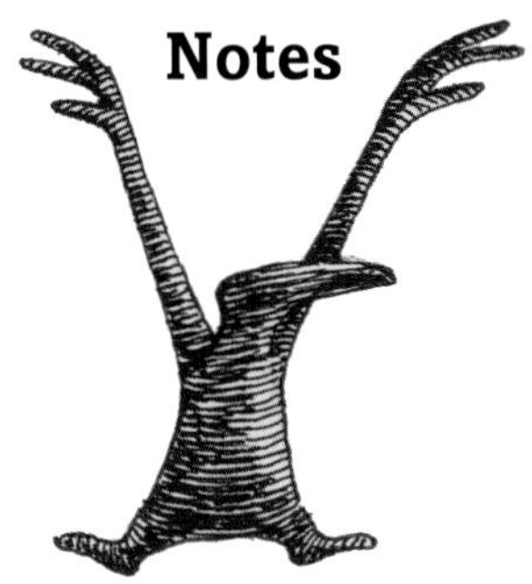

Gorey's Worlds

1. Gorey's bequest to the Wadsworth Atheneum consists of seventy three artworks. Archival records and photographs indicate that he owned other works of art, some of which are in private hands, either with friends or having been sold at auction. In terms of existing scholarship on Gorey, Clifford Ross and Karen Wilkin were among the first to explore and discuss the affinities between Gorey's work and the artists he admired. See *The World of Edward Gorey*, ed. Clifford Ross and Karen Wilkin (New York: Harry N. Abrams, 1996).

2. For more on Edward Gorey's deep admiration for the ballet and Balanchine, see Robert Greskovic's essay in this book. Gorey never met Balanchine, but he and Kirstein became friends and worked together on several ballet-related projects. The most notable was a piece commemorating the fiftieth season of the ballet, titled *The Lavender Leotard: or, Going a Lot to the New York City Ballet*. Through Kirstein, Gorey may have heard updates on the Wadsworth Atheneum's major acquisitions and exhibitions related to the ballet.

3. Kirstein's classmate Edward Warburg was the third founder. For an in-depth history of how Austin and Kirstein brought Balanchine to Hartford, and the disappointing outcome, see chapter 10 in Eugene Gaddis, *The Magician of the Modern: Chick Austin and the Transformation of the Arts in America* (New York: Alfred A. Knopf, 2000), 198–220.

4. Selma G. Lanes, *Through the Looking Glass: Further Adventures and Misadventures in the Realm of Children's Literature* (Boston: D. R. Godine, 2004), 111.

5. Gorey summered in Barnstable in an attic room in a family house before buying his own house. My thanks go to Edward Gorey's cousin Skee Morton and Ken Morton, her son, for sharing their time and recollections about Gorey on the Cape.

6. These postcards are now in the collection of the Edward Gorey Charitable Trust.

7. Thank you to Robert Greskovic, who accompanied Gorey on this trip to Hartford, for sharing this information with me, as well as so many other valuable insights and observations about Gorey's interest in the ballet.

8. Walter Benjamin and Edmund Jephcott, *Reflections: Essays, Aphorisms, Autobiographical Writings* (New York: Schocken, 1986), 154.

9. Ibid., 155.

10. Keith D. Mano, "Edward Gorey Inhabits an Odd World of Tiny Drawings, Fussy Cats and 'Doomed Enterprises,'" *People*, July 3, 1978.

11. The Munch print is part of the Gorey bequest and is discussed in Arnold Arluke's essay in this book. Two Balthus

drawings are in the Gorey bequest and will be discussed later in this essay.

12. Mel Gussow, "At Home with: Edward Gorey; a Little Blood Goes a Long Way," *New York Times*, April 21, 1994. For more on Gorey's personal library, now housed at San Diego State University, see Linda Salem, "The Edward Gorey Personal Library: Evidencing Insights," in *Frontiers in American Children's Literature* (Newcastle upon Tyne: Cambridge Scholars Publishing, 2016), chapter 15.

13. In McDermott's view of Gorey's studio, hanging to the left of the work table are two prints in the Wadsworth's bequest: Eugène Delacroix's *Tiger Sleeping in the Desert* (fig. 3.14) and an engraving of a dragon by an unidentified artist (fig. 4.9). Some of these objects—such as tassels and finials—find their way into Gorey's stories. Representing a pioneering look at these affinities was *Edward Gorey's Cabinet of Curiosities*, the first exhibition on Gorey's collections and his interest in *Wunderkammer*, at the Edward Gorey House in 2017. http://www.edwardgoreyhouse.org/our-2017-exhibit.

14. Elizabeth Smith Brownstein, *If This House Could Talk* (New York: Simon & Schuster, 1999), 222.

15. For example, see Edward Gorey, *Les Passmenteries Horribles* (1977), *Les Urnes Utiles* (1980), and *Les Echanges Malandreux* (1985). Stories such as *The Listing Attic* (1954) and *The Blue Aspic* (1968) are written in English but also include French words or phrases in the text.

16. Two of these drawings are now part of the Edward Gorey bequest at the Wadsworth Atheneum. The third remains unlocated.

17. Thank you to Linda Salem, the librarian for the Edward Gorey Personal Library at SDSU Library, for her research on Balthus books in Gorey's library. Peter F. Neumeyer, *Floating Worlds: The Letters of Edward Gorey and Peter F. Neumeyer* (San Francisco: Pomegranate, 2011), 122. See also Clifford Ross, "Interview with Edward Gorey," in *The World of Edward Gorey*, ed. Clifford Ross and Karen Wilkin (New York: Harry N. Abrams, 1996), 18.

18. For a closer look at connections among Gorey, Balthus, and surrealism, see Kevin Shortsleeve's essay in this book.

19. See catalogue numbers P194–195 and D418–D422 in Virginie Monnier and Jean Clair, *Balthus: Catalogue Raisonné of the Complete Works* (New York: Harry N. Abrams, 1999).

20. John Russell, *Balthus* (London: Arts Council of Great Britain, 1968), 11.

21. The two soldiers were different: the Spahi is cavalry and the Zouave is infantry. Their uniforms were slightly different and primarily distinguished by color and headwear.

22. Gorey also owned a Bonnard print, *Last Light* (*Dernier reflet*), 1926–27, and a pencil sketch by Vuillard of trees which were part of his bequest to the museum. Bonnard and Vuillard were called Intimists because of their predilection for intimate domestic scenes. Colta Ives, Helen Giambruni, and Sasha M. Newman, *Pierre Bonnard: The Graphic Art* (New York: Harry N. Abrams, 1989), 79.

23. The receipt for the Bonnard is dated October 31, 1977. The date of Gorey's acquisition of the Vuillard drawing has yet to be confirmed.

24. "Edward Gorey: Proust Questionnaire," *Vanity Fair*, October 1997.

25. Edward Gorey to Robert Greskovic, September 13, 1985. Collection of Robert Greskovic.

26. In addition to the five prints in the Gorey bequest at the Wadsworth, I am aware of two others that he owned.

27. James Leo Yarnall, "Meryon's Mystical Transformations," *Art Bulletin* 61, no. 2 (June 1979): 289–300, 291. Yarnall's article goes into greater detail about the multileveled political, magical, and psychological meaning of Meryon's prints.

28. Philip Gilbert Hamerton, *Old Paris: Twenty Etchings by Charles Meryon* (Liverpool: Henry Young & Sons, 1914).

29. Meryon's first biographer, Philippe Burty, described the artist's painful years, "années douloureuses," when he was diagnosed with chronic lypomania (melancholia) accompanied by delirium and hallucinations, in *Charles Méryon, Sailor, Engraver, and Etcher: A Memoir and Complete Descriptive Catalogue of His Works* (London: Fine Art Society, 1879). Several of the artists Gorey admired and collected, such as Balthus, Charles Burchfield, and Edvard Munch, suffered from nervous breakdowns and/or clinical psychological conditions.

30. Stefanie Heraeus and Deborah Laurie Cohen, "Artists and the Dream in Nineteenth-Century Paris: Towards a Prehistory of Surrealism," *History Workshop Journal*, no. 48 (Autumn 1999): 151–68, 161.

31. When Gorey purchased these prints from the Lee Witkin Gallery, collecting photography was still in its early stages. Alexandra Mezey, "Selling Photography as Art Put Lee Witkin in the Picture," *People*, April 9, 1979. http://people.com/archive/selling-photography-as-art-put-lee-witkin-in-the-picture-vol-11-no-14/feed/. Witkin later became Berenice Abbott's dealer in the mid-1970s.

32. In a conversation with Ross, Gorey noted the haunting quality of Atget's work, *The World of Edward Gorey*, 15.

33. Clark Worswick, *Berenice Abbott/Eugène Atget* (Arena Editions, 2002), 23. In Paris, Abbott worked with the pioneering art dealer Julien Levy to rescue Atget's vast archive of thousands of prints and negatives. She later made new photographic prints from select negatives.

34. Gorey, *The Fantod Pack* (New York: Gotham Book Mart, 1995). The word "fantod" signifies a state of worry or nervous anxiety, irritability.

35. Berenice Abbott, *The World of Atget* (New York: Putnam, 1964), xvii.

36. See, for example, various female figures in *The Prune People*, *The Wuggly Ump*, and *The Curious Sofa*.

37. These receipts are in the Edward Gorey Charitable Trust.

38. Alexander Theroux, *The Strange Case of Edward Gorey* (Seattle: Fantagraphics, 2011), 159.

39. For a closer look at Gorey's treatment of animals, see Arnold Arluke's essay in this book.

40. J. Benjamin Townsend, *Charles Burchfield's Journals* (Albany: State University of New York Press, 1993), 332.

41. The technique was also referred to as Grecian painting because it resembled the effect of paintings discovered on the walls of ancient Grecian palaces. I am grateful to Shelley Langdale for sharing her time and insights on this material in Gorey's collection. For more on the genre, see Shelley Langdale, "The Enchantment of the Magic Lake: The Origin and Iconography of a Nineteenth-Century Sandpaper Drawing," *Folk Art* (Winter 1998/99): 52–63, 55, and *Darkness Like a Dream: Nineteenth-Century Sandpaper Drawings from the Collections of Randall and Tanya Holton and Matt Mullican and Valerie Smith*, exh. cat. (New York: The Drawing Center, 1999).

42. Gorey told Kevin McDermott that he was "attracted to them early in the game." McDermott, *Elephant House or, The Home of Edward Gorey* (San Francisco: Pomegranate, 2003), n.p. In Edward Gorey's archive is a handwritten receipt dated February 19, 1979, for three unidentified sand paintings, totaling $190.

43. Langdale, "The Enchantment of the Magic Lake," 55. Other versions of *The Magic Lake* are in the Martha and Maxim Karolik collection, Museum of Fine Arts, Boston; in the Smithsonian American Art Museum; and in several private collections.

44. My thanks to Andreas Brown for bringing this valentine and so many other valuable archival materials to my attention.

45. See also Meryon's *Le Ministère de la Marine*, fig. 1.12.

46. At the time of his death, Evans had created four thousand alternative world stamps, representing forty-two imagined

countries. Willy Eisenhart, *The World of Donald Evans* (New York: Harlin Quist Books, 1980), 15.

47. The other two Donald Evans works are in private collections. I thank Bill Evans for assisting my research on this fascinating artist.

48. Eisenhart, *The World of Donald Evans*, 68. Of note, Evans, like Gorey, loved wordplay and used a pseudonym, Doke Emmonds, in college.

49. For a discussion of Baxter's and Booth's works, see Kevin Shortsleeve's essay in this book.

50. Clifford Ross, email with the author, March 26, 2017, and in-person interview by the author, the artist's studio, March 15, 2016.

51. Ibid.

52. There is one York in the Gorey bequest; the seven other works are privately owned. Roberta Smith, "Albert York, Reclusive Landscape Painter, Dies at 80," *New York Times*, November 1, 2009.

53. Bill Berkson, "The Idylls of Albert York," *Art in America*, September 1988, 172–77.

54. Barry Schwabsky, "Artists Keeping Secrets: The Eloquent Silences of Albert York and Judith Scott." *Nation*, December 9, 2014.

The Man Who Wanted to Be Entertained

1. Once the NYCB moved, in 1964, from New York's City Center of Music and Drama to Lincoln Center's New York State Theater, Ted's seat of choice remained A,1, in the theater's Second Ring, i.e., front row, on the aisle.

2. *Nutcracker* (Full length version. Chor: George Balanchine after Lev Ivanov; mus: Petr Chaikovskii; lib: Marius Petipa after Dumas's Casse noisette; scen: Horace Armistead; cos: Barbara Karinska; lighting: Jean Rosenthal. First perf: U.S.: New York City, City Center, February 2, 1954, New York City Ballet. First perf. of revised version: New York City, New York State Theatre, December 11, 1964, New York City Ballet, scen & lighting: Rouben Ter-Arutunian; cos: Barbara Karinska.) ballet.

3. Peg Churchill, "Balanchine Modest on Ranking Ballet: 'We're What We Are,'" *Schenectady Gazette*, July 26, 1969.

4. *Coppélia* (chor: George Balanchine and Alexandra Danilova after Marius Petipa; mus: Leo Delibes; scen & cos: Rouben Ter-Arutunian; lighting: Ronald Bates. First perf: New York, Saratoga Springs, Saratoga Performing Arts Center, July 17, 1974, New York City Ballet). ballet.

5. *Don Quixote* (chor: George Balanchine; mus: Nicolas Nabokov; scen, cos & light: Esteban Francés. First perf: New York, State Theatre, May 28, 1965, New York City Ballet Company). ballet.

6. Arlene Croce, "Edward Gorey," *Ballet Review*. 28, no. 2 (2000): 23.

7. Tobi Tobias, "Balletgorey," *Dance Magazine*, January 1974, 67–71.

8. *Rocky Horror Picture Show*, dir. Jim Sharman, 1 hr. 40 min., 20th Century Fox. 1975.

9. Arlene Croce, *After-Images* (New York: Vintage Books, 1979), 395.

10. Robert Doty, *Extraordinary Realities* (New York: Dodd, Meade & Company, 1973), 8.

11. Peter F. Neumeyer, ed., *Floating Worlds: The Letters of Edward Gorey and Peter Neumeyer* (San Francisco: Pomegranate, 2011), 39.

12. Toni Bentley, *Costumes by Karinska* (New York: Harry N. Abrams, 1995), 6.

13. It should be noted here that Ted's 1978 Tony award for the Broadway production of *Dracula* was for his costume design, not his somewhat better-known, and much more documented, set designs. *Dracula* (written by Hamilton Deane from the novel of the same name by Bram Stoker. Opened New York, Martin Beck Theater, October 20, 1977).

14. *Bacchanale* (chor: Leonide Massine, mus: Richard Wagner, [Venusberg music from Tannhäuser], lib & scen: Salvador Dalí [based on the Venusberg scene of Tannhäuser], cos.: Barbara Karinska. Ballet Russe de Monte Carlo, 1939.) ballet.

15. *Schéhérazade* (chor: Michel Fokine; mus: Nikolai Rimski-Korsakov; lib: Alexandre Benois or Léon Bakst; scen & cos: Léon Bakst. First perf: France: Paris, Théâtre Nationale de l'Opera, June 4, 1910, Les Ballets Russes.) ballet.

16. Bentley, *Costumes by Karinska*, 41.

17. Gorey, *The Object-Lesson* (Garden City, NY: Doubleday, 1958).

18. *Apollo* (Original title: *Apollon musagète*. Chor: George Balanchine; mus: Igor Stravinsky; scen: André Bauchant; cos: André Bauchant. First perf: Paris, Théâtre Sarah Bernhardt, June 12, 1928, Ballets russes de Diaghilev.) ballet.

19. For the history of how Chick Austin and Lincoln Kirstein collaborated to bring George Balanchine from Russia to Hartford, see chapter 10 in Eugene Gaddis, *The Magician of the Modern: Chick Austin and the Transformation of the Arts in America* (New York: Alfred A. Knopf, 2000).

20. Lincoln Kirstein, Diaries (typescript), October 8, 1934, 34.

21. *Jewels* (chor: George Balanchine; mus: Peter Ilich Tchaikovsky, Gabriel Fauré, Igor Stravinsky; scen: Peter Harvey; cos: Barbara Karinska. Ballet in three parts. The music for Emeralds from G. Fauré's Pelléas et Mélisande and Shylock; the music for Rubies from I. Stravinsky's Capriccio for piano and orchestra; the music for Diamonds from P. Tchaikovsky's Symphony no. 3 in D major. First perf: New York, New York State Theater, April 13, 1967, New York City Ballet.) ballet.

22. *Episodes* (A work in 2 parts: Episodes I: Choreography by Martha Graham; Episodes II: Choreography by George Balanchine; Mus: Anton von Webern, Music for Episodes I: Passacaglia, Opus 1 & Six pieces, Opus 6; Music for Episodes II: Symphony, Opus 21; Five pieces, Opus 10; Concerto, Opus 24; Variations, Opus 30; and Ricercata in 6 voices from Bach's Musical offering: Scen: David Hays; cos: Karinska, for Episodes I. First perf: New York, City Center, May 14, 1959, New York City Ballet Company and Martha Graham and Dance Company.) ballet.

23. *Liebeslieder Walzer* (chor: George Balanchine; mus: Johannes Brahms, Liebeslieder Walzer, op. 52 and 65; scen: David Hays; cos: Barbara Karinska. First perf: New York, City Center, November 22, 1960, New York City Ballet Company.) ballet.

24. *A Midsummer Night's Dream* (chor: George Balanchine; mus: Felix Mendelssohn-Bartholdy; lib: William Shakespeare; scen: David Hays; cos: Barbara Karinska. First perf: New York, City Center, January 17, 1962, New York City Ballet Company.) ballet.

25. *La Valse* (chor: George Balanchine; mus: Maurice Ravel, Valses nobles et sentimentales and La valse; cos: Barbara Karinska; lighting: Jean Rosenthal. First perf: New York, City Center, February 20, 1951, New York City Ballet.) ballet.

26. *Orpheus* (chor: George Balanchine; mus: Igor Stravinsky; scen & cos: Isamu Noguchi. First perf: New York, City Center, April 28, 1948, Ballet Society.) ballet.

27. Gorey, *The Gilded Bat* (New York: Simon and Schuster, 1966).

28. *Agon* (chor: George Balanchine; mus: Igor Stravinsky; lighting: Nananne Porcher. First perf: New York, City Center, November 27, 1957, New York City Ballet, as a preview in a benefit program for the March of Dimes; official premiere: December 1, 1957.) ballet.

29. The twenty-seventh plate of *The Lavender Leotard* shows a male and female dancer in costuming related to designs Karinska provided for *Who Cares?*, Balanchine's 1970

Gershwin-inspired ballet; the woman wears a short-skirted leotard, similar to the one on the book's cover, where for the first publication Gorey hand-tinted the skirt a slightly different shade of lavender from that of the costume's torso. The caption reads, "I sometimes think if I see that lavender leotard with the little skirt that doesn't quite match in one more ballet . . ."

30. *Bourrée Fantasque* (chor: George Balanchine; mus: Emmanuel Chabrier; scen & cos: Barbara Karinska. First perf: New York, City Center, December 1, 1949, New York City Ballet.) ballet.

31. Gorey, "Recollecting Diana Adams," *Ballet Review* 21, no. 3 (1993): 21–24.

32. Ted passed along to me a paperback copy of a book about Noh about which he was most enthusiastic: *On the Art of the No Drama: The Major Treatises of Zeami*, ed. Masakazu Yamazaki, trans. J. Thomas Rimer (Princeton, NJ: Princeton University Press, 1984).

33. *Diggity* (chor: Paul Taylor; mus: Donald York; scen: Alex Katz; lighting: Mark Litvin. First perf: Washington, DC, National Theatre, November 15–20, 1978, Paul Taylor Dance Company.) dance.

34. *Dust* (chor: Paul Taylor; mus: Francis Poulenc, Concert champêtre; scen: Gene Moore; lighting: Jennifer Tipton. First perf: New York, City Center 55th St. Theater, June 1, 1977, Paul Taylor Dance Company.) dance.

35. *Nightshade* (chor: Paul Taylor; mus: Alexander Scriabin, Piano sonata no. 10; Two poems; Vers la flamme; cos: Gene Moore; lighting: Jennifer Tipton. First perf: New York, City Center Dance Theater, April 19, 1979, Paul Taylor Dance Company.) dance.

36. Ted's love of cats is well documented in his interviews and his work, but he was not a "cat person" at the expense of a fondness for dogs. He once noted the heart-tugging effect dogs could have on one: "They can look so down-trodden," he observed.

37. *When We Were Very Young* (chor: Twyla Tharp; mus: John Simon; text: Thomas Babe; set: Santo Loquasto. First perf: New York, Winter Garden Theatre, March 26, 1980, Twyla Tharp and Dancers.) dance.

38. *Murder* (chor & written by David Gordon; mus: Hector Berlioz, 1st movement of Symphonie funèbre et triomphale, op. 15; scen & cos: Edward Gorey; lighting: Allen Lee Hughes. First perf: San Francisco, War Memorial Opera House, February 27, 1986, American Ballet Theatre. First New York perf: Metropolitan Opera House, May 5, 1986, American Ballet Theatre.) dance.

39. *Ballet Review* 7, nos. 2 and 3 (1978–79): 64–117.

40. The text submitted by him was credited, in his own words, as follows: "Editor's Note: The above document appears through the courtesy of EDWARD GOREY (Xerox of original, which has lots of blurry photographs, on request)."

41. Gorey, *The Remembered Visit: A Story Taken from Life* (New York: Simon and Schuster, 1965).

42. Space does not permit detailing the theater works Edward Gorey oversaw while he was in NYC, most prominently of *Gorey Stories*, subtitled *An Entertainment with Music*, which eventually played on Broadway in 1978, where it was classified as a "play with music." The two-act show closed after its opening night, owing in part to the fact that there was a newspaper strike on at the time. Regardless of its fate, the show remained a rare enthusiasm of his, rare because Gorey felt, "It was the only time I appreciated my own work," eventually adding, "In the later previews for Broadway, I thought it was the best ensemble acting I have ever seen in my life." See Richard Dyer's "The Poison Penman," *Boston Globe*, April 1, 1984.

43. *Babe*, dir. Chris Noonan, 1 hr. 31 min. Universal Pictures. 1995.

44. Carol Verburg, *Edward Gorey Plays Cape Cod—Puppets, People, Places & Plots*. (San Francisco: Boom Books, 2011).

45. The Edward Gorey House is a museum and center devoted to Ted's life and work. It is open to the public seasonally. For more information, visit http://www.edwardgoreyhouse.org/about-gorey-house.

Understanding Gorey's Human-Animal World

1. Adrian Franklin, *Animals and Modern Cultures: A Sociology of Human-Animal Relations in Modernity* (London: Sage, 1999).

2. Sari Mäenpää, "Sailors and Their Pets: Men and Their Companion Animals Aboard Early Twentieth-Century Finnish Sailing Ships," *International Journal of Maritime History* 28 (2016): 480–95.

3. Jean Veevers, "The Social Meaning of Pets: Alternative Roles for Companion Animals," *Marriage & Family Review* 8 (1985): 11–30.

4. Clinton Sanders, *Understanding Dogs* (Philadelphia: Temple University Press, 1999), 10.

5. James Serpell, *In the Company of Animals* (Cambridge: Cambridge University Press, 1996).

6. Gail Melson, *Why the Wild Things Are: Animals in the Lives of Children* (Cambridge: Harvard University Press, 2009).

7. Arnold Arluke, "Animal Assisted Activity as a Social Experience," in *Handbook for Animal Assisted Therapy*, ed. A. Fine (London: Academic Press, 2010), 401–19.

8. Edward Gorey, *The Osbick Bird* (New York: Fantod Press, 1970).

9. Dieter Petzold, "Beasts and Monsters in MacDonald's Fantasy Stories," *North Wind: A Journal of George MacDonald Studies* 14 (1995): 4–21.

10. Edward Gorey, *The Utter Zoo*, vol. 1. (New York: Meredith Press, 1967).

11. Michael Lynch, "Sacrifice and the Transformation of the Animal Body into a Scientific Object: Laboratory Culture and Ritual Practice in the Neurosciences," *Social Studies of Science* 18 (1988): 267.

12. Edward Gorey, *The Gashlycrumb Tinies: Or, After the Outing* (New York: Simon and Schuster, 1963).

13. Paul Rüsse and Karita Nuut, "Rehepapp and Robin Hood: Tricksters or Heroes?" *Interlitteraria* 21 (2016): 130–42.

14. Edward Gorey, *The Doubtful Guest* (Garden City: Doubleday & Company, Inc., 1957).

15. Kevin Shortsleeve, "Edward Gorey, Children's Literature, and Nonsense Verse," *Children's Literature Association Quarterly* 27, no. 1 (Spring 2002): 27–39.

16. Michael Heyman and Kevin Shortsleeve, "Nonsense," in *Keywords for Children's Literature*, ed. Philip Nel and Lissa Paul (New York: NYU Press, 2011), 165–69.

17. Pru Hobson-West, "Beasts and Boundaries: An Introduction to Animals in Sociology, Science and Society," *Qualitative Sociology Review* 3 (2007): 23–41.

18. Gill Bliss, "Animals with Attitude: Finding a Place for Animated Animals," *Proceedings of the Conference on Critical Perspectives on Animals in Society* (University of Exeter, March 10, 2012), 37–44.

19. Claude Lévi-Strauss, *Totemism* (Boston: Beacon Press, 1963), 89.

20. Elizabeth Lawrence, "Cultural Perceptions of Differences between People and Animals: A Key to Understanding Human Animal Relationships," *Journal of American Culture* 18 (1995): 75–82.

21. Eden Lackner, "A Monstrous Childhood: Edward Gorey's Influence on Tim Burton's *The Melancholy Death of Oyster Boy*," in *The Works of Tim Burton: Margins to Mainstream*, ed. Jeffrey Andrew Weinstock (New York: Palgrave Macmillan, 2013), 151–64.

Edward Gorey: Nonsense, Surrealism, and Silent Matter

1. Stephen Schiff, "Edward Gorey and the Tao of Nonsense," *New Yorker*, November 9, 1992, 89.

2. Tobi Tobias, "Balletgorey," *Dance Magazine*, January 1974, 67–71.

3. Peter Neumeyer, *Floating Worlds: The Letters of Edward Gorey and Peter Neumeyer* (San Francisco: Pomegranate, 2011), 39.

4. Ibid., 201.

5. Schiff, "Edward Gorey and the Tao of Nonsense," 154.

6. Lewis Carroll, "Jabberwocky," in *Through the Looking-Glass and What Alice Found There*, *The Complete Works of Lewis Carroll* (New York: Penguin, 1988), 140.

7. Samuel Foote, "The Great Panjandrum," in *The Chatto Book of Nonsense Poetry*, ed. Hugh Haughton (London: Chatto and Windus, 1988), 159.

8. Robert Dahlin, "Conversations with Edward Gorey," in *Conversations with Writers*, vol. 1, 1977.

9. Gorey, "The Object-Lesson," in *Amphigorey* (New York: Perigee, 1972), n.p.

10. "One dark day in the middle of the night, / Two dead boys got up to fight. / Back to back, they faced each other, / Drew out their swords and shot each other . . ." Mary and Herbert Knapp, *One Potato, Two Potato: The Folklore of American Children* (New York: W. W. Norton, 1976), 97–98.

11. Gorey, "The Epiplectic Bicycle," in *Amphigorey Also* (New York: Harcourt Brace, 1983), n.p.

12. Gorey, "The Untitled Book," in *Amphigorey Too* (New York: G. P. Putnam's Sons, 1975), n.p.

13. Kevin Shortsleeve, "Edward Gorey, Children's Literature and Nonsense Verse," *Children's Literature Association Quarterly* 27, no. 1 (Spring 2002): 34.

14. Edward Lear, *The Dong with a Luminous Nose*, illustrated by Edward Gorey (New York: Young Scott Books, 1969), n.p.

15. Gorey, "The Iron Tonic," in *Amphigorey Too* (New York: G. P. Putnam's Sons, 1975), n.p.

16. Karen Wilkin, "Mr. Earbrass Jots Down a Few Visual Notes," in *The World of Edward Gorey*, ed. Clifford Ross and Karen Wilkin (New York: Harry N. Abrams, 1996), 51.

17. "Edward Gorey, Eccentric Illustrator," *London Times*, April 18, 2000, 25.

18. Alison Lurie, "On Edward Gorey," *New York Review of Books*, May 25, 2000, 20.

19. Hendrik van Leeuwen, "The Liaison of Visual and Written Nonsense," *Explorations in the Field of Nonsense*, ed. Wim Tigges (Amsterdam: Rodopi, 1987), 80.

20. Andreas Brown, interview with the author by telephone, early January 2001.

21. Edward Lear, *The Jumblies*, illustrated by Edward Gorey (New York: Young Scott Books, 1968), n.p.

22. "CatEgory," in *Amphigorey Again* (New York: Harcourt, 2006), n.p.

23. Tobias, "Balletgorey," 71.

24. Neumeyer, *Floating Worlds*, 177. Gorey told Neumeyer he bought it for a dollar. See also Monroe essay, p. 5 (fig. 1.2b).

25. Dick Cavett, "The Dick Cavett Show with Edward Gorey," *WNET*, New York, November 30, 1977, and Richard Dyer, "The Poison Penman," *Boston Globe*, April 1, 1984, 44.

26. Martin Gardner, "Notes," *The Annotated Alice: The Definitive Edition* (New York: Penguin, 2001), 163. Uccello's dragon, however, was not acquired by the National Gallery until 1959, eighty-eight years after *Through the Looking-Glass* was published.

27. Tobias, "Balletgorey," 71.

28. Thank you to Elizabeth Barbeau of the Wadsworth Atheneum Museum of Art for pointing this out to me.

29. "Edward Gorey: Proust Questionnaire," *Vanity Fair*, October 1997.

30. Neumeyer, *Floating Worlds*, 122 and 183.

31. See Nicholas Weber, *Balthus: A Biography* (New York: Knopf, 1999), or Sabine Rewald, *Balthus: Cats and Girls* (New York: The Metropolitan Museum of Art, 2013), 15.

32. Rewald, *Balthus: Cats and Girls*, 16.

33. Nadja Hansen, "Balthus: *Cats and Girls*—Interview with Curator Sabine Rewald," http://www.metmuseum.org/blogs/now-at-the-met/features/2013/sabine-rewald-interview, n.p.

34. Rewald, *Balthus: Cats and Girls*, 16.

35. Wilkin, "Mr. Earbrass Jots Down a Few Visual Notes," 97.

36. Hansen, "Balthus: *Cats and Girls*," n.p.

37. Ibid.

38. Rewald, *Balthus: Cats and Girls*, 49.

39. Ibid.

40. Neumeyer, *Floating Worlds*, 227.

41. Wilkin, "Mr. Earbrass Jots Down a Few Visual Notes," 69.

42. Jane Doonan, "Realism and Surrealism in Wonderland: John Tenniel and Anthony Brown," *Signal* 58 (January 1989): 19, and Lisa Ede, "Edward Lear's Limericks and Their Illustrations," in *Explorations in the Field of Nonsense*, ed. Wim Tigges (Amsterdam: Rodopi, 1987), 116.

43. Van Leeuwen, "The Liaison of Visual and Written Nonsense," 89.

44. James Thurber, "A Trochee (left) encountering a Spondee," in *The Beast in Me and Other Animals* (New York: Queens House, 1948). Gorey owned an original James Thurber drawing, accession number 2001.13.67.

45. Clifford Ross, "Interview with Edward Gorey," in *The World of Edward Gorey*, ed. Clifford Ross and Karen Wilkin (New York: Harry N. Abrams, 1996), 12.

46. Alexander Theroux, *The Strange Case of Edward Gorey* (Seattle: Fantagraphics Books, 2000), 40.

47. Ross, "Interview with Edward Gorey," 12.

48. Lewis Carroll, "Poeta Fit, Non Nascitur," in *Phantasmagoria, The Complete Works of Lewis Carroll* (New York: Penguin, 1988), 790.

49. Glenn Baxter, interview by email with Erin Monroe, August 9, 2015.

50. G. K. Chesterton, "A Defense of Nonsense," in *The Defendant* (London: J. M. Dent and Sons, 1901), 68.

51. Michael Holquist, "What Is a Boojum? Nonsense and Modernism," *Yale French Studies*, no. 96 (1969): 100–117.

52. Juliet Dusinberre, *Alice to the Lighthouse: Children's Books and Radical Experiments in Art* (Basingstoke, Hampshire: Macmillan, 1987).

53. Virginia Woolf, "Mr. Bennett and Mrs. Brown," in *The Virginia Woolf Reader*, ed. Mitchell A. Leaska (New York: Harcourt, Brace, Jovanovich, 1984), 194.

54. Ibid., 197.

55. Ibid., 199.

56. Gorey, *The Black Doll* (New York: Gotham Book Mart and Gallery, 1973), 7.

57. Jane Merrill Filstrup, "An Interview with Edward St. John Gorey at the Gotham Book Mart," *The Lion and the Unicorn* 2, no. 1 (1978): 32.

58. Wilkin, "Mr. Earbrass Jots Down a Few Visual Notes," 97.

59. André Breton, "On Surrealism in Its Living Works," in *Manifestoes of Surrealism* (Ann Arbor: University of Michigan Press, 1969), 297–98.

60. André Breton, *Surrealism and Painting*, trans. Simon Watson Taylor (Boston: MFA Publishers, 1965), 5.

61. Ibid., 5–6.

62. Alfred Jarry, "Le Homard et la Boîte de Corned-Beef que Portait Le Docteur Faustroll en Sautoir," in *The Chatto Book of Nonsense Poetry*, ed. Hugh Haughton (London: Chatto and Windus, 1988), 352.

63. James Leo Yarnall, "Meryon's Mystical Transformations," *Art Bulletin* 61, no. 2 (June 1979): 293. For more on Gorey's collection of Meryon prints, see Erin Monroe's essay in this book.

64. Yarnall, "Meryon's Mystical Transformations," 292.

65. Filstrup, "An Interview with Edward St. John Gorey at the Gotham Book Mart," 84.

66. Wilkin, "Mr. Earbrass Jots Down a Few Visual Notes," 90.

About the Authors

Arnold Arluke, Professor Emeritus of Sociology and Anthropology at Northeastern University, is a Senior Research Fellow at the Tufts Center for Animals and Public Policy.

Robert Greskovic is a dance critic who writes for the *Wall Street Journal*. He was a personal friend of Edward Gorey's and frequently attended performances of New York City Ballet and other dance companies with him.

Erin Monroe is the Robert H. Schutz Jr. Associate Curator of American Painting and Sculpture at the Wadsworth Atheneum Museum of Art and curator of the exhibition *Gorey's Worlds*.

Kevin Shortsleeve is Associate Professor of English at Christopher Newport University and has published academic studies on Edward Gorey, Dr. Seuss, Walt Disney, and nonsense literature.

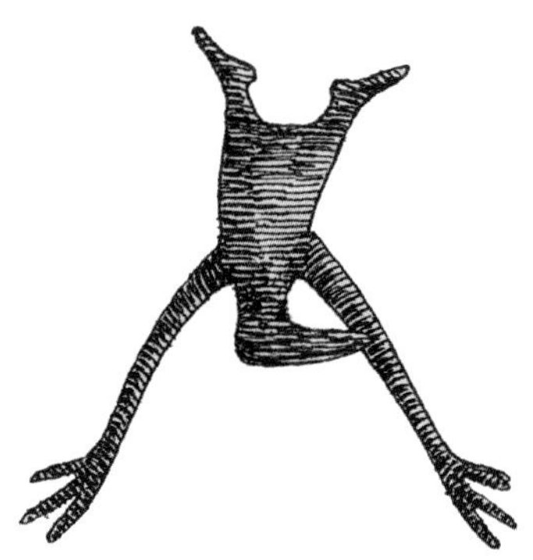

Index

Note: Illustrations are indicated by page numbers in italic type.

Photo Credits

Figbash Acrobate Alphabet [A to Z] by Edward Gorey scattered throughout. New York: Fantod Press, 1994.

Frontispiece. Clifford Ross (American, b. 1952), *Edward Gorey at Home*, 1997. Archival pigment print on paper, 14 × 11 in. (35.6 × 27.9 cm). Collection of the artist.

P. iv. Edward Gorey, "Notes pertaining to *The Blue Aspic*," c. 1967. Graphite, pen and ink, and watercolor on personalized stationery, 7 × 4½ in. (17.8 × 11.4 cm). The Edward Gorey Charitable Trust.

P. 150. Clifford Ross, *Edward Gorey Performing Ballet, on Walkway Above Cranberry Bog, Yarmouth Port, MA*, 1997. Archival pigment print on paper, 14 × 11 in. (35.6 × 27.9 cm). Collection of the artist.

Image courtesy of the Art Institute of Chicago (Fig. 4.19)

© 2017 Artists Rights Society (ARS), New York (Figs. 1.8, 3.17, 4.21)

© 2017 Artists Rights Society (ARS), New York/ADAGP, Paris (Figs. 1.7, 2.9a, 2.9b, 2.10a, 2.10b, 4.16, 4.18a)

© Balthus (Figs. 1.3, 1.5, 4.12)

© Harry Benson (Figs. 1.1, 3.1, 4.1)

Images courtesy of Bridgeman Images (Figs. 4.12, 4.21)

© Steven Caras, All rights reserved (Fig. 2.1)

Reproduced with permission of the Charles E. Burchfield Foundation (Figs. 1.25, 1.27, 1.28)

Images courtesy of Columbia University Rare Book and Manuscript Library, Alpern Collection (Figs. 1.44, 2.5)

Image courtesy of Condé Nast (Fig. 3.2)

Reproduced with permission of The Dance Research Foundation, publishers of *Ballet Review* (Fig. 2.19)

© The Edward Gorey Charitable Trust (all reproductions of Edward Gorey's artwork and text)

© Estate of Donald Evans (Fig. 1.39)

© 2017 C. Herscovici/Artists Rights Society (ARS), New York (Fig. 4.21)

© Kevin McDermott (Figs. 1.2a, 1.2b, 1.29)

Digital Image © The Museum of Modern Art/Licensed by SCALA/Art Resource, NY (Fig. 4.16)

Image courtesy of the Rare Books & Manuscripts Library of the Ohio State University Libraries (Fig. 4.14)

Photography by Allen Phillips (Figs. 1.4, 1.6–1.15, 1.17, 1.19–1.24, 1.26–1.28, 1.30–1.33, 1.35–1.37, 1.39–1.42a, 1.43, 2.4, 2.6, 2.9a, 2.9b–2.19, 3.4, 3.6–3.10a, 3.14–3.17, 4.2–4.7, 4.9–4.10, 4.13, 4.15a, 4.25b, 4.18a, 4.18b, 4.20, 4.22)

© Pomegranate (Figs. 1.16, 1.18, 1.25, 1.34, 1.38, 2.8, 3.3, 3.5, 3.10b, 3.12, 3.13, 4.6a, 4.6b, 4.11, 4.17, 4.23)

© Clifford Ross (frontispiece, Fig. 1.40, p. 150)

Photograph by Maurice Seymour courtesy of Ronald Seymour (Fig. 2.7)

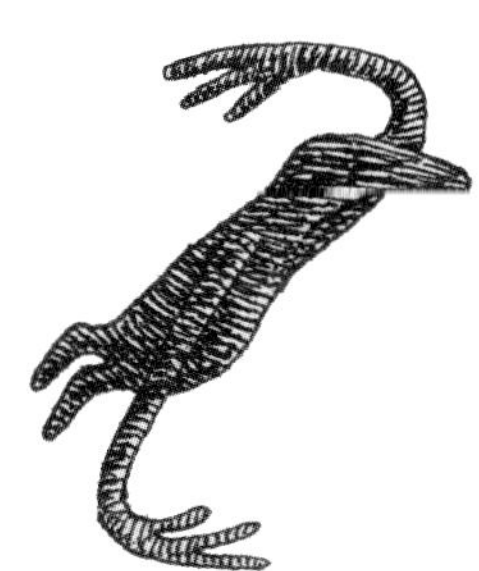

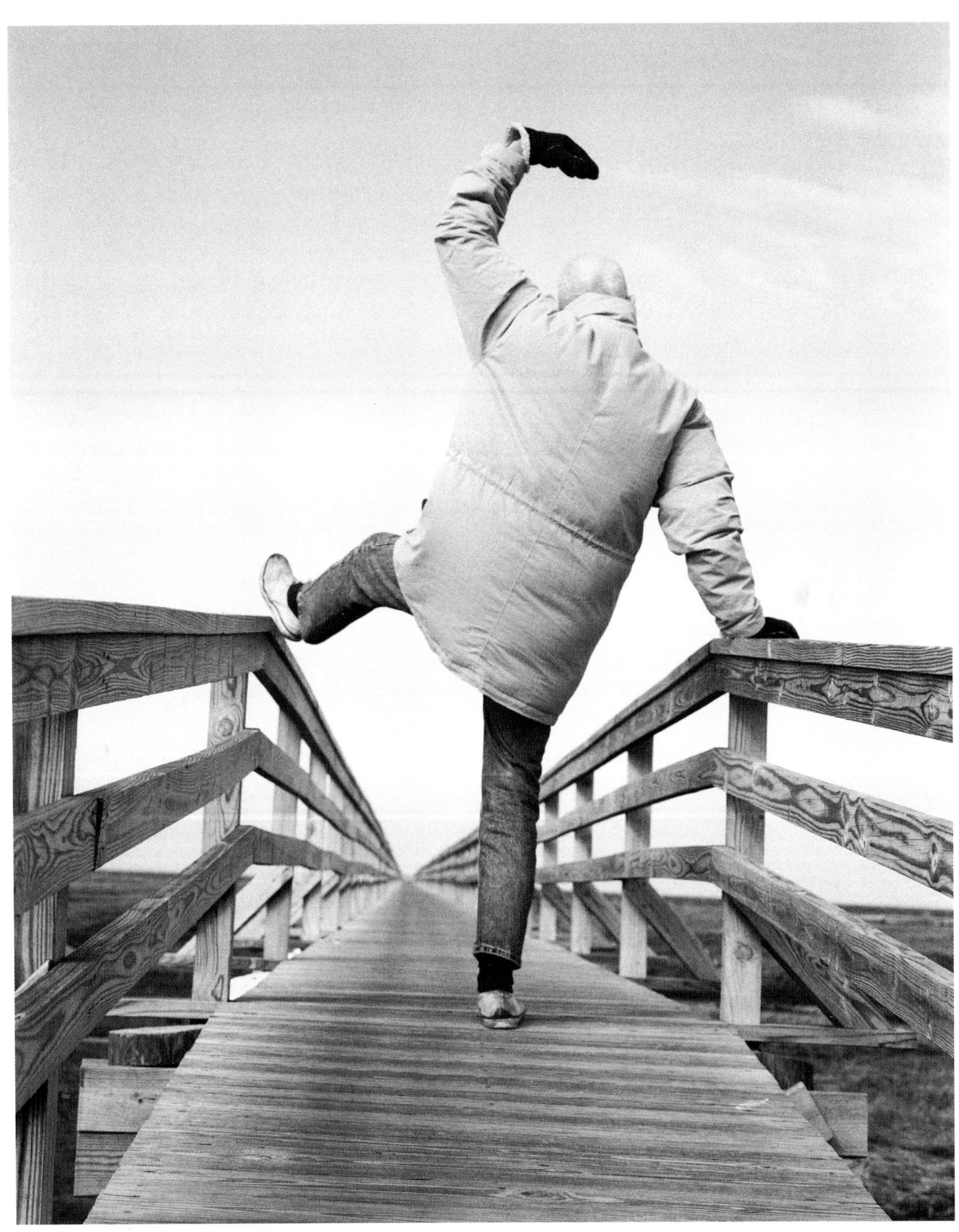

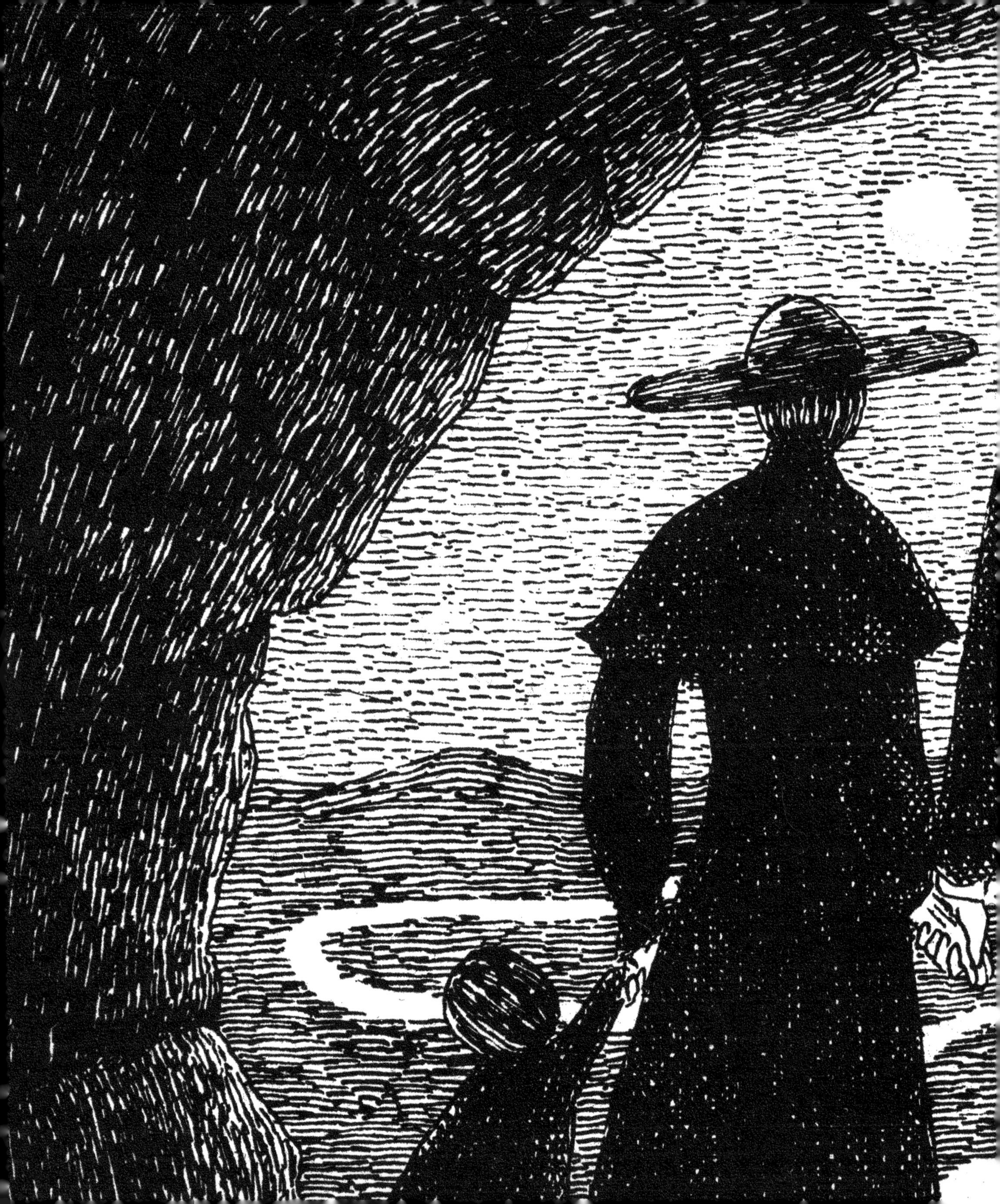